José María Heredia
in New York,
1823–1825

José María Heredia in New York, 1823–1825

*An Exiled Cuban Poet in the Age of Revolution,
Selected Letters and Verse*

Edited, Translated, and with an Introduction by
Frederick Luciani

Cover image: *The Bay of New York taken from Brooklyn Heights* (ca. 1820) by William Guy Wall. The Edward W. C. Arnold Collection of New York Prints, Maps, and Pictures, Bequest of Edward W. C. Arnold, 1954. The Metropolitan Museum of Art, New York.

Published by State University of New York Press, Albany

© 2020 State University of New York

All rights reserved

No part of this book may be used or reproduced in any manner whatsoever without written permission. No part of this book may be stored in a retrieval system or transmitted in any form or by any means including electronic, electrostatic, magnetic tape, mechanical, photocopying, recording, or otherwise without the prior permission in writing of the publisher.

For information, contact State University of New York Press, Albany, NY
www.sunypress.edu

Library of Congress Cataloging-in-Publication Data

Name: Luciani, Frederick, author.
Title: José María Heredia in New York, 1823–1825: an exiled Cuban poet in the age of revolution, selected letters and verse / Frederick Luciani, author.
Description: Albany : State University of New York Press, [2020] | Includes bibliographical references and index.
Identifiers: ISBN 9781438479835 (hardcover : alk. paper) | ISBN 9781438479842 (pbk. : alk. paper) | ISBN 9781438479859 (ebook)
Further information is available at the Library of Congress.

Library of Congress Control Number: 2020937126

10 9 8 7 6 5 4 3 2 1

A translation dwells in exile. It cannot return.

—Willis Barnstone

Contents

Acknowledgments	ix
Introduction	1
The Life of José María Heredia	1
Heredia and Exile	8
Heredia as Travel Writer	13
Heredia and Nineteenth-Century Inter-American Literary Relations	18
The Translations in this Volume	22
Selected Letters, 1823–1825	33
Selected Verse, 1823–1825	167
To Emilia	169
The Pleasures of Melancholy	179
Athens and Palmyra	197
To Washington	201
Niagara	207
Project	215
The Exile's Hymn	219
Return to the South	227
Immortality	233
Notes	235
Works Cited	265
Index	271

Acknowledgments

The editor and translator of this volume gratefully acknowledges the counsel and encouragement of Rolena Adorno, Raquel Chang-Rodríguez, Carol Delaney, Nancy Farriss, John Gallucci, Roberto González Echevarría, Nina Scott, and Nancy Vogeley. He thanks Miguel Delgado, Mónica Escudero Moro, Roger Hecht, Kenneth Mills, and Chrystian Zegarra for invitations to share his work on Heredia in various venues; Mirta Yáñez for her kind interest in the project; Ulises Castro Núñez and Paul White for their fellowship during research trips in Spain, Cuba, and the United States; and Matthew DeLaMater for suggesting a path to publication.

Sabbatical time from Colgate University and support from Colgate's Research Council were an essential help for the completion of this project. Research was greatly facilitated by Nancy Machado Lorenzo and Carlos Valenciaga of the Biblioteca Nacional José Martí, and Amanda Moreno and Martin Tsang of the Cuban Heritage Collection at the University of Miami Libraries.

Special thanks to Jacinto Regalado for his unflagging enthusiasm for this project, for his careful reading of the manuscript, and for his collaborative wordsmithing. His help and support have improved the introduction and translations beyond measure.

Introduction

The Life of José María Heredia

Early on a Monday evening in April 1824, a young Cuban gentleman wound his way in nervous excitement through the streets of New York toward the park in front of City Hall. His spoken English was halting—he had arrived in the city as a political exile just a few months before—but he read it very well, and he had noticed an unsettling announcement in the New York papers. A public demonstration in support of DeWitt Clinton, and against the state legislators who had removed him as president of the Erie Canal Commission, would be held that day at five o'clock. The young man's own experience as a participant in a thwarted rebellion against Spanish rule in Cuba, and the draconian crackdown that had followed, made him fear the worst for this demonstration: a riot or a violent confrontation with police. He had to see for himself how such a protest would unfold in the country in which he had found refuge.

In the park the young man witnessed a scene that left him shaking his head in slightly incredulous relief. As he would recount in a letter to his uncle in Cuba, the demonstration began when a speaker got up on a table to give a vehement speech in support of Clinton. Some toughs from an opposing party elbowed their way through the crowd and upset the table, tumbling the speaker to the ground. Unhurt and unfazed, he dusted himself off, climbed onto the table again and continued his oration, this time with a cordon of allies surrounding the table to keep the opposition at bay. After he concluded his speech, an agreement was made to send a delegation to Clinton and express, on behalf of the people of New York, support for him and displeasure with the state legislature's unjust action. The proclamation thus framed, the crowd dispersed with some minor scuffling among the contending factions, but nary a sign of a public official or law enforcement officer during the entire episode. There was nothing to fear: this new republic may have been born of revolution, but its institutions and rough-hewn citizens seemed to have an uncanny capacity for containing and channeling partisan passions.

It is not surprising that the young man who witnessed that demonstration before New York's City Hall should have had an instinctive fear of a spark that might ignite political and social turmoil. José María Heredia (Cuba 1803–Mexico 1839) was a true child of the Age of Revolution, and his short and eventful life was marked decisively by the upheavals on the American continent as new republics struggled to emerge from the old colonial order.[1] He was born in Santiago de Cuba on December 31, 1803; being born there was itself a consequence of revolution. His parents, José Francisco Heredia y Mieses and María de la Merced Heredia y Campuzano, were members of the same extended family of landowners in the island colony of Santo Domingo; the family traced its American roots to the Spanish *conquistador* Pedro de Heredia. In the wake of the Treaty of Basel, which conceded the Spanish portion of Hispaniola to France in 1795, José Francisco and María de la Merced, like many others of their race and class, fled Santo Domingo before the invading forces of Toussaint Louverture, fearing that the violence of the Haitian Revolution might engulf the whole island.

The erudite and principled José Francisco was to play out the rest of his life as a loyal subject of the Spanish crown, in judicial and administrative posts in Pensacola in Spanish Florida, Venezuela, and Mexico. He occupied these posts against the backdrop of two related struggles for independence: that of Spain as it fought a war of liberation against the forces of Napoleon, which invaded the Peninsula in 1808; and that of the Spanish colonies against the mother country, precipitated by the usurpation of the Spanish throne by Napoleon's brother Joseph Bonaparte, who ruled Spain as José I from 1808 to 1813. The Heredia family—José Francisco; María de la Merced; their eldest child, José María; and his four sisters[2]—crisscrossed the Caribbean and Gulf of Mexico during the twilight years of Spanish rule on the American mainland, suffering separation, shipwreck, and flight before advancing insurgent armies. José Francisco was no admirer of revolution; as administrator in Venezuela, he witnessed its excesses and ravages.

José Francisco provided his son with a fine education in the classics, in literature and languages, and in the principles of the Catholic faith. He also instilled in his son a lifelong reverence for the rule of law, although politically José María would come to diverge from his father's conservative tendencies.³ Because of his father's multiple postings, José María spent most of his early years outside the land of his birth. Yet his sense of *patria*, initially linked with a Spain in the throes of its own liberation efforts and experiments in constitutional rule, was to become bound with his Cuban identity. As a law student in Havana, he breathed the air of uneasy excitement that the island colony was experiencing as ripples of the mainland independence struggles found their way to its shores. Emotional identification with Cuba, discontent with the island's colonial status, and a commitment to the principles of constitutional democracy were to be essential elements of Heredia's thought and wellsprings for the patriotic verses through which he would give voice to the struggle for Cuban independence.

The year 1820 found the Heredia family in Mexico, where José Francisco occupied a Spanish government post; when he died suddenly, his wife and children returned to Cuba. The family settled in Matanzas, a small coastal city and provincial capital. While far from wealthy—the death of José Francisco left his wife and children in some financial difficulty—the Heredias were well connected among Cuba's *criollo* elite, and surrounded by a prosperous extended family. That family included María de la Merced's younger brother Ignacio, a lawyer and coffee planter with whom José María was exceptionally close. In Havana, José María finished the study of law; in June of 1823 he was awarded his degree, and he prepared to take up practice.

By then, Heredia was gaining attention within his circle and beyond as a gifted poet. His early compositions give a sense of his amorous infatuations and political idealism, and his adaptations of French and Latin works suggest the scope of his erudition and a desire to hone his talent by imitating literary models. A few of these early works show that, although he was barely more than an adolescent, Heredia was approaching full command of his art. His poem "En el teocalli de Cholula," begun in Mexico when he was only sixteen, is a striking example.⁴ A meditation upon the ruins of a pre-Hispanic temple, it is considered among Heredia's most accomplished works. It contains the elements that distinguish his best poetry: a precise observation of landscape, a sure handling of lexicon and meter, a sweeping historical vision, a stern moral sensibility, and an Americanist scope that transcends classical and European paradigms.

In his late teenage years in Cuba, Heredia forged friendships that would sustain him for the rest of his short life. One of these was especially intense and would prove decisive for his poetic career and legacy.

Domingo del Monte (1804–1853) was a key figure in Cuban thought and letters in the first half of the nineteenth century. Like Heredia, he was trained in law and keenly interested in literature. Del Monte was to make his mark principally as editor and critic, as a patron and champion of Cuban writers, and as the host of gatherings of the island's most prominent intellectuals and writers. No one was more important than Del Monte in the editing, sponsoring, and dissemination of Heredia's poetry. Although separated geographically after 1823, the two men would have a close, if complicated, lifelong friendship.[5]

These, then, were the circumstances of Heredia's life during the last months of 1823, as his twentieth birthday neared. He was a newly credentialed and well-connected lawyer; the potential breadwinner for his widowed mother and younger sisters; a well-educated young man of varied intellectual interests; a poet discovering his voice and making a name for himself in Cuban literary circles; a political idealist *au courant* with evolving events in Europe and the American mainland; and an energetic roustabout, buoyed by the companionship of Domingo del Monte and other young Cubans who were living heady days of political change. All signs must have pointed toward a future of success and happiness.

But Heredia's life was about to take a sudden turn. Given his ideals and his social environment, perhaps it was inevitable that he would be caught up in the pro-independence agitation then sweeping Cuba. In July 1823, government authorities became aware of an island-wide conspiracy with masonic affiliations known as the *Soles y Rayos de Bolívar*, whose aim was to foment armed rebellion against Spanish rule. More than six hundred individuals across the island were implicated in the plot. Heredia had been active in the Matanzas cell of the *Soles*, known as the *Caballeros Racionales*. In a bid for leniency, three fellow members of the *Caballeros* denounced him as an important figure in the group, and in early November an order was issued for his arrest. But Heredia had gone into hiding; through the intercession of a young friend, Josefa ("Pepilla") Arango (the "Emilia" to whom Heredia would address a letter from exile and a major poem, both contained herein), he found refuge on the Arango family plantation near Matanzas. After a week there, he slipped out of the island in disguise aboard the American ship *Galaxy* bound for Boston. His separation from Cuba, which would continue almost uninterrupted for the rest of his life, had begun.[6]

Heredia endured the rough passage north bundled in the coat that the *Galaxy*'s captain loaned him. He reached a snowy Boston on

December 4, 1823, and within a few days ran across fellow conspirators Luciano Ramos and Miguel María Caraballo, the first of what would be an expanding group of Cuban expatriates with whom he would share lodgings, travels, and adventures. The three young men soon moved to New York City, where Heredia would live for most of the rest of his twenty months in the United States.[7] In New York, Heredia was better able to receive letters from home, thanks to the ship traffic between that city and Cuban ports, and through the good offices of countryman Cristóbal Madan, an employee at the trading firm of Goodhue & Co. Moreover, Leonardo Santos Suárez, Tomás Gener, and Félix Varela had arrived in New York just a week before; these three Cuban delegates to the Spanish *Cortes* had fled Spain, charged with treason upon the dissolution of that body by Ferdinand VII and the end of Spain's experiment in constitutional rule. These and companions from elsewhere in Spanish America would provide Heredia with friendship, moral support, and a reprieve from his forced immersion in the English language. If Heredia also engaged in any political machinations with fellow expatriates, they left little or no documentary trace.

Heredia's struggles with English made securing employment in New York difficult. A monthly stipend that his Uncle Ignacio sent from Cuba kept him financially afloat, and toward the end of his stay he also obtained a salary, room, and board as a Spanish teacher at a private school in the city. His modest resources were sufficient to purchase books, to take advantage of cultural opportunities—years later he would recall a stirring performance of *Richard III* in New York—and for travels in the summer of 1824. Although relatively free of financial worries, Heredia still faced physical and psychological challenges. The northern winters aggravated his predisposition to consumptive illnesses; in the winter of 1825, his condition was grave. He worried for the well-being of his mother and sisters in Cuba. He felt bitterness over the betrayal he had suffered at the hands of fellow conspirators. He anxiously awaited the outcome of the judicial hearings on the island regarding the *Soles y Rayos* plot and the fate of those implicated in it. And he felt a certain cultural alienation in the United States coupled with fierce nostalgia for the land from which he had been torn—as *destierro* and *desterrado*, his words of choice for describing his situation, vigorously express.

Despite these difficulties, Heredia maintained an intense rhythm of intellectual activity during his months in New York; arguably, this was to be the most productive phase of his poetic career. Between November

1823 and September 1825, he composed such major works as "A Emilia," "Placeres de la Melancolía," and his signature work, "Niágara." The last of these, composed at the falls, and the aforementioned "En el teocalli de Cholula," are the two poems that have secured Heredia an essential place in the canon of Spanish American literature. He expressed his civic sensibilities, shaped now by the experience of living in a free republic, in compositions like "A Washington," perhaps composed at Mount Vernon. His translations into Spanish of Ossian, Alfieri, and others reflected his expanded readings in world literature, especially of authors associated with international Romanticism. Heredia kept up to date with literary and other topics through English-language publications like the *North American Review*, and he frequented New York's publishing houses and booksellers. Crowning these months of literary activity, in the summer of 1825 Heredia published the first collection of his works: *Poesías* (New York: Behr and Kahl). It is not surprising that he was able to publish his poetry in Spanish in the United States; a vigorous, often politically charged Spanish-language press existed in Philadelphia and New York in the 1820s.[8] Through Domingo del Monte, copies of Heredia's *Poesías* were to reach prominent readers and reviewers in the Spanish-speaking world, thus greatly expanding his literary reputation.

In December 1824, Heredia received word that the legal case against the *Soles y Rayos* conspirators had been decided, and that he was among those sentenced to banishment from Cuba and exile to Spain. The doors to his homeland now officially closed, and with the prospect of continued difficulties living in the United States, Heredia left for Mexico in August 1825. The recently elected President Guadalupe Victoria—Mexico's first after the adoption of the Constitution of 1824—had offered Heredia a passport for his relocation to the new republic. En route, catching sight of Cuban shores from the rail of his ship, he penned another signature poem, "Himno del desterrado." By mid-October, he was welcomed in Mexico City by Victoria, who would offer him his patronage during his four-year term in office. Heredia was given a position in the government's *Secretaría de Estado* and would go on to serve in judicial posts in the State of Mexico, as a *diputado* in that state's congress, and in significant positions in cultural and educational institutions.

In 1827, Heredia married Jacoba Yáñez, the daughter of an old friend of his father in Mexico, and they began a family. His literary activity continued unabated, even if his most innovative and productive years as a poet already were behind him. His adaptations of French tragedies were performed in Mexico; he edited and published several literary journals, to which he contributed reviews, essays, stories, and poetry; and he advanced an ambitious intellectual project, his *Lecciones de Historia Universal* (1831). In 1832, an expanded and revised edition of his *Poesías* was published in two volumes in the city of Toluca. In the preface to this edition, Heredia noted the changes of fortune and occupation that he had undergone at his young age:

> The whirlwind of revolution has forced me to traverse, in a short time, a vast distance, and at age twenty-five I have been, with greater or lesser success, a lawyer, a soldier, a traveler, a language professor, a diplomat, a journalist, a magistrate, a historian and a poet. All my writings surely have suffered because of the strange volatility of my fate. (*Poesías* 1832, 1, 4)

In the 1830s, Heredia was caught up in the chaos that plagued Mexico after Victoria's presidency; on more than one occasion he was compelled to take up arms in favor of one faction or another. It seems that he was subject to suspicion and persecution from all sides. As a Cuban, he still was technically a Spanish subject, and therefore some questioned his loyalty to the Mexican republic. As an outspoken defender of democratic liberalism and the rule of law, he ran afoul of many in this period of aggressive political opportunism in Mexico. Moreover, Heredia's troubles with Spanish authorities in Cuba only worsened; he was accused of association with the *Gran Legión del Águila Negra* conspiracy of the late 1820s, another pro-Cuban independence plot linked to freemasonry and based in Mexico. This time the colonial government in Cuba sentenced Heredia to death and the confiscation of his possessions, which made his dream of a return to his native island all the more improbable. His placement in Mexican government and judicial posts at a young age did not endear him to all, and his career path was often blocked. This had serious financial consequences for Heredia and his growing family, as did the irregular payment of government salaries in situations of near-anarchy. His health was delicate, as was that of his wife, and the couple lost three of their six children to childhood diseases.[9]

Heredia's prospects for reunion with his mother and sisters brightened when the widow of Ferdinand VII, María Cristina de Borbón, acting as regent, issued an amnesty decree for Spanish political exiles. While the terms of the decree alone were not sufficient for Heredia to return to

Cuba, they did inspire him to seek permission to do so. In 1836, through direct contact with the island's governor, Captain General Miguel Tacón, Heredia was granted a two-month visit. Leaving Jacoba and their children in Mexico, Heredia arrived in Havana in November 1836 and stayed, mostly in Matanzas, until January 1837. Upon his return to Mexico, he faced continued difficulties: declining health, the loss of a government post because of a new requirement that its holders be native-born Mexicans, and the failure of the government to pay salaries owed to functionaries, leaving the Heredia family in even more dire financial straits. Heredia's final months were spent scraping by, and on May 7, 1839, at age thirty-five, he finally succumbed to the consumptive illness that had plagued him since his teens. His widow and children moved to Cuba in 1844, where Jacoba died within a month, leaving her two daughters and one son in the care of her mother-in-law and the extended Heredia family.

Heredia and Exile

Heredia's death inspired an elegy by the Cuban poet Gertrudis Gómez de Avellaneda (1814–1873), whose "A la muerte del célebre poeta cubano D. José María Heredia" (1841) addresses Cuba and asks:

> Who will sing your breezes and your palm trees,
> Your fiery sun, your brilliant sky?
> [. . .]
> He clamored for you in his cruel exile,
> And now perfidious fortune condemns
> His cold remains in foreign soil to lie . . .[10]

For Cubans of his and later generations, Heredia was the poet who first and most vividly expressed a sense of Cuban nationhood, linked indissolubly to the island's landscapes and to the poet's exilic condition. For it was from the distance of his *destierro* that Heredia evoked, in his imagination and from the depths of his ethical and political consciousness, a homeland that combined, in his words, "of the natural world, loveliness, / of the moral world, depravity" ("The Exile's Hymn," included herein).

The degree to which Heredia's verses were an inspiration for pro-independence Cubans of his generation cannot be overstated. The phenomenon was recorded by Cuban writer Cirilo Villaverde (1812–1894) in his antislavery novel *Cecilia Valdés*, first published in 1839. In a passage that explains the grip that censorship had on Cuba in the 1820s and 1830s, and the efforts of Félix Varela and others to incite independence sentiments on the island through journalistic writings from abroad, Villaverde notes the far greater impact of Heredia's poetry:

> The patriotic verses of that famous poet exercised a greater and more general influence on the minds of youth. . . . His "Himno del desterrado" of 1825 aroused keen enthusiasm in Havana; many learned it by heart and a goodly number repeated it whenever the occasion came their way to do so without endangering their personal freedom.[11]

Not only did Heredia's patriotic poems become instant classics; the poet himself soon acquired a halo of martyrdom. To a considerable degree this was self-generated; it arose from his poems that linked longing for his homeland, self-pity for his exilic state, patriotic fervor, and the fantasy of dying a hero's death in the battle for Cuban independence. Even close friends like Del Monte, it seems, clung to the idea of Heredia as the exiled poet-martyr, a figure of both passion and pathos. This idea could lead only to disappointment when more complex reality impinged upon the idealized image, burnished by distance, that they had of him.

That reality is revealed in Heredia's letters, which give a more tangled view of his political sentiments and his life in exile. When Heredia fled Cuba in late 1823 as authorities were rounding up members of the *Soles y Rayos de Bolívar* groups, mutual incriminations and efforts at self-exculpation among the conspirators were common. Perhaps induced by a combination of principle and panic, on the eve of his escape Heredia composed a letter to Francisco Hernández Morejón, the primary judge in the legal proceedings against the *Caballeros Racionales*. In this letter (included herein), Heredia claimed that he had broken with that group almost a year before. Moreover, he asserted, when he was associated with the *Caballeros*, they only had "endeavored peacefully to prepare public opinion for independence." He conceded that others in the conspiracy may have had darker intentions—alluding to "civil war" and perhaps hinting at a slave revolt—but he had no direct knowledge of it. The tone and content of the letter diverge considerably from that of Heredia's militantly patriotic verse. In it one hears not the firebrand poet, but the young lawyer hoping to influence the outcome of his case by carefully parsing his views and actions. The letter was soon published, and was not well received by some in Heredia's circle.[12]

A similar ambivalence can be detected in the personal letters that Heredia wrote during his New York exile. When expressing his political and personal convictions, he is by turns defiant and tepid, steadfast and disillusioned, self-pitying and self-aggrandizing. The complexity of his sentiments is exemplified in a letter he wrote to his Uncle Ignacio in February 1824, while he was still awaiting word of the resolution of his case:

> I am convinced that our fellow men are not worthy of the sacrifices that one makes for them; but the harm has already been done, and at the end of the day it is a beautiful and sublime thing to be a martyr for the human race, for having committed an error common to generous souls in all times and places, an error that, like me, befell Demosthenes, Cato and Washington.
>
> However, the disillusionment that I have acquired will serve to help me reform my conduct in future, and if justice is done me, I will go back over to your faction, at least until the next life shows me that there is some greater or lesser chance of perfectibility, since, having lived in Matanzas and New York, I know there is little chance of that on this earth.

It would seem that a number of things contributed to this ambivalence: realization of the full consequences of his actions, the collapse of solidarity among the *Caballeros*, the stress of life in exile, and greater experience in a world of flawed social and political arrangements. At the same time, personal letters like this are of limited value as reflections of Heredia's truest feelings; they were not official statements of political opinion, but expressions of a transient state of mind. Moreover, like any letter writer, Heredia took into consideration the viewpoints and sensibilities of his addressee—in this case, those of a respected uncle who evidently was not quite on the same political page as his nephew. To this must be added the fact that Heredia knew that some of his letters were being intercepted by the authorities in Cuba, which required him to be extremely careful about what he wrote. He needed to protect himself while his legal case was still pending and to avoid incriminating those to whom or about whom he was writing.

These factors must explain the lacunae in Heredia's letters regarding aspects of his life in New York. For example, he names most of his fellow expatriates sparingly and innocuously, as roommates, traveling companions, and so on. He alludes a few times to the former delegates to the Spanish *Cortes*, Tomás Gener and Leonardo Santos Suárez, but does not mention the formidable political visionary Félix Varela at all. Nor does Heredia speak of the Argentine José Antonio Miralla, who also fled Cuba for New York in 1823 because of his implication in pro-independence activities, and with whom, we know from other contexts, Heredia almost certainly engaged during his time in that city. Only Antonio Betancourt, one of the three *Caballeros Racionales* who implicated Heredia as a prominent member of the group and thus precipitated the order for his arrest, receives more expansive treatment in Heredia's letters. Betancourt turned up in New York one month after Heredia's arrival, and Heredia is acerbic, if ultimately magnanimous, in his depiction of him. The freeness with which he portrays Betancourt suggests that Heredia saw no need to shield a man by whom he considered himself betrayed.

Besides soft-pedaling his interactions with current or former political agitators, in his letters Heredia assured his mother that he was keeping safely away from political writings and activities. It is difficult to determine if that was entirely true. In a February 1824 letter to Ignacio, Heredia describes his daily routine with this tantalizing passage:

> I am up with the birds at eight, have breakfast at eight-thirty, and if there is no rain or snow, I go out at nine-thirty or ten. I wander around, here and there, until three o'clock, when I return for lunch. I go back out at four, until teatime at seven, after which, if the night is mild, I go out to visit some friend, or to visit with due precaution some mathematical conventicle, but almost always I remain at home studying or writing, have supper at ten, and turn in at eleven. I regularly walk five or six miles when I go out.

The casual allusion to the "mathematical conventicle" visited with "due precaution" easily escapes notice. The phrase may imply that Heredia was quietly attending meetings of Freemasons in New York. Given the masonic character of the *Caballeros Racionales* of which he had been a member and of the *Gran Legión del Águila Negra* with which later he may have been involved, Heredia's association with freemasonry is undeniable even if its extent and duration is not well documented.[13] In any case, the cryptic reference in Heredia's letter may indicate that, through such networks, he engaged in pro-Cuban independence intrigue during his months in New York.

A full assessment of the evolution of Heredia's political views during his subsequent exile in Mexico would be a complex task. Certainly in republican Mexico, with his fate already sealed vis-à-vis the colonial authorities in Cuba, he felt freer to speak his mind on political matters. The 1832 edition of his poetry published in Toluca restored some of the more incendiary verses that he had suppressed in the 1825 New York edition, and he remained vocal and eloquent as essayist, orator, and delegate. Yet his personal letters suggest that he fell victim to considerable disillusionment in the last decade of his life, even as he strove to maintain the highest degree of probity as a magistrate and participant in Mexican politics. Given the prolonged turmoil that he witnessed in Mexico, and the material adversity that this caused Heredia and his young family, it is hard to imagine how he could have avoided bitterness and skepticism about the prospects for successful republican government in Spanish America.

This provides a context for a second controversial letter that Heredia wrote in April 1836. In it, he asked the governor of Cuba, Captain General Miguel Tacón, for permission to visit his family on the island. The letter contains the following passage:

> It is true that twelve years ago, the independence of Cuba was the most fervent of my vows, and that in order to achieve it I would have sacrificed happily my life's blood. But the calamities and misfortunes that I have witnessed for the past eight years have greatly modified my opinions, and today I would regard as criminal any attempt to transplant to fortunate and opulent Cuba the ills that afflict the American continent.[14]

Heredia could not have been more explicit in his disavowal of his former pro-independence sentiments, and a number of his old acquaintances on the island reacted as one might expect. When he arrived in Cuba, Heredia was largely shunned by Del Monte and others, whose correspondence gives a sense of just how displeased they were. In a letter to Heredia, Del Monte called him a "fallen angel," and in a letter to another of their group,

Del Monte reported that Heredia had "lost his immense patriotic-poetic prestige to such a degree that the young people [of the island] avoided seeing and having dealings with him."[15] Del Monte's wording confirms the extent to which Heredia, from the convenient distance of exile, had become an iconic figure for the younger, progressive sector in Cuba. As such, he was expected to be pure and unwavering in his patriotic fervor and, in a sense, in his suffering and martyrdom.

The dissatisfaction that Del Monte and others of his generation felt with the real, complex, and contradictory José María Heredia has echoed in twentieth- and twenty-first century biographies and commentaries. Scholars often have felt compelled either to excuse or reproach him for his perceived apostasy in his letters to Hernández Morejón in 1823 and to Tacón in 1836. As in Heredia's lifetime, the poet has continued to precede and preempt the man; the fiery zeal of his verses can still tempt readers to a sympathetic identification bordering on hero worship, and from there to disappointment with a more complicated reality. Perhaps only those who have suffered prolonged displacement can view Heredia's actions as a consequence of the impossible choices imposed by exile itself, rather than through a lens of moral judgment.

Heredia as Travel Writer

Between November 1829 and March 1830, a series of travel letters that Heredia wrote to his Uncle Ignacio appeared in a journal for women published by Domingo del Monte in Havana: *La Moda o Recreo Semanal del Bello Sexo*. Del Monte provided a preface to the first installment, announcing the series and reminding his readers of the literary prestige of the author:

> Merely by mentioning the name *Heredia*, we are sure to spark the interest of our amiable subscribers. The *Cuban poet*, whose beautiful compositions are known by heart by nearly all *Habaneros* with any level of education, and whose fame now extends to Europe, wrote the letters from which we have extracted these fragments during his residence in the United States in 1823 and 1824. He did not write them to be published, but rather to give a friend of his an idea of that country. Therefore it should be no surprise that in

these letters one finds the occasional negligence of style which, admittedly, is a sure sign of friendship and trust. Despite this, and the fact that these letters are written in *humble prose*, it will not be forgotten that their author is the sublime singer of Niagara and of the tempests of the torrid zone, especially when some grandiose object appears before him and arouses the genius to which, to the glory of his homeland, is owed works of such felicitous inspiration.[16]

A comparison of the letters adapted for *La Moda* with their originals reveals that Del Monte eliminated their personal content—including any reference to Ignacio Heredia as addressee—and lightly revised them for style.[17] In edited form, these letters, originally written to amuse Ignacio during tranquil afternoons in his coffee grove, became minutely descriptive travelogues, composed with considerable stylistic polish despite Del Monte's fussy claims to the contrary. While it is not clear if Heredia knew that, through his uncle and his friend, his letters would appear in print, their quality suggests that he had publication at least in the back of his mind.

The letters describe Heredia's sea voyage from Cuba, the city of Boston, his trip to Philadelphia in April 1824 with passages on the New Jersey estate of Joseph Bonaparte and the city of New York, and his visit to New Haven, Connecticut, and environs. But the most remarkable series of travel letters are those that Heredia wrote between June 7 and June 17, 1824, recounting his trip to Niagara Falls. These letters take the reader from the streets of New York, up the Hudson River valley by steamship to Albany and Troy, and across the interior of New York State by stagecoach and canal boat to the Niagara frontier. Heredia notes historical curiosities, aspects of American culture and character, and advances in technology, transportation, and communications. He includes the occasional amusing anecdote; for all his seriousness of purpose and careful cataloguing of what he saw, Heredia, accompanied by friend Juan de Acosta, had sheer fun on this trip.

The Niagara letters are striking in their evocation of the beauty of the landscapes along the way, culminating in a rapturous description of the falls. They are important complements to Heredia's signature poem "Niágara," showing a similar gift for vivid description, the same penchant for emotional identification with nature and melancholy introspection, and the same preoccupation with the natural sublime. In fact, the word *sublime*, dear to Romantic sensibilities, echoes insistently throughout the letters and the poem. Along with its companion term *picturesque*, the word was becoming intimately linked with the landscapes of New York State: the Hudson Valley; the Catskill Mountains, which provided a conveniently proximate "wilderness"; the deeply forested interior of the state, which was opening to settlement; and of course Niagara itself. Admired as the most spectacular natural attraction in North America before the wonders of the Far West became widely known, the falls were, at the time of Heredia's journey in 1824, increasingly accessible to travelers from the Eastern Seaboard. Heredia followed a route that already was hallowed by travel writers, novelists, and poets, and which, beginning just a year later with Thomas Cole, would inspire the Hudson River School of landscape painters.[18]

Heredia prepared for his trip by reading widely. He consulted geography books, atlases, and travel guides. For his discussion of the Erie Canal, he cites articles from the *North American Review*, which he carried with him on his journey. He also had at hand John Howison's *Sketches of Upper Canada* (1821), from which he quotes at length for the description of the falls, translating into Spanish. More broadly, Heredia's readings in international Romanticism preceded and even shaped his journey. François-René de Chateaubriand's novel *Atala* (1801), which drew on that author's travels in North America in 1791, appears to have been a major influence. In a letter written a month before his trip, Heredia advised his mother to tell his sister Ignacia to read the description of the falls in that novel; he mentions in a letter from Niagara that Chateaubriand's description of the Niagara River is both beautiful and accurate; and scholars have traced specific influences of Chateaubriand's text on Heredia's verse "Niágara." It is telling that *Atala's* idealized and sentimentalized rendering of the North American wilderness was present in Heredia's mind. It suggests the degree to which his trip was motivated by things beyond the curiosity of the average tourist—things that the Romantic aesthetic and vision of life emphasized, like the search for the exotic and the primitive, and a yearning for extreme sensation.

But the journey to Niagara in 1824 was a far cry from that of 1791. The New York State interior, which thirty years before had been a wilderness crossed by rough roads, populated by Native Americans and dotted by forts, now was becoming settled farmland, with towns springing up along the banks of the Erie Canal, as Heredia puts it, "as if by magic." What had been a bone-jarring stagecoach journey taking weeks was now a relatively comfortable trip by packet boat taking just a few days.

Heredia reveled in the ease and speed of his trip, and his letters discuss the canal as a great work of engineering and a transformative conduit for the movement of people and goods. Besides its commercial function, the canal was now part of a larger tourist infrastructure—the first in the United States—which included Hudson River steamboats with regular service, hotels in the Catskills and in spas north of Albany, and facilities for visitors at Niagara. The packet boats that plied the canal were floating hotels, from which one could watch varied sights drift by while eating off imported English china, as Heredia notes. At Niagara, one could pass the night at one of the comfortable new hotels or have refreshments and play billiards at an establishment just a short stroll from the edge of the precipice. Heredia is matter-of-fact in noting such amenities, accepting that the trip to Niagara was becoming less an adventure for the intrepid and more an excursion for the ordinary tourist.

Thus, although Heredia's imagination was roused by a Romantic vision of the American wilderness, and he was able to give free rein to this vision in his verse "Niágara" and in passages of the corresponding letters, his understanding of the United States was also pragmatic and forward looking. He saw that the young nation was undergoing rapid demographic and technological change, and that advances in transportation and communications were "overthrowing the tyranny of distance" in the westward-expanding republic.[19] The Erie Canal was for him a striking example of the economic and technological development that was achievable in a republic of free citizens.[20] He was the direct beneficiary of the burgeoning publication and journalistic industries in the United States of the 1820s; his access to books in diverse languages in New York, and his opportunity to publish his own works there in his native Spanish, had a significant effect upon his literary trajectory. His letters take note of institutions of higher learning and culture, like Yale College and the Philadelphia Museum, and even of humbler indicators of the diffusion of literacy and culture in the American hinterland, like the curious library boat that plied the Erie Canal.

Heredia's admiration for the United States was clearly influenced by individual Americans he knew. While his difficulties with English and other challenges during his stay prevented him from completely overcoming his outsider status, he had amiable associations with people like the skipper who loaned him warm clothing on the voyage to Boston and remained an important ally, the New York bookbinders and booksellers whose shops he haunted, and the shipping merchants on whose services he depended for communication with home. Heredia must have been on very good terms as well with his students at the school where he taught Spanish for a few months. His New York edition of *Poesías* includes a brief preface in English expressing hope that the volume will help Americans learn Spanish, a "little service of an exiled youth," offered as "an expression of gratitude for the asylum he has found in this happy country!"

Indeed, such friendly acquaintances helped Heredia to view the culture and character of his country of refuge in an almost unfailingly positive light. His letters suggest a special appreciation for what he perceived as the pragmatism and unflappability of Americans. He notes their capacity for organizing for action in a peaceable and autonomous way, whether fighting fires in Philadelphia or protesting politically in New York. He observes a keen sense of justice and egalitarianism in the Americans around him, evident in his anecdotes of the New York demonstration against the wrong done to DeWitt Clinton,[21] and the reprimand given to the expatriate Joseph Bonaparte by his proletarian New Jersey neighbors. Such examples seem to reflect Heredia's belief in the beneficial effect that republican governments have on the private and civic virtue of individual citizens. He was charmed as well by the neoclassical confections by which the young United States gestured toward an imagined august past: a bank building in Philadelphia that replicated the Parthenon; backwoods towns in upstate New York that carried lofty names from antiquity, like Utica, Rome, Syracuse, and Palmyra.

Heredia's observations of the American character were not without touches of ironic detachment. His letters offer a few trenchant anecdotes of Yankee competitiveness—for example, that of a frantic and pointless race between canal boat captains—and shrewdness in business dealings. But in general his letters show a disinclination to overtly criticize any important aspect of American life and culture. For example, despite the anti-slavery sentiments that he expressed elsewhere,[22] his extant letters make no mention of slavery in the United States. In a letter of June 1824, while describing the pleasant landscapes along the Erie Canal, he writes: "At the same time that I admired them with pleasure, I felt free of the iron hand that pressed my heart in the fields of Cuba when I remembered that their bounty was born of the sweat, at times of the blood, of so many miserable slaves." While it was true that the small family farms of upstate New York did not depend upon massive use of slave labor like in the American South, Heredia surely knew that slavery existed in the United States. Indeed, the state of New York would not definitively abolish it until 1827. Yet he was silent on this matter, as he was on other social and economic ills that he must have witnessed during his North American stay. His cherished ideal of republican government and its moral benefits may have compelled him to omit any discrepant elements. Especially in his travel letters, which he perhaps knew might be published in Cuba, he may have desired to present such an idealized image of the United States as an example for Spanish American nations as they attempted to forge an emancipated future.

Heredia and Nineteenth-Century Inter-American Literary Relations

In a letter of June 29, 1825, Heredia told his mother that he was sending along three copies of his *Poesías*, just off the New York presses, and that another batch would soon be on its way to Cuba. Fewer than six weeks later, an anonymous review of the book appeared in Spanish in the *New York American* newspaper.[23] In a preface to the review, the editors explained that they were publishing "the critique, as it was communicated for this paper, without, as [they] first thought of doing, translating it," noting that "those whose knowledge of the Spanish would enable them to relish the extracts from [the] poems" contained in the review "would also like to read in the same tongue the opinions which a Spaniard entertains of them." The review, evidently written by someone who knew Heredia's circumstances very well, is unreserved in its praise. It ends with the following wish: "May fortune treat him more kindly; but in the honorable expatriation occasioned by his constant, generous efforts on behalf of liberty, and amidst all the troubles that the enemies of his homeland may cause him, he should be as sure of the appreciation of good men as he is of the hatred of despots." The editors echoed the reviewer's praise: "We willingly add our testimony to that of the writer of the critique, as to the merits of this little volume, which we have read with much gratification. There are throughout, in the poems which compose it, traits of the truest genius . . ."

That summer of 1825 saw Heredia engaged in another work for publication: a translation of the speech that Massachusetts congressman and famed orator Daniel Webster delivered at the Bunker Hill monument in Boston on June 17, commemorating the fiftieth anniversary of the iconic Revolutionary War battle. The speech celebrated not only the Revolution, but also the freedom, progress, and prosperity of the American republic since. Heredia must have been particularly stirred by the passages of Webster's oration that extolled the independence struggles on the South American continent. His translation was published in New York by mid-August, and soon was reviewed anonymously in the *United States Literary Gazette*. The reviewer recognized the salubrious effect that Webster's speech, rendered in Spanish, would have on South American readers: "This oration will make them know better, and respect more, the early founders and martyrs of American liberty. It will do honour to our country, and good to South America." The reviewer also saw the speech as potentially useful to North American readers: "Señor Heredia, of New York, is a gentleman who has executed, in our opinion extremely well, the task of translator. We recommend the work to those who are studying Spanish; and we recommend, also, that they use the original, to ascertain the doubtful meaning of a word in the translation, just as freely as they would use a dictionary."[24]

In August, Heredia departed for Mexico, never to return to the United States. But his recent publications continued to stir some interest in New York and Boston. In January 1827, an anonymously translated version of "Niágara" appeared in the *United States Review and Literary Gazette*. This new journal, the successor to the *United States Literary Gazette*, was edited by William Cullen Bryant, on his way to recognition as his country's foremost poet. Around this time Bryant embarked upon the serious study of the Spanish language and developed what would be a lifelong interest in Spanish and Spanish American literature.[25] The translation of "Niágara" was soon credited to him—and indeed sometimes is today—and it was widely assumed that he and Heredia had been personally acquainted in New York. The matter was debated by twentieth-century scholars until documents emerged showing that the translation of "Niágara" was executed mostly by a friend of Bryant's, with some retouching provided by the latter, and that Bryant and Heredia had never met.[26] In any case, this English rendering of the poem was to have a long life of its own. In 1827 a lengthy fragment of it appeared in the first edition of *The National Reader*, a textbook for American schoolchildren, and in subsequent multiple editions. Longfellow included it in his seminal collection *The Poets and Poetry of Europe* (1845), and it has appeared in other anthologies from the mid-nineteenth century to the present day—sometimes, in recent years, as an example of early Latino literature in the United States. The venerable status of this translation is confirmed by a bronze plaque dedicated to

Heredia at Niagara Falls, bearing an excerpt of the translated poem, on the parapet at Table Rock on the Canadian side.

These three episodes in the literary career of Heredia—the 1825 Spanish-language review of his *Poesías*, his 1825 published translation of Daniel Webster's Bunker Hill speech, and the auspicious 1827 publication of the English translation of his "Niágara"—reflect a broader phenomenon: the rich cross-cultural and cross-linguistic relations between the Anglophone and Hispanic worlds in the 1820s, with special import for inter-American literary relations.[27] During that decade, Andrés Bello engaged in intense intellectual and literary activity in England, where he was to publish, among other things, the influential *Repertorio americano* (1826). Washington Irving embarked upon travels in Spain, one result of which was his celebrated *Tales of the Alhambra* (1832), which effectively introduced the idea of Romantic Spain to the Anglo-American world. Félix Varela began an important trajectory of Spanish-language publishing in Philadelphia and New York, including the pro-independence journal *El Habanero* (1824–1826). George Ticknor, having returned from extensive travels in Europe, devised the first syllabus for the study of Spanish literature at Harvard (1823). In the United States, sketches and news from Spain and Spanish America appeared frequently in the *United States Literary Gazette* and similar publications, as did reviews of books published in Spanish and reviews of Spanish and English grammars for those seeking to learn either language.

The phenomenon reflected a number of factors. The upheavals caused by Napoleon's invasion of Spain, Spain's thwarted interval of constitutional rule, and the Spanish American wars of independence all resulted in the emigration or exile of influential Spaniards and Spanish Americans to England and the United States. Anglo-American Romantics like Irving fell under the spell of Spain's heroic past and "primitive" present, tinged with Orientalist exoticism. The incipient age of steam and the development of canal systems in the 1820s made movement within and among nations more practicable. A sense of solidarity arose among many Anglo and Spanish Americans resulting from their similar independence struggles and subsequent processes of national self-definition. That solidarity sometimes was expressed in poetry. In his "La victoria de Junín, Canto a Bolívar" of 1825, the Ecuadorian poet José Joaquín Olmedo called for the newly liberated South American nations to receive "the sacred kiss of fraternal friendship"[28] of their North American neighbor (Hills 73). In turn, writers in the United States like James Gates Percival saw the nascent South

American republics as "sister[s] in freedom," and called for "one fraternal band" of nations that would "spurn the chains / that tyrants forge," as Percival wrote in his 1821 "Ode on the Emancipation of South America" (403). Within this general picture of North- and South-American solidarity, Cuba was a special case. Still in the grip of Spain, it inspired particular concern in the United States, where debates about its future, including potential annexation, were prevalent, as they were in Cuba itself.[29]

These trends converged in Heredia, his experience living and writing in the United States, and his early reception by literary North Americans. As already noted, his letters and correspondence express almost unqualified admiration for the United States, and he regarded its republican government and institutions as a model for Cuba and the rest of Spanish America. During his time in exile, he strove to learn English and became much more familiar with recent literature written in that language, some of which he translated into Spanish. Through recreational travel, he indulged his curiosity about North American geography, technology, culture, and manners, and in his travel letters he endeavored to interpret these for a Cuban reader. Publication possibilities in Spanish in New York, and increased interest in showcasing works translated from other languages into English in North American periodicals, gave Heredia for a time a select and favorably disposed audience in the United States.

However, other factors conspired to allow Heredia and his work only partial integration with the Anglo-American literary world of the 1820s. For all his curiosity about his country of refuge, Heredia knew that he was just passing through. While he read English well enough to produce good translations and be influenced by American and English authors, he did not have sufficient conversational mastery of the language to engage with New York literary circles. He was hindered by his frequent ill health, his preoccupation with his legal status in Cuba, his limited professional prospects in the United States, and his overall situation as a cultural outsider. His gaze always turned nostalgically toward Cuba, or longingly toward a life in a Spanish-speaking country where the full range of his talents might flourish. While his poetry attracted the notice of English-language readers and those with some ability in Spanish in the United States, by the time that attention began to manifest itself in print Heredia had already left the country, never to return. Thus, aside from "Niágara," which was to have a long anthologized life, the interest that Heredia and his works stirred in the United States was relatively narrow and short-lived.[30] For these reasons, his place in the history of inter-American literary relations was correspondingly limited, if of some enduring resonance. Perhaps the present volume will contribute to a renewed understanding and appreciation of José María Heredia in the United States and beyond.

The Translations in This Volume

The present volume gathers a significant portion of José María Heredia's correspondence and poetry for the first time in English translation.[31] The period to which these letters and verses correspond—the twenty months that Heredia spent in the United States from November 1823 to September 1825—is not an arbitrary choice. Heredia produced much of his best poetic work during his stay in New York, along with an important body of travel letters. The letters he sent to family and friends in Cuba during these months tell a story with a certain narrative arc. They chronicle his flight from Cuba to escape arrest; his tribulations, travels, and personal evolution during his life in exile in the United States; and his departure for Mexico when his health and ambitions demanded a more favorable climate and culture. Most were penned in New York City, where Heredia lived a few blocks from a waterfront that saw significant ship traffic with Havana and Matanzas, and among a small colony of Cuban expatriates whose frequent comings and goings facilitated his communication with home. But because his letters and those of his correspondents often went astray or were intercepted, Heredia found himself obliged to reiterate things in multiple letters; the present volume omits a number from this period whose content duplicates that of others.

The letters vary greatly in length and character. Some are expansive, meticulously crafted, and of real literary merit, while others are short and hastily written. Letters written to Heredia during this period mostly have not survived, yet the content of the letters that he received from his mother and from his Uncle Ignacio, especially, often can be surmised based on Heredia's responses. The tone of his letters is strongly suggestive of the nature of his relationship with his correspondents, and to some extent even reveals aspects of their personalities.

The majority of the letters that Heredia wrote from New York were addressed to his mother. María de la Merced was about forty years old when her son fled Cuba, leaving her with modest resources to run a household with four young daughters and some domestic slaves. Having shared her husband's precarious existence when he was a crown official in a time of revolution, she was alert to the dangers faced by her son as a failed insurrectionist on the lam. She clearly disagreed with him as to whether he should stay in the United States or move on to Europe or South America. In letter after letter, with increasing urgency, Heredia begged his mother to send his law diploma so that he could move to a warmer climate and make a living there, citing the devastating effects of the northern winters on his health. But María de la Merced evidently felt that Heredia was safer in the United States than in countries in revolutionary or post-revolutionary turmoil; moreover, her dream that her son might be granted a pardon would be foiled should he relocate to a country in open rebellion to Spain. Heredia waited until his mother gave him express permission to relocate to Mexico before he did so. Both culture and the family dynamic probably explain his obedience, although in many ways he was resolute and self-sufficient beyond his years.

On other matters, Heredia was more forceful and directive with his mother, giving her stern advice on how she should deal with friends and relations, on how and where she should invest her money, and on how she should regard his actions that led to his conviction in the *Soles y Rayos* conspiracy. It is clear that María de la Merced had expressed worry that her son's letter to Hernández Morejón had served only to further entangle and compromise him. After her son was sentenced to exile in Spain, she urged him to accept the pardon that family friends were prepared to seek for him. Heredia firmly rejected both notions, defending the integrity of his letter to the judge and refusing to accept a pardon that might be seen as an admission of guilt. Heredia argues from a position of scrupulous principle, backed by his legal training. María de la Merced may have heard echoes of her husband's voice in her son's letters, and in some ways seems to have deferred to him as head of the household.

Ignacio Heredia Campuzano was about eight years older than his nephew José María, and the two shared an intense, fraternal friendship. While Heredia regarded his uncle with great respect, his letters to him are more expansive and less formal than those to his mother. Both men were lawyers by training, and had many acquaintances and experiences in common. Heredia's letters to Ignacio thus have frequent inside allusions and jokes, and at times a certain "man of the world" quality. The two shared a love of traveling, and among Heredia's best-crafted letters are those he wrote to Ignacio describing his journeys in the northeast United States. In his letters, Heredia returned repeatedly to a place and scene that he held dear: a table set up in the shade of his uncle's coffee grove, where the two men had spent many happy hours in conversation. Heredia imagined his uncle there, reading aloud his nephew's long, descriptive letters, and answering them in turn at siesta time on Sunday afternoons. The spot also is evoked in Heredia's emotional dedication to Ignacio of his New York *Poesías* (1825).[32] The memory of blissful afternoons shared with his uncle in that cherished place must have sustained the young Heredia through many a freezing New York night and bout of illness.

The first letter that Heredia wrote from the United States at the end of November 1823 was to his friend Pepilla Arango, the young woman whose family had provided him refuge at their plantation at the time of the order for his arrest. In its content and highly literary quality, the letter is a prose complement to the epistolary poem "To Emilia" (also included in the present volume). It is filled with emotional hyperbole and melodrama. Heredia gives a florid account of his clandestine departure from Matanzas, his voyage on the *Galaxy*, and his first encounter with the desolate winter landscapes of New England. He crafts a kind of Gothic tale with himself as its ill-fated hero, while Pepilla is his *amiga dulcísima*, his benefactress and the object of his chaste devotion. None of Heredia's other extant letters have quite the tone and technique of this one; he seems to filter his own experience through his readings in literature.

Heredia's letter to close friend Silvestre Luis Alfonso y Soler in Havana (February 28, 1824) gives a brief account of his escape from Cuba, his situation in New York, and his desire to publish his poetry there. The letter is one of thirteen from Heredia to Alfonso that survive from what must have been a steady correspondence from the time the two young men met in Havana around 1819 until Alfonso's death in 1828 at age twenty-six. When Heredia wrote Alfonso this letter, he apparently did not know that his friend would soon join him in New York.[33] Alfonso would prove to be a great source of support during difficult times, including the serious illness that Heredia suffered in the winter of 1824–1825. Heredia's letter to Alfonso included herein contains political and personal confidences, and gives evidence of the great trust and affection between the two.[34]

Heredia's letter (July 10, 1824) to Cristóbal Madan, the employee of Goodhue & Co. who was of such help to fellow Cuban expatriates in New York,[35] is expeditious and playful. As he asks for his assistance with some practical matters relating to the delivery of mail and books, Heredia addresses Madan as the "Consul" and teases him for the good-heartedness that constantly makes him the object of such requests. In a self-deprecating way, Heredia even tries out his "makeshift" English on him.

Heredia's letter to Domingo del Monte from New York (March 15, 1825) reflects a difficult chapter in their friendship. At the time of his flight from Cuba, Heredia had reason to believe that Del Monte, in league with his persecutors, had betrayed him. It took several years of pained correspondence, interspersed with resentful silences and hampered by letters lost or crossed in the mail, for the matter to be cleared up and the two friends to reconcile. The tone of the letter included in this volume—the only one that Heredia wrote to Del Monte from New York that survives—is dignified and wounded. The letter has rhetorical flourishes and flashes of erudition that give a sense of the intellectual tenor of the relationship between the two, and that suggest a desire on Heredia's part to impress a friend whose judgment he greatly respected.[36]

The present volume annotates Heredia's correspondence with notes that identify persons, places and other references. With the advantage of having consulted some of the original manuscripts or early manuscript copies of Heredia's letters in the Escoto Collection at Harvard's Houghton Library and in the Biblioteca Nacional José Martí in Havana, this editor has been able to correct a number of mistakes that appear in previous editions of Heredia's correspondence published in Spanish. Each letter is headed with an indication of its addressee, followed by the letter's sources using the following abbreviations: *Escoto*, *BNJM* (Biblioteca Nacional José Martí), *Moda* (*La Moda o Recreo Semanal del Bello Sexo*), and *Augier*, the last of these for the nearly complete collection of Heredia's letters published by Ángel Augier, embracing the full span of Heredia's life (Heredia, *Epistolario*).

The nine poems chosen for translation in this volume all have an autobiographical dimension that complements the story told in Heredia's letters. The first, "A Emilia," is an epistolary poem addressed to Pepilla Arango (Emilia being a poetic pseudonym). Like Heredia's November 1823 letter to Pepilla from Massachusetts, it gives evidence of the high esteem in which Heredia held her—an affection that went beyond gratitude. In an 1826 letter sent from Mexico, Heredia reminded his mother that he would never forget that "without [Pepilla], he would have died on the gallows or, even worse, in the depths of a Spanish dungeon." He assured his mother that he never had matrimonial designs on Pepilla, but that they were joined forever by a "sweeter and more enduring" bond. In a letter sent a year later to a friend, Heredia admitted that, if he had a sufficient fortune and were not in exile, he would offer Pepilla his hand in marriage.[37]

Details of the poem date its composition to sometime after April 1824. That month, the prominent conspirator of the *Caballeros Racionales* group, Dr. Juan José Hernández y Cano, died soon upon release from a Havana prison, some said by poisoning. This is the "dear, departed friend" whose death Heredia laments in the poem. There are other highly charged political elements in the poem as well, including the poet's denunciation of slavery in Cuba, his impassioned call to Cubans to stand up to "vile tyrants," and his declared intent to take up arms in the independence struggle. These militant sentiments probably explain why Heredia chose to exclude the poem from the 1825 New York edition of his *Poesías*. "A Emilia" first appeared in the 1832 Toluca edition, in which Heredia, then resigned to likely permanent exile from Cuba, included his more combative poems and restored stanzas he had previously suppressed.

Heredia's "Placeres de la melancolía" offers a compendium of Romantic topics, woven in autobiographical threads under the overarching theme of Melancholy. The title echoes that of Thomas Warton's 1745 poem "The Pleasures of Melancholy," but its chief inspiration most likely was Milton's "Il Penseroso" (1645). In that poem, Milton invokes Melancholy as goddess and muse, as does Heredia, although for the Cuban poet Melancholy also is personified as mother, wife, lover, and friend—womanly figures who offer him a "balm of consolation and peace." While Milton may have been Heredia's most immediate influence, ultimately his poem harks back to Robert Burton's *The Anatomy of Melancholy* (1621), a kind of urtext for Romantics who treated the theme, like Keats in his 1819 "Ode on Melancholy."

In "Placeres de la melancolía," melancholy and contemplation are intimately linked. The poet reflects upon moments of his past, present, and future life with sadness commingled with the consolation derived from reflection itself. These moments include his solitary and dreamy childhood, his adolescence marked by erotic dissipation, his mourning for his father, his suffering in exile and yearning for his homeland, his longing for an "ideal wife" with whom he might enjoy a "sweeter and more lasting" kind of love, and his restless desire to travel to the Old World and meditate upon the ruins of lost civilizations.

Heredia returned to the theme of ancient ruins—a favorite of the Romantics—in "Atenas y Palmira." The poem clearly is an adaptation of a segment of the aforementioned "The Pleasures of Melancholy" by Warton, a fact that was not acknowledged in the 1832 Toluca edition in which the poem first appeared, and which heretofore has not been noted by Heredia scholars. While he introduces some changes (like contrasting Athens with Palmyra instead of Persepolis), Heredia follows the sequence of images and ideas in Warton's poem point by point. The scarcity of rhyme in "Atenas y Palmira" approaches blank verse, surely another influence from Warton. Indeed, Heredia's adaptation possibly was an experiment in blank verse composition.[38]

Heredia may have composed "Atenas y Palmira" during his time in New York. An annotation in an early manuscript draft of the poem indicates that it was written "after seeing the panoramas of Athens and Palmyra."[39] Because Heredia never visited the lands of antiquity, the word *panoramas* must refer not to real landscapes, but to painted ones. Significantly, in 1824 John Vanderlyn's "Rotunda" in New York City displayed a 360-degree painting of Athens and surroundings.[40] Heredia, who lived a short walk from the Rotunda, surely would have wanted to see such a novelty. Thus, "Atenas y Palmira" may have been inspired both by a painting in the round of ancient splendors and by Warton's poem in English, which offered Heredia rich imagery and the example of a freer metric form in which he evidently had an interest.

The next two poems correspond to Heredia's summer travels in 1824. "A Washington" is presented as an apostrophe delivered at the first president's tomb. When it appeared in the Toluca edition, it bore the subtitle "escrita en Monte-Vernon" and the year of composition (1824). In February of that year, Heredia wrote his uncle Ignacio about his spring travel plans, which included a trip to Philadelphia, Baltimore, and Washington. The Philadelphia leg of that journey is amply described in subsequent letters, but no mention of travels farther south appears in Heredia's extant correspondence. Accordingly, the indication that the poem was written in situ might be taken with a grain of salt. But even if Heredia never visited Washington's gravesite, the sense of moment and place that his poem conveys is vivid, and its sentiments are undoubtedly heartfelt.

Heredia's admiration for Washington was unqualified. In the American founding father he saw a model of the personal and civic virtue that was necessary for the success of a republican form of government as well as a result of it. He mentioned Washington repeatedly in correspondence, and he devoted several essays to him. His sources probably included early biographies like John Marshall's influential one of 1803–1807, and patriotic poetry like that of Philip Freneau, who also eulogized the first president. Heredia's poem begins with the proverbial "first in war, first in peace, first in the hearts of his countrymen" coined by Henry Lee in his 1799 "Funeral Oration on the Death of General Washington." From such sources the poem draws the conventional high points of the Virginian's life and career: his resolution in battle, his temperance in abjuring absolute power, his wisdom as president, his noble retirement at Mount Vernon.

Reading Heredia's "Niágara" in tandem with his letters to Ignacio of June 1824 gives the sense that the poem was the inevitable outcome—perhaps even a primary motive—of his trip to the Niagara frontier. Through his readings before and during the trip, Heredia was well prepared to encounter the "natural sublime" at Niagara, and when he did, it demanded an immediate response in poetic form. The opening lines describe the moment of inspiration through which the poem comes into being, as the poet takes up the lyre, the "divine gift" of poetry now restored to him. In the corresponding letter, Heredia claimed that he had in fact "hurriedly composed" "Niágara" at the edge of the falls. Two pieces of evidence suggest that this was not just a Romantic pose. The first is that with his letter Heredia enclosed a copy of the poem for Ignacio. The second is that during that same summer, Heredia's fellow exile Tomás Gener saw the poem inscribed in the author's hand in a guest book at the falls.[41] If, as it seems, the poem came into being almost fully formed, it is a remarkable instance of swift and assured composition by a young poet.

Heredia's "Proyecto," first published in the 1832 Toluca edition but dating from his New York stay, offers a fantasy of transformation, freedom, and revenge. The speaker imagines becoming a corsair on the high seas to escape a world in the grip of tyranny, and to prey upon the aristocrats who have been the agents of that oppression. The poem is melodramatic and fanciful, but its vehement condemnation of despotism and corruption is consistent with convictions that Heredia held throughout his life.

With "Proyecto," Heredia perhaps wanted to try his hand at a topic with significant precedents in Romantic literature: that of the pirate antihero. As several scholars have noted, he may have been inspired by Lord Byron's "The Corsair" (1814).[42] He also may have known Sir Walter Scott's *The Pirate* (1822) and James Fenimore Cooper's nautical romance *The Pilot* (1824). In any case, pirates were not just a literary topic for Heredia. His correspondence from New York reveals that he was constantly planning some sea voyage or another and was well aware of the real privateers and *filibusteros* who plagued Atlantic shipping.[43] Whatever his sources of inspiration, Heredia showed a flair for nautical themes, as in his letters describing his tempestuous voyage north upon escape from Cuba, and in the set piece in "Niágara" in which he describes having reveled in the danger of a storm at sea.

Heredia composed the "Himno del desterrado" during his sea voyage from New York to Mexico. As the schooner *Chasseur* threaded the Florida Straits, he caught sight of the northern coast of Cuba and the peak known as the *Pan de Matanzas*, a familiar landmark for *matanceros*. That moment was the catalyst for Heredia's poem, with its vigorous expression of the range of his emotions as an exile, from melancholy nostalgia to militant patriotism. The poem contrasts Cuba's physical beauty with the tyranny under which it suffers; Heredia decries the moral degradation of his homeland and exhorts his countrymen to take up arms for independence.

Heredia published "Himno del desterrado" in a Mexican newspaper within weeks of his arrival.[44] The definitive version appeared in the 1832 Toluca edition, and, as already noted, Villaverde's *Cecilia Valdés* comments on the great impact that it had upon an entire generation of pro-independence Cubans in the 1830s. Nor did the poem go unnoticed in nineteenth-century North American literary circles. An English translation of a portion of it appeared in a survey of works by various Spanish American poets in the *North American Review* in 1849. In that survey, the anonymous reviewer and translator says of Heredia that "as a patriot, his sufferings, bravely incurred and calmly borne in her behalf, testify even more loudly than his eloquent words to the depths and strength of affection with which he clung to the best hopes for his country."[45]

Heredia composed his "Vuelta al Sur" on that same sea voyage from New York to Mexico. The poem describes the sense of physical and emotional well-being that the poet experiences as the ship enters tropical latitudes. As in "Niágara," the poet's natural surroundings stir poetic inspiration, and he once more reaches for his lyre—now *Cuba*'s lyre, whose broken strings are made whole by the warm breezes that caress it. But the tone of the poem does not remain languorous; the poet feels the ardor of his youth revived by the sun of the tropics, an ardor now transformed into patriotic passion.

When the poem first appeared in a Mexican journal in 1827, it contained four stanzas that Heredia omitted from the Toluca edition.[46] Perhaps the references in these stanzas to his recent banishment from Cuba and to his impetuous eagerness to take up arms for Cuban independence were more relevant when he composed the poem than they were in 1832, when Heredia had settled into a new life in Mexico as a married man with children. The translation in the present volume includes these stanzas in italics, so as to restore the original coherence of the poem and to capture more fully the vehemence of Heredia's feelings when he wrote it.

The sonnet "Inmortalidad" takes up a theme that Heredia returned to throughout his career. "Niágara" closes with the hope that the poet's verses will prove as eternal as the great cataract itself; the poet imagines a kind of after-death apotheosis in which he will continue to hear the "echoes of his fame." In "A Emilia" and "Vuelta al Sur," the poet imagines eternal fame gained through a glorious death as poet-warrior and martyr for Cuban independence. In an 1829 essay, Heredia would explore the meaning and purpose of posthumous fame, linking it with virtue: fame can be the recompense for a virtuous life, and the vehicle for passing virtue on from generation to generation. In a poem of 1834, also titled "Inmortalidad," Heredia would offer a lengthy and systematic argument for the existence of an immortal soul.[47] In the sonnet included in the present volume, Heredia expresses the idea succinctly and artfully, and in a way that reveals a fundamental religious faith that his letters mention only in passing.

For all nine poems, the translator has endeavored to choose compatible metrical forms and rhyme schemes in English that might elevate the translations from merely accurate renderings to aesthetically pleasing poems in their own right.

The first seven poems are *silvas*, a preferred verse form for Heredia and his generation. The *silva* consists of predominantly hendecasyllabic lines mixed with some heptasyllabic lines in no fixed order, with occasional rhyme. Heredia's *silvas* show considerable variation in the predominance of the hendecasyllables, including sometimes to the exclusion of heptasyllables, as in "A Emilia." The presence of rhyme varies considerably as well, from the rather insistent rhymes of "Proyecto" to the virtual blank verse of "Atenas y Palmira."

For the translation of the *silvas* "A Emilia," "Placeres de la melancolía," "Atenas y Palmira," and "A Washington," the translator has chosen freely combined pentameter and trimeter lines that settle mostly into an iambic rhythm, and with rhymes that arise opportunely. For "Niágara," the translator has elected freely combined tetrameter and trimeter lines with occasional rhyme, which offer a somewhat more streamlined rendering of the poem compared both to Heredia's original *silva* and to the 1827 translation associated with Bryant. For the *silva* "Proyecto," the translator has chosen the "ballad stanza"—quatrains in which the first and third unrhymed lines have four stresses, and the second and fourth rhyming lines have three. This gives the poem a faster pace and more persistent rhythm than in Heredia's original. Use of the ballad stanza was suggested by two classics of English-language poetry with a maritime theme: Coleridge's "Rime of the Ancient Mariner" (1798) and Longfellow's "The Wreck of the Hesperus" (1842).

"Himno del desterrado" and "Vuelta al Sur" are written in decasyllabic lines in the *octava italiana* or *octava aguda* metric form. The translation of "Himno del desterrado" uses quatrains in pentameter with rhymes in the even-numbered lines, while that of "Vuelta al Sur" is once more in ballad stanza, reflecting the poem's maritime theme. The translation of "Inmortalidad" follows the structure of the Petrarchan sonnet.

For the poems, as for the letters, the translator has endeavored to use language that is neither falsely archaic nor anachronistically modern. Poetic license in the form of departures from standard syntax or the use of contractions like "o'er" or "where'er" has been necessary to maintain meter and rhyme schemes. As always with translating poetry, the balance between fidelity to the meaning of the original and the aesthetic autonomy of the new rendering has been a judgment call; the facing original Spanish and translated English versions of the poems will allow readers to assess the decisions made by the translator in this regard.[48] Unless otherwise indicated, the editor is responsible for all the translations that appear in the present volume, including in the notes.

In a letter of October 14, 1826, Domingo del Monte urged Heredia to turn from translating French and Italian tragedies to writing more original works of his own. He reminded his friend that "the translator's glory is a meager one; if the work is pleasing, the author is divine, and if not, the translator is infernal" (Heredia, *Epistolario* 283). While that adage has some truth to it, it is not the whole story. However meager the glory, the rewards of translation are great when working with an author like José María Heredia. His youthful letters and verses were the outpourings of a prodigious mind and a sensitive and generous soul. For this translator, he has been the best of travel companions.

Selected Letters, 1823–1825

To Francisco Hernández Morejón[1] [Augier no. 24]

Matanzas, November 6, 1823

Señor Don Francisco Hernández Morejón

My Dear Sir:
   As I depart this city in order to safeguard my freedom, threatened as I am by proceedings in which you have a role, I feel I must make this declaration of the reasons that compel me to take this step, so that the latter will not be interpreted in a way that is more unfavorable than it merits. Don Juan Guillermo Aranguren has told me that he and his brother-in-law Don Antonio Betancourt[2] have denounced me as a member of a secret society which is being prosecuted, called the *Caballeros Racionales*. Upon receiving this news I knew that my imprisonment was inevitable, since those two witnesses were themselves more than deserving of it.[3] It is said that these proceedings are directed against a conspiracy discovered in Havana, and which is accused of preparing a scene of horror the very semblance of which is sufficient to make any righteous man tremble with indignation and fright.[4] My integrity has not allowed me to countenance the prospect of finding myself mingled in prison with men to whom such abominable and horrifying plans have been attributed. It is true that some overheated theories of social improvement may have induced me to fall into error, but my soul is not stained with sanguinary projects, nor is it susceptible

to them. I do not know if the others who are accused are in the same situation as I, since almost a year ago I broke off all close contact with the *Racionales*, a group I believed to be defunct. When I knew them, they only endeavored peacefully to prepare public opinion for independence. That should appear in the proceedings.

But while these proceedings unfold and remove the veil from your eyes, and show me as I truly am, I wish to preserve my liberty in a foreign country. It is painful for me to go to breathe the air of any place other than my homeland. Along the happy banks of the San Juan River I am leaving behind . . . suffice it to say a good mother who is drowning in tears of affliction.[5] But necessity so orders things, and the sacrifice must be made. Oh! That sacrifice is sufficiently rigorous punishment for my offenses such as they are, whose origin must be pardonable in the eyes of the thoughtful man who will gauge correctly the steps taken by a youth of eighteen years upon the slippery ground of the times in which we live, in which diverging ideas of patriotism have tripped up even more experienced men. Not even the faintest idea of contributing to a conflagration of my country in civil war ever entered my heart. Sweet-tempered and sensitive by nature and upbringing, and as befits my years, how could I look without horror upon a future of frightful calamities, such as those that always accompany such wars? No one who knows me could believe me capable of such a thing, and I cannot hold myself in lesser esteem because of a misplaced notion that, while now subjecting me to misfortune, does not close the door to the correction of my error, which is limited to the dimensions I have indicated.

I reiterate that time will find me innocent and will make you see that that is true, and that I have not deserved the misfortune that has befallen me, despite the poor light in which the indictment may have made me appear.

The day will come when I will return to this city and devote myself to my peaceful occupations in the bosom of my family, but I do not wish to await that day in a jail cell. I beg you then that you see fit to give this letter all possible publicity so as to realize the effect indicated at the outset, and that you add this original to the judicial documents so that at every point the motives for my flight are on record, a flight made necessary by the news that I received from Aranguren and by impulses of conscience overwhelmed by the horrendous crimes that have been planned.

Since it is to be feared that some of those who accuse me in the future will include me in their reports to try to gain some benefit, believing that they cannot harm me with their slander since I am absent, I also beg that, upon interrogating them, if it falls within your authority, you read them this letter, so that they will know that as soon as the criminal proceedings have concluded, or before if I have been able exactly to assess the accusations, I will appear in person to clear my name, and since it will be easy to refute anyone who has lied, I will be implacable in the pursuit of my slanderers.

I have the honor of according you the consideration and respect with which I remain your most humble servant,

José María Heredia

To Josefa ("Pepilla") Arango y Manzano[6] [Augier no. 25]

Tarpaulin Cove, November 31, 1823[7]

My Dear Friend:

I shall begin to fulfill my promise to write you about the land of my exile, although I have not yet reached the end of my journey. Surrounded by strangers with their barbarous and incomprehensible tongue, and distressed by the frozen silence of this climate, I take pen in hand in the eager hope that to speak with you, my rescuer, my sweet friend, my sister in love, will help me to forget the horror of my present situation, if just for a few moments.

I shall not attempt to portray here the terrible days of my banishment. Were you not there to view them yourself, and did you not join in my afflictions and dangers with the most intense sympathy? Every time that I see the moon resplendent in the purest of skies, and its rays refracted in the tranquil surface of the waters, I shall remember the last night that I spent on the banks of the San Juan River. I shall hear again the long-desired signal, and see the celestial young woman who, with the most affectionate attentions, tempered the horrors of my situation. I shall see her hide her tears and extend her hand to me in a final farewell. I shall feel, beating upon my desperate heart, that of my benefactress, and I will feel the fragile little boat that evaded the vengeance of tyrants tremble beneath my feet.

I departed in silence from that beloved and ill-fated land, and, seated in the prow of that flimsy boat, I could scarcely sort out my feelings: my eyes rested in turn upon the city where so many loved ones wept for me, and upon the fortress[8] in which the most savage and insolent tyranny had imprisoned my unfortunate friends and had a cell ready for me. I felt moved simultaneously by tenderness and rage; my eyes were incapable of tears, my head was a burning volcano, and an inferno and death were in my heart.

More than once I felt tempted to throw myself into the sea and end my life, and I believe that all that dissuaded me was the prospect of dying unavenged. Bloody, ruinous designs presented themselves to my mind, and in them alone could I find a kind of dreadful relief. I am horrified now to remember what I might have been capable of in those terrible moments.

I spent the night on board, not many yards from that awful fortress, gazing at the lights burning in some of its cells. At dawn we weighed anchor, and I trembled when I saw the sails unfurl and, filling with a fresh wind, carry me out to sea. The ship ran aground, and amid the general confusion, I felt a kind of secret joy in finding my escape temporarily thwarted. But the damage was repaired and I spent all the next day seated in the stern of the ship, staring dully at the shore receding in the distance. As evening fell, the shoreline disappeared entirely, and only the Pan de Matanzas[9] was yet visible, like a shoal in the midst of the sea. In turn it was enveloped by the shadows of night, and still I strove to penetrate them with my vision, and to catch a farewell glimpse of the land of my birth. A flash of lightning revealed it to me for the last time.

What can I tell you of the sea journey? We were beset by the gales typical of the season, which were followed by great calms in which the churning sea still evoked the past storm. The early winter cold was uncomfortable to all, and most of all to me, since I was dressed as lightly as in our own torrid climate. Perhaps I would have perished had it not been for the humanity of the captain, who loaned me some of his own clothing.

I never have felt less afraid of the perils of the sea. I always have found a kind of pleasure in contemplating the furor of its unchained, roiling elements, and I never have heard the crash of thunder above me without feeling an intense, sublime emotion. But now amid the storm in all its fury, I spent hours at a time seated in the stern, gazing at the enraged sea or at the sky covered with fearsome clouds, sometimes laughing at the struggles of the crew, their confusion and their shouting. It was not that way when I arrived from Puerto Príncipe just four months ago, and a fortunate and tranquil future seemed to open before me.[10] Doubtlessly the value of life diminishes greatly for the man who has fallen into misfortune, who sees his existence only fraught with crimes and sorrows, and who regards the grave as his refuge from the storms of the world and the injustices of men.

The headwinds that prevented us from rounding Cape Cod compelled us to make anchor here, in one of the small islands near Falmouth, on the coast of Massachusetts. I went ashore and saw with horror just what winter is. A river was frozen. The countryside seemed to have been consumed by a recent fire. Not a single blade of grass alleviated the vision of such frightful aridness. Not a soul was to be seen, nor animal, nor insect. The only two buildings upon which my eyes could rest—a lighthouse and the keeper's cottage, entirely closed up—looked like tombs. To expand the picture that I am painting for you, I saw a sky covered in clouds whose uncertain horizon blended with a sea enveloped in fog . . . I stood there shuddering, believing I was with Milton in that immense solitude where the throne of death rises up.[11]

Without a doubt this terrible scene did much to cool the enthusiasm with which I greeted the land of liberty, which offers an immense refuge to all the oppressed of the world, and where that man of clear conscience, beneath the aegis of wise legislation, can raise his brow to the sun, and has only to fear the law which, protecting the innocent, is unerring and relentless in the remedying of his wrongs.

I went to have a look at the lighthouse, which is tended by a sailor who lost his leg in a naval combat during the last war with the British. His grateful homeland thus provides for his sustenance, and compensates him for the blood he shed on its behalf. The tidiness of his quarters, his own cleanliness and that of his wife and children, whose robust appearance bespoke their health and good fortune, and a small barn in which there was a cow and lots of fowl, did much to dissipate the sad impression that the first glimpse of his wooden leg had left me with. He clambered up the stairs of the lighthouse with the greatest agility. My own limbs, stiff with cold, prevented me from keeping up with him, and two or three times he stopped to wait for me. Gazing at me with pity, and taking one of my frozen hands in his, he spoke to me some affectionate and incomprehensible words.

The horrible cold weather has compelled me to take refuge indoors before a consoling fire. I shall finish this letter and then browse through some newspapers of which I will not understand a single syllable. Except for the chance to observe the curious dress and manners of these people, I shall be consumed by tedium in this absolute isolation.

Goodbye, my Emilia.
—H

To Ignacio Heredia Campuzano [BNJM; *Moda*; *Augier* no. 26]

Boston, December 4, 1823

Much loved Ignacio:

I did not want to embrace you when we parted, because I was afraid that my resolve would fail that ultimate test, and that it would be impossible for me to tear myself away from a land in which I was leaving behind so many loved ones. That feeling was so strong in me, that even as I crossed the dock to board ship, I had no fear that I would be discovered, and ruined. At that moment, prison almost seemed less distressing than to embark upon that trip. And I abandoned myself to my fate with neither hope nor trepidation. Once on board, I did not go below until the moment of departure, and then only because a small sailboat was heading toward us, and the captain was fearful. Our ship ran aground, and there was a great commotion. I returned to deck and stayed there until the morning, with my eyes set on Matanzas and the fortress . . .

The first three days out, we had beautiful weather. Then we were assailed by furious headwinds, or were becalmed but with rough seas that tore our sails. And on the 27th of the month at 40° latitude, we encountered such a deep freeze that the seawater congealed as the waves broke on deck, and formed sheets of ice that made it difficult for the crew to maneuver. Through sheer effort we arrived at an island called Nantucket; there we took on a pilot, but he got drunk and heaven knows why we didn't end up in pieces on the shore that night. We were obliged to backtrack about 15 leagues and make anchorage off another little island, where everything was frozen solid. For more on that, I will enclose a copy of my diary,[12] so that you and our friend Don Pedro can amuse yourselves with it in the coffee grove, the memory of which is not the least of my torments.

This morning we arrived at this port, and by chance I came across Bacon's merchant house.[13] I presented him with the bill of exchange and he accepted it. After that I went with the captain, a worthy fellow in every way, to his boarding house, where I had dinner, and where his landlady told me in French, through another resident, that I could stay there as long as I wanted, which, as long as money changed hands, I already knew to be the case. As you used to say, money is the universal language. They have shown me to a very nice room, with a fine bed, and all for five dollars a week. I have established myself, then, in the house of Mistress MacCondray, Brattle Street number 15. After tea, I retired to my room to write you and share with you some of my observations.

I have not yet made a decision regarding a trip to New York or Philadelphia. The cold in those cities is just about what it is here; and en route I would be exposed fully to it. Charleston is where the climate is more benign, but from here to there is some 500 leagues, a distance not so easily traveled in winter. I plan to stay here for a while, and if the weather turns much colder, I will resign myself to being a recluse next to the fire, and spend my time tackling the English language head-on, or have a go at my poetry.[14]

The worst thing is that I am deprived of my books. If my banishment is to continue even for one year, please ship them to me via Atkins, directed to Bacon, for him to deliver them to me. In any case, send me by the same channels, as soon as you can, the printed papers and manuscripts that were in the black trunk. If I have departed by then, Bacon will send them to me wherever I am.

Boston is a great city, and in its order and cleanliness, very beautiful. All the houses are of three or four stories, made of brick or cut stone and covered with shingled roofs, and all with glazed windows. The streets are wide and perfectly paved, with raised brick sidewalks on either side, to separate pedestrians from carriages. There is an infinite number of the latter, and the horses that pull them seem to me to be bigger and stronger than those of Cuba, although that may be a false impression. The streets are full of people at every hour of the day, and even so there is not the kind of clamor that you find in the streets of Havana. Of course, there are no black pushcart drivers here. I have never seen such pretty girls as I have today. If you had been in Boston, you never would have said what you did regarding Matanzas, about losing the notion of beauty. Although for all that, the famous *ship* doesn't exactly seem to you to be a sack of hay.[15]

December 5

All that I can say about the bed I spent the night in is what you have said of your bed in Bordeaux. Lunch was good, and I have found myself wandering aimlessly the streets of Boston, like a booby.[16]

The cold weather is still bearable, and hasn't affected me much. I do have a cold, although so does just about everyone else I see. It's a bad season.

What a beautiful city! I have been surprised above all by the great order that reigns in it. All of the houses have engraved plaques of copper or wood that indicate the name and occupation of their inhabitants, which is an excellent custom, and greatly facilitates business dealings.

Everyone seems employed, and I have not yet seen a beggar, nor even anyone who shows the signs of poverty or neglect. What a fortunate country, despite its harsh climate, blessed with Heaven's most benign favor.

I will close this letter and give it to Bacon so that he can send it along at the first opportunity. Please continue to write me via New York, directing your letters to H. Goodhue & Co. for them to send on to me, which can be done via that flatterer who went to the coffee grove with Bodan.[17]

Don't let them whitewash the state of my affairs. Speak with all frankness, and don't omit even the smallest details. And let me know about *the Ship*.

I am not sending a copy. One will accompany another much longer letter on the *Galaxy* which is returning your way in a few days. That will be a safer occasion to do so.

If this letter should arrive before the *Galaxy*, which I much doubt, I ask that you go to see those who gave me refuge, and convey to them my regards and gratitude.[18] I will write them via the *Galaxy*, but not now because the communication would be risky.

I don't know if you will be able to understand these last paragraphs, because the ink is almost frozen. I have nothing to tell you for Chea . . .[19] My regards and congratulations to Don Joaquín, to Félix Lanas, to Señor de la Riva, to Don Juan José Pérez, to Balboa, to Veguilla, to my dear tutor, to the great Abus, and to Don Pedro Hernández.

And remembrances to Abreu, to *the Ship*, to Josefa and Isabelita (tell them I think about them every evening at the hour of our social gatherings), and to Don Pedro and Dalcour. What a string of names! There is hardly anyone in Matanzas who does not matter to me.

Good-bye, don't forget me, and remember that my foremost vow is to return to Matanzas and live with you, since without that my happiness never will be complete.

Your most loving
José María

I have no need to tell you to embrace Rueda[20] for me. Don't forget to tell me all about the conspiracy hearings and how they are going.

Oh human misery! How many have been taken prisoner, if the judge has been made aware of who the chapter members are this year?[21] I forgot to mention that a certain *flatterer* has come to tell me that he would be *most pleased if I would want to go to Buenos Aires, for which trip he would provide free passage, aboard a handsome frigate that will be leaving this port in 8 days.*[22] You can surmise my answer. It seems as if the sailors have spoken about my *escape*. I am running out of paper, but not of the desire to write you. Good-bye.

December 18

By now you will have gotten an update in the letter that I sent Mother, including my decision to leave for Philadelphia. I don't know which merchant Bacon will recommend to me for sending letters, but for now continue to do so via Goodhue & Co. in New York, for them to send on to me in Philadelphia, or here via Bacon, since you can't imagine how anxious I am to hear about my family and affairs. When I can, I will let you know the name of the Philadelphia merchant.

Hold on to my books and papers until further notice. Letters to Philadelphia could be sent via Latting,[23] who will write to Miguel Caraballo.

Good-bye. From wherever it is, I will write you and love you,

José Mª

There is nothing more uncomfortable than writing here.

Bacon has not given me a letter for Philadelphia. I suppose there is no better letter of recommendation than bank notes. Write me in Philadelphia via Latting, and send me a recommendation for some merchant there. We leave in one hour.

Good-bye. I am sending back my mattress and pillow, which are only a nuisance, via Captain Harding.

To María de la Merced Heredia y Campuzano [BNJM; Augier no. 27]

Boston, December 5, 1823

My dearest Mother:

Yesterday I arrived in this city, and I am fine. The cold is still bearable, and it has not affected me as much as I feared. In Ignacio's letter you will have read about my doubts regarding moving somewhere else. I am here now, and to relocate to a different climate would mean traveling 500 or 600 leagues, which this time of year would be arduous.

It is true that I am not among Spanish speakers here, but I get by with French and Italian, and this way I will learn English more quickly. I already am starting to speak a few words, like a parrot.

What can I say regarding my emotions? You well know how it felt to part from Matanzas and leave behind my family, my studies and my friends. But not for a moment do I regret having preferred exile to crime and infamy. I don't think that this can last long, and then, when I return to Cuba, I will carry with me the glorious reputation of someone whose honesty has been refined in the crucible of such painful trials. And I have satisfied my own curiosity regarding the extent of the soundness of my principles.

December 6

I have gone to see the merchant to whom I was recommended, to give him a letter and another for Ignacio, and he told me that there will be no chance to send them until the packet boat leaves; and that a ship left yesterday. You can imagine how distressed I was to think that you might be upset, wondering if something had happened to me. But the captain put my mind somewhat at ease when he told me that he had written to A . . .[24] to say that everyone had arrived safe and sound. Since I don't speak the language, I imagine that this will happen to me again more than once. Please don't worry, and don't attribute it to neglect or indifference on my part.

December 16

For the last four to six days it has been snowing furiously, the snow is a yard deep in the streets, and the only way to clear a path is with picks and shovels. The carriages have exchanged their wheels for runners, upon which they glide over the snow at incredible speed. But there are days like today with no snowfall, and the sun, although it doesn't warm, shines brilliantly, the air is serene, and it is pleasant to walk. But you must go along carefully, because it would be very easy to fall and break your neck, since all the streets are covered with snow packed as hard as iron.

At dinnertime the Captain appeared with Luciano Ramos, whom he came across in a café. You can imagine how happy I was to find myself with my old comrade and countryman. It had been a month or more since I had spoken real Spanish. We have resolved never to separate, since fate has reunited us, and to help each other whatever comes our way.[25]

I caught a cold, but it has run its course, and Luciano is amazed at how well I look, a thousand times better than in Matanzas. And in fact I feel very well and I am even getting some color, I'm not sure if from the candles or from the brandy and cider that I habitually drink. Upon the advice of my innkeepers, I have not had a drop of water for the last twelve days, and the cider that they ply us with agrees with me very well. My only fear is that if I remain here in the North, I will end up worse than a jailhouse drunk.

December 17

It is a beautiful day today and we have gone out to take a walk. Luciano and I ran across Miguel María Caraballo[26] in the street, so the gang of exiles has grown. It is a great consolation for us to be among people we know and who speak the same language, and we will be able to aid each other in any misfortune that may befall us.

December 18

This morning we have resolved to go tomorrow to New York, and from there to Philadelphia, where it isn't so cold, although the difference isn't much, and we will be closer to Havana. From here we will take a coach to Providence, about 40 miles, and it will cost us $3. From there by steamship to New York for $10, so for $13 plus whatever our meals cost us on the way to Providence, we will have traveled the 100 leagues or so from here to New York, and for four or five dollars more we can be in Philadelphia, another hundred miles to the south. How wonderful!

Good-bye, dear Mother, and I will write you from wherever when I can, and please don't fail to write me as well, via the channels that Ignacio will indicate to you. Love to my sisters, especially my dear Ignacia,[27] to a certain individual,[28] to my aunt Francisca, to Magdalena[29] and to Abus, and the others at home, nor do I forget Pachis.[30] Be tranquil regarding my fate and give your blessing to your most loving son

José Mª

Ignacia: I don't write you because with the cold here it is very uncomfortable to do so. But do write me, and remember me to the Lamars, the Delmontes, and to Veguilla.

To María de la Merced Heredia y Campuzano [BNJM; Augier no. 28]

Boston, December 19, 1823

My dearest Mother:

Today Luciano Ramos, Miguel Caraballo and I leave for Philadelphia, fleeing from this climate. The details of how we were reunited are contained in another letter in the care of Captain Harding of the *Galaxy*, but since I don't want you ever to be deprived of my news, I am sending you these few lines via the frigate *Madison*, to tell you that I am fine and to indicate the channels by which I have written at greater length, which here is difficult to do, since my hand is so stiff with cold.

Please don't fail to write me via Bacon, since he will send your letters along to Philadelphia. There I will join up with Acosta, who is an excellent fellow.[31] This country is so inexpensive, that I reckon that with 40 or 50 dollars monthly I will be able to live very well, since room and board and excellent laundry cost only $25.

I am very well, and am getting along just fine with the cold, which I am not afraid of. It is atrocious, but has to give way a little when one is dressed with a layer of flannel underneath, another of wool, and a cloak above.

Via the *Galaxy* I have written to the Marchioness and A[32] . . . The letters are going in the care of Atkins.

I tremble a bit when I stop to think about my reversals of fortune, but when I remind myself that I have not been at fault, that these temporary adversities will spare me from infamy and eternal regret, I feel full of strength and resolve, and my only hope is that you feel the same.

I have written Ignacio at length via the *Galaxy*, and I believe that that letter will arrive before this one. I will not write him now because it is almost time for us to leave.

My affectionate regards to Doña María, my sisters and the others at home, and Rueda. And don't be distressed; remember that virtue doing battle with misfortune is the most beautiful spectacle on earth, and is pleasing to God. Be happy and until we meet again, give your blessing to your most loving son

José Mª

To María de la Merced Heredia y Campuzano [Augier no. 29]

New York, December 24, 1823

My dearest Mother:

I arrived in this city the day before yesterday, and find myself among Gener and others from Cuba, for which reason I have resolved to stay here, at least for now.[33]

The cold is unbelievable; all one can do is to stay inside on snowy and rainy days. I am deprived of my books, but it is easy to obtain them in *circulating* libraries, as they call them here, which for one dollar per month loan me all that I want.

In Boston I had given you instructions to write me in Philadelphia, but be advised that now you should write me here in New York, via Goodhue or Gener.

I could give you a very long account of the details of my trip from Boston to here, but it is uncomfortable to write in this cold, and I will just say that in two and a half days we traveled 250 miles, or more than 83 leagues, in excellent coaches, for 13½ dollars. Along the way we found excellent inns in which to have breakfast, lunch or dinner, and to sleep in perfect comfort. The speed of travel here is incredible. The coach flies along, and every five leagues they change the four horses. From Boston to here we went through more than 160 of them.

Another motive for staying here is the constant communication that there is with Havana, by which I will be able to have news from home easily and frequently. I still have had none, which has made me very displeased.

Please do not fail to write me by any channels, since that is the greatest pleasure that my heart can have in these circumstances.

The fellow in charge of dispatching this letter is urging me to finish. Remember me to all those who have not forgotten me, and do not be distressed by our separation, which I hope will end soon.

Your most loving son
José Mª

To María de la Merced Heredia y Campuzano [Augier no. 30]

New York, January 4, 1824

My dearest Mother:

I have written you several times from Boston, but as yet have not gotten any word from home, which has me very uncomfortable.

My life here is quite dismal, in this country whose language I can't understand for all I try, and whose customs are so different from ours. If I were not waiting to hear how things turn out, by now I would have gone on to Italy or France. But I may do so still if the current situation continues, since this climate is unbearable.

I am longing to receive a letter from you, so please do not fail to write me by any channels, since that would be the greatest consolation for me amid all this turmoil.

I haven't discarded the idea of taking a trip to Santo Domingo, to see if I might derive some benefit from what we have there, but right now the weather is very bad for sailing, and every day the gazettes are full of news of shipwrecks, and so I haven't wanted to risk it. And anyway I would be quite lost there, and if here two months have gone by without my receiving any word from my family, how would it be there?[34]

I have seen the two sons of Aunt Belén, Ignacio and Joaquín, who are in school here.[35]

Good-bye. I have nothing more to add. You can read the rest in the letter that I sent Ignacio. My affectionate regards to my dear sisters, my aunt Francisca, and remember me as well to the servants,[36] the Delmontes and the Lamars, and the Rueda family. And take good care, don't worry about anything, and be happy as you deserve to be, and let your most loving son suffer in your stead.

José M^a

I am living at no. 44 Broadway, if you want to indicate that on the envelope.

To María de la Merced Heredia y Campuzano [Augier no. 31]

New York, January 17, 1824

My dearest Mother:

I have written you countless letters in the two months since we parted, but have not yet had the pleasure of receiving any news from home.

I already have explained to you my determination to stay here, since it is the busiest port in the United States, and thus I will have greater opportunity to hear from my family.

It is pointless to insist, Mother, how anxious I am to receive news about the state of your health, and that of my sisters and other family.

Although I had planned to go to Philadelphia to live, as I wrote you from Boston, I have discarded that option, for the reason indicated above, and because it is so dismal to travel in winter.

I have asked you for my diploma, and hope that you will send it to me, retaining a sworn copy in case it gets lost. I think not having my diploma with me has me so uneasy because I realize that it might come to pass that I find myself deprived of that means of subsistence, the fruit of my lifetime of labor, and be obligated to look for more humiliating and dangerous employment.

I am not progressing in English as quickly as I would like, and pronunciation is a terrible obstacle for me. I barely have begun to say a few words in the more than a month that I have been in North America.

The cold is as one would imagine, given that this is New York in mid-January. But I am enduring it with good spirit, thanks to the clothing store that I wear upon my person: wool socks, flannel undershorts and shirt, a white shirt, wool pants, tie, vest and jacket, studded boots, a cloak and hat or fur cap. That is what I wear on the street, and at home as well, except for the cloak. I forgot to mention my gloves.

Clothing here is just as expensive as in Havana, if not more. A wool frock coat and pants have cost me 36 dollars.

I have nothing else to tell you. Don't fear for my health, which so far, thank God, is better than I could have hoped, and even if I should fall ill, I have friends here who would help me and care for me with an interest inspired by our common fate and misfortune.

My regards and affection to my dear Ignacia, Coptun, a certain individual, and even the disgrace of nature,[37] and to Magdalena, Manuel and my Aunt Francisca, regards to Rueda and to those who remember me, and be assured of the tender love of your son

José M^a

*To María de la Merced Heredia y Campuzano and
Ignacio Heredia Campuzano* [Augier no. 32]

New York, January 24, 1824

My dearest Mother:

Although I have written you a thousand times, I am writing you these few lines to tell you that I continue in good health, and thus calm any apprehensions that you may have.

Today Betancourt[38] arrived, and I don't know if it is my virtue or my foolishness, but I have been unable able to condemn him. He is a poor wretch, and I am incapable of hating anyone.

I can't think of anything else to tell you, since it is pointless to repeat that my foremost vow is to return to the bosom of my family.

Remember me to my dear sisters, to Chea, my Aunt Francisca and the Rueda family, and be as happy as your most loving son prays to God for you to be.

José Mª

Dearest Ignacio:

I am longing to have a letter from you, to know something of my fate, and to have the pleasure of hearing your voice, even if by way of the pen.

I already have requested from you my books and my diploma; with the former, send me as well a volume of French tragedies that is in the armoire, and contains among other things *Hamlet* and *Macbeth*.[39]

I wish to know if you want me to go to Europe, which would make me very happy.

Good-bye, please write me at length, and give my regards to my true *friends* and acquaintances, an embrace for Chea, and receive the heartfelt friendship of your

José Mª

To María de la Merced Heredia y Campuzano [Augier no. 34]

New York, February 21, 1824

My dearest Mother,

I have been disappointed not to receive a letter from you along with the one I received from Ignacio, dated January 24, but I am consoled by the news that you are in good health and visiting Aunt María de los Ángeles[40] in Havana.

I am quite well, thank God, and even when I have been under the weather, the young woman in the boarding house in which I live has attended to me with the greatest care and concern, such that I scarcely have been troubled by being ill far from home.

Please tell Aunt Francisca that I have directed a letter that she sent me for Santiago, along with another that I wrote him, to Santo Domingo, via a merchant house that tomorrow or the day after will dispatch a ship for there.[41]

I have instructed the bearer of this letter, a friend who shared a room with me for ten months, to see you in person, and to satisfy your curiosity regarding me, as I could never do by letter. Through him you will be able to learn about my life here, what the cold is like, and so forth.[42]

When it comes to learning English, I must be the most dull-witted person in the world. I hardly have begun to speak a word in the two and a half months that I have been contending with this family.[43]

I would love to be able to send you and the girls something, but there is nothing here that one can't obtain in Matanzas or Havana, everything is very expensive, and you know how hopeless I am when it comes to shopping. Perhaps when Jaime Tió departs for Cuba, I will send along a barrel of apples, which is about all that can't be had there.

There is no need to tell you how much I long to see you and embrace you, but also that I am well able to endure these undeserved misfortunes. I just want to know how all of this is going to come out, so as not to become an idle simpleton. I have tried to learn some profession, but none of these rascals here will take me on without the proper credentials. However, I have my eye on a bookbinder friend, who will teach me his craft whether he wants to or not.

The boarding house in which I live is excellent: first rate in the decency and quality and character of its residents, and we are very well treated. But since nothing can be perfect in this world, there is a blasted Frenchman here, deaf as a post, who is driving me absolutely crazy.

Give my love to my sisters, my aunt Francisca, Magdalena and the great Arbus. Tell Ignacia to write me, and to give Pepilla my news; my affectionate regards to Rueda and family, and the Delmontes and Lamars. Take good care, and be as happy as your loving son desires.

José M.ª

Do Diatifas, Coptum and a certain individual remember me much? What have they said regarding my trip? Does a certain individual have much to say?

Tell Magdalena that when she writes to Micaela Sterling[44] she should include the enclosed.

New York, February 21, 1824

Much loved Ignacio:

With inexpressible pleasure I received your letter of January 25, in response to mine of December 24. I don't know to what to attribute the lack of the letters from Boston, unless it was the delayed departure of the brigantine *Galaxy*.

You may be assured that I have been most indignant to learn of Perucho's court appearance and that Herrera and Arango have been imprisoned.[45] What iniquitous mystery is afoot there? Is it supposed that they had something to do with the *Soles*? Tell me why? If there have been such evil souls as I imagine, I shall finally know for sure the depths to which a degenerate and frenzied man can descend.

You complain about the brevity of my letters, and vaunt the length of yours, without considering that everything you tell me is of the greatest interest and import to me, while I don't have much to say except that I am well and that you should write me. I would like to tell you about all the things you ask me, but you well know that my letters are prone to go astray before they arrive in your hands, and could contain this or that paragraph that would be the cause of grief and affliction.[46]

As for my personal news, this is my regimen: I am living in the boarding house of a Frenchman at 88 Maiden Lane, where for six and a half dollars per week, I am treated perfectly, including a fire for my room. They say that there are other places that offer rooms for five or even four dollars, but one has to be careful, since they don't serve roasted meat, that is *roast beef*, with potatoes at noon, and as much bread as you want with codfish in the morning, and hot water with three or four drops of milk, which is what they call tea, in the evening. Anyway, such is life, and also you have to pay two dollars a week for the fire, and there goes all your money. In Boston it wasn't that way.

I am up with the birds at eight, have breakfast at eight-thirty, and if there is no rain or snow, I go out at nine-thirty or ten. I wander around, here and there, until three o'clock, when I return for lunch. I go back out at four, until teatime at seven, after which, if the night is mild, I go out to visit some friend, or to visit with due precaution some mathematical conventicle,[47] but almost always I remain at home studying or writing, have supper at ten, and turn in at eleven. I regularly walk five or six miles when I go out.

What bothers me most is my ineptitude for learning English. Even after two months of continuous work, I barely can say a few words, despite the effort a young lady here in the boarding house, and others in the house Navarro[48] is staying at, have put into teaching me. And to think that that idiot Dr. Lanas, as Chea says, thought he would teach you English in Matanzas in no time at all. I'm afraid that my scant progress has something to do with being in the company of other Spanish speakers, and I am thinking of spending some time out in the country in the spring, to see if I can make some headway in understanding these "Muslims."

In that same season I am thinking of going to Philadelphia, which would cost only 20 *reales* when the steamboats are operating,[49] and to Baltimore and Washington which are a bit farther away, and also to see the famous falls of the Mohawk and Niagara, which are both in this state of New York.

I have presented the letter from Latting to Howland,[50] and he has made me a thousand offers of help. I will begin to collect the monthly stipend on the first of March.

Regarding my books: I had told you in a previous letter not to send all of them, but just the ones I indicated in a list, but you didn't receive it and shipped off all of them, even the French newspapers in bindings, which have cost me $10 in fees, even though I declared in customs that they were for my own personal use, and the shorts cost me 15 *reales*.[51] Someone there told me that I should file an appeal with the governor, and offered to put me in touch with a lawyer, but since I know the kind of people I am dealing with, and had seen that a notary charged Juan de Acosta $14 for a marriage license for his daughter, I gave up on the whole matter and shelled out the money.[52] The same old story. And now you know—don't send me anything again, not even a pin.

Let us speak now of the most praiseworthy Betancourt.[53] The day he came to me, almost crying, he only inspired in me a kind of contemptuous pity. He tried to exculpate himself, and I told him not to speak of things whose memory would only confound him and shame him in his own eyes. He took that however he took it, and even attempted to take a room in the boarding house in which I had been staying, but by then I had moved. Then he began to come around here, with the pretext of seeing Luciano Ramos and Miguel Caraballo, who live with me. We almost always insult him, railing against those who turned themselves in and gave testimony, and since he is shameless, he says that we are right and that he is worthless. In truth, I don't think he understands half of what we say, since he is almost always *in Boston*.[54]

I must tell you about an incident that occurred three or four days ago. Betancourt went to spend the night in a bordello, and in the morning he tried to leave without paying his *quantum-vobis*, under the pretext that he hadn't done anything. They locked him in, he broke out using the fireplace tongs, and he went cursing to tell it all to Juan de Acosta, with whom he lives in the same room. You can imagine what a bender he was on. Now he has proclaimed that instead of going whoring, he is going to become an onanist. "Watch out!" Acosta has told him, scandalized. "Watch out, for if I see you do such a thing, I'll beat the lust out of you with a riding crop!" The poor fellow is terrified, and says that New York is going to be swept out to sea, like Callao.[55]

A friend and fellow boarder, who is in charge of this letter, will tell you other things that I prefer not to write about. I have instructed him to go and see you, and he will speak with you at length.[56]

I will send you, with Jaime Tió who will be leaving for Matanzas in a few days, some essays that I have written about the customs and laws of the people here. I am not going to send them now, because you can't imagine how difficult it is to write in this cold, no matter how close one gets to the fire. My handwriting says it all; it is so messy that I'm not sure if you will understand this letter.

I can't forgive you for not telling me any news about *the Ship*, Josefa, Isabel, Rita, and other acquaintances. How is Farantis getting along? How about the new coffee plantation of Don Pedro and company? What news is there from Jesús María, which I so sorely miss?[57] How is it faring under Pelayo and company? Tell me everything, you who live beneath a blessed sky, where it is not painful to write because there is no cold to make your fingers stiff, where one feels better and, in a manner of speaking, more in possession of life. See here, the tiniest details are a delight for this unfortunate exile. I have read your letter a hundred times, and always with newfound pleasure.

Along with this letter I am sending another one for Don José de Arango, and two more enclosed in it, one for the Marchioness and one for Pepilla.

There is no need for me to express my gratitude for your favors. You know me well, and that is enough.

I am thinking as well of sending Pepilla Arango a copy of *Telémaco* that I am having elegantly bound.[58] I'm not telling her that I am sending it, because I'm not sure they will have it ready in time.

Good-bye. You can't complain this time that I have shortchanged you with this letter. An embrace for Chea, my best regards to Don Pedro, Rueda, Nicolás, Don Joaquín, Lamadriz and family and Pancho Abreu, greetings on my behalf to Estanislao and the girls, remember me to Balbona, one-eyed Alfonso, and the other boys of the profession, Veguilla, Don Pedro Hernández, and give Sotico[59] a pull on the ears. As for you, keep well, write me at length, and be as happy as I desire you to be.

Your most loving,
José Mª

I am not sending the receipt,[60] because here they are as expensive as they are there, but if there are none to be had, let me know.

Indicate on the envelope of my letters that they are going in the care of Mr. Howland, whose first initials Latting will give you, so that he can pick them up, since the mail here is a mess.[61]

My roommate Miguel Caraballo sends you regards; we speak of you always.

February 24

After I had sealed this letter, they brought me yours of the first of this month, which has brought me inexpressible joy, not only because I have been brought up to date about you and the others at home, but also because throughout the letter you have let me know that you take pleasure in corresponding from afar with this scoundrel, and that your thoughts turn to the delightful Jesús María, where we whiled away so many happy hours.

Your story has amused me a great deal, and you will see here that I have anticipated your desire to know mine.

So Doña Mencía de Mosquera has finally gone off to look for sons-in-law worthy of her glorious lineage, which she could not find in Matanzas! It seems that once I left, the last obstacle fell that kept her from moving, which as you know I helped you to thwart on the various occasions when it came up.

I am so glad that my letters from Boston got to you. Upon my soul, if it were not for the discomfort of writing here, I would have worn you out with my letters, and the briefest would have been like that of December 4. I would like to share all my observations with you, but since I don't know English well, my fear is that they would be imprecise and even erroneous. However, when the Catalonians[62] head back your way, I will send some along, and the notes from my trip.

I am convinced that our fellow men are not worthy of the sacrifices that one makes for them; but the harm has already been done, and at the end of the day it is a beautiful and sublime thing to be a martyr for the human race, for having committed an error common to generous souls in all times and places, an error that, like me, befell Demosthenes, Cato and Washington.

However, the disillusionment that I have acquired will serve to help me reform my conduct in future, and if justice is done me, I will go back over to your faction, at least until the next life shows me that there is some greater or lesser chance of perfectibility, since, having lived in Matanzas and New York, I know there is little chance of that on this earth.

What has me most worn down is the climate here, and I am thinking that if things continue this way, and I cannot return to Matanzas before next winter, I would do well to go and spend it in Italy, where I can get by as well as here, and see that classic land of natural beauty, and the remnants of all the sublime things that mankind's enthusiasm for the good has produced, and in addition live in a climate more similar to that of the land of my birth. Just imagine this scoundrel speaking Italian and eating macaroni in Naples or Venice, or meditating with emotion upon the ruins of the Eternal City.

If you could hear me speaking English with all the seriousness of people here, you would have a good laugh. If you saw what a terrifying face I make when unwitting people ask me for anything the least bit unusual, you would be frightened yourself.

I have already told you that this villain is planning to visit Niagara Falls, once the cold weather ends. Imagine me there among the savages.

You should write me directly here, or else via Philadelphia, but not via Charleston, unless it is something urgent, because the letters that arrive here from so far south cost a fortune. Your last one cost me two and a half dollars. What is more, every day ships arrive here from Matanzas and from Havana, and everything can be coordinated to save some money.

Some days ago I went to see Western's[63] brother, and he showed me a letter from him, in which he praised me to the skies. He invited me to take tea with him and I went, but I have not gone back, because of this confounded cold weather. Right now all the streets are covered with snow, and instead of carriages everyone goes about in sleighs like in Russia, which glide along at amazing speed.

I have begun a translation of Ossian, and I will see if I can interest some bookseller in it. The original is in prose, but it has seemed to me that that sublime song of the Caledonian bard should be restored to poetry, and so I am translating it in blank verse.[64]

It is inconceivable that we have no translation of this rival of Homer. I will send along a poem or two with the Catalonians, for you to look over.

Even though Mother may go to Havana, as you know my inclination is for Matanzas, since I am more and more aware of my need to live at your side, and I miss you always. But we will see how that goes; let's not get ahead of ourselves.

You can't complain of my brevity, since this letter if anything is longer than your last. You see, since your complaints fill up so much paper, you feel very proud of yourself thinking that you have written a good deal. But so it goes, and I am resigned to it.

My regards to Señor de la Riva. Do you know, it makes me laugh when I think how he would get along in the conventicles here, and how strange he would look strolling along Broadway?[65]

I have received nothing from Rouvier's brother-in-law, nor have I seen him.

Good-bye, my brother: be well, and don't forget your most loving friend and nephew,

José Mª

I am enclosing the letter to Arango, unopened: read it, and seal the flaps before delivering it.

February 28

I have just learned that Jaime Tió is leaving tomorrow, and so I have decided to send this with him, along with the two books for Pepilla. I had the misfortune to choose a bookbinder who was a dirty old drunk, and he did not do the kind of job that I would have wished and that the beauty of the editions required. He left smudges from his filthy hand on the first page, which has me quite annoyed.

I also am sending some little books that old man Guardia had loaned me, and which were sent along with mine. Please return them to him, since I don't want that vile man to go shooting off his mouth about me.

The hurried departure of the Catalonians will not permit me to send the papers that I mentioned, which need to be copied over, and the Ossian needs to be annotated, because if not you will not understand it because of the connections and mutual references among the poems. My brain is not up to that right now.

The Catalonians will tell you how I have become an Englishman, both in speaking and in knocking back the brandy and beer.

Tell Mother that you have received this letter, since even though I have written her, it is possible that she has not received my letters.

Good-bye, give my best regards to Chea. And be as happy as I wish you to be.

Your grateful
José Mª

To Silvestre Luis Alfonso y Soler[66] [Augier no. 36]

New York, February 28, 1824

My dearest Silvestre:

When you last wrote me, asking for news about the events in Matanzas, they were preparing the order of imprisonment that was to strike me like a thunderbolt. I scarcely had time to look for refuge, which a most generous friend offered me. Eight days later I boarded ship amid the greatest danger, and my disguise and my calmness allowed me to slip past, without being recognized, those who were frantically looking for me. So here I am, so bedeviled by the cold weather that I envy the lot of those who were imprisoned, and I can assure you that it was only so that I would not have to swallow insults that I didn't wait around to be captured.

You will be aware that hundreds of the *Racionales* in Matanzas turned themselves in. The blackguards! They almost make me regret having once believed in my lofty sentiments.

Mother is there in Havana, and since the bearer of this letter will not be able easily to deliver another that I have written her, I beg you to be in charge of delivering it to the home of Señor Franco, to whom it is addressed on the outer envelope.

How is Lola? And the celestial nymph of the Yumurí?[67] You know, the memory of her, and that of Luz, often serve to beautify, somehow, the hours of my banishment.

Do let me know how they are, if they have married, etc., since you know how interested I am.

I am going to attempt to publish my poems here, the erotic and the moral ones; as for the patriotic ones, I don't want even to make a clean copy of them. See if you can find me some subscribers among our friends, and I will send you some copies. In said edition I will include some poems of Ossian translated in verse from English prose versions.

Good-bye, my friend. My regards to Tatao, Céspedes[68] and our other comrades. Please write me, and don't forget your true friend

José Mª

To Ignacio Heredia Campuzano [BNJM; Augier no. 37]

New York, March 6, 1824

Much loved Ignacio:

I have just learned on the street that a ship that I thought would be slow to depart for Matanzas is about to set sail, so I am writing you these few lines hurriedly to let you know that I am well and have not forgotten you.

I wrote you a long letter three or four days ago, and sent it with Jaime Tió, and included a letter for that friend of mine and his family, and several books.[69]

I then received a letter from Mother in Havana, dated February 6, in which she tells me that no one has named me in the indictment and that Franco has told her that he sees no reason why I should not go.[70] But as you have well said, I should be wary of such news. I can't write her now because I am in a rush, but please write her and tell her that I am fine and am not going anywhere. And tell her that she should take consolation in that fact, and tell Ignacia not to be upset, since the thought of that torments me more than any of my own sorrows and afflictions. If possible, please include this letter, or copy it for her. I will write to her at length at the first opportunity.

I also received your note dated February 13, and I pledge to you the same, that my promise is sacred, and that whatever my suffering here, even at the risk of death, I will remain in the United States until my fate is decided, unless the legal proceedings should drag on until next winter; but even in that case, I would go to spend the winter in Charleston or Savannah, unless you were to give me permission to go to Santo Domingo. So please rest easy on that count, and don't leave me troubled with the thought that you may be worried.

Tell Aunt Francisca that I have dispatched her letters through a merchant house that is sending a ship tomorrow to Santo Domingo.

Despite the haste with which I write, you will note by my handwriting that the horrible months of January and February have passed. What bitter hours they have cost me! Now that the weather has turned milder, I have begun to feel, for the first time since I arrived in the United States, that I am still in full possession of life. Can you imagine the horror of the situation in which I have found myself, in this awful climate, thinking about my family's afflictions and contemplating the injustice of men, tormented in equal measures by my body's ailments and my soul's agitation? You who know me well can conceive of my suffering. Finally it seems that winter is giving way and, thank God, I can hope to live.

On the first of this month I took possession, through Howland, of the first stipend of $50.[71]

Please don't fail to write me, noting on the envelope that you are sending the letter in care of Howland. In that way, I will still receive your letters easily even when I am not in the city.

Next month I am planning to go to Philadelphia, and when I return, to the countryside, which must be very beautiful. I think I am becoming fatigued by the company and turmoil of my fellow men, even more so when they are crowded together and stirred up as they are in big cities. But always address your letters to me here in New York.

My mother tells me that A . . . had written a commentary about my letter to Pancho Hernández,[72] and I would like to see it. If you can send me a copy, I will be most grateful.

With a friend who is soon leaving for Havana, I am going to send to Mother some picture cards representing public buildings and other views of this city, and I will ask her to send them on to you with my observations.

Please tell A . . . and family that I never forget them, and if I do not write them always it is only because it is not safe to do so, and I am afraid of implicating them. Give my regards to all my acquaintances, affectionate ones to Chea and to Don Pedro, and warm greetings to Rueda and family, not forgetting the great secretary.

Good-bye, my true friend. Don't forget me, write me, and know that you have the heart of your most loving

José María.

I don't know if you will be able to understand this letter, since I have written it in less time than it will take you to read it, so as not to miss the chance to send it. You guessed the motives of Doña Mencía for going to Havana: *aristocracy*, she tells me, along with the story of Merced Angulo's wedding.

To María de la Merced Heredia y Campuzano [BNJM; Augier no. 38]

New York, March 8, 1824

Dearest Mother:

I received with the greatest pleasure your letter of February 6, the first that I have had from you since I left Matanzas. Please set aside your fears that I may go to Caracas or Mexico. I would have no motive to go there besides the insufferable rigor of the climate here, and with regard to the latter, things are getting better; soon winter will be over. I have never been ambitious, and as long as I can be here I will go nowhere else. But if matters have not been settled by next winter, you must give me permission to spend it in a more benign climate, like that of Italy or one of the southern states like Carolina or Louisiana, since although I made it through this last winter, in the next I may not live to tell the tale.

I wrote to Ignacio the day before yesterday, and because I was in a hurry to do so, I was unable to write you, and I knew that I would be able to do so on this occasion. I didn't want to bother the bearer of this letter with further delays.

The best way to guarantee our communication in the future will be for you to give me the name of some merchant friend of Franco, who might take responsibility for the letters, because any sent by mail from here run the risk of going astray. You have only to address your letters thusly:

> J. M. Heredia, Esq.
> Maiden Lane No. 88
> New York

In that way they will be delivered to me from the establishment of the consignee. Please do not forego any chance you have to write me about the state of the conspiracy hearings. Some sinister news is circulating here about them, including that the Audiencia was moving to Havana to render judgment, and that the prisoners were being held in the most rigorous conditions. If you can't write, then ask Ignacia to do so, or Magdalena or that rascal Antonio Angulo, who doesn't seem to be good for anything but addressing envelopes.[73] Has Abus remained with Ignacio?

I have begun to speak some English, but so little that I become frustrated with myself. I don't know if you know that Ignacio has arranged for a merchant here to pay me $50 every month, of which I have taken the first installments. The poor fellow![74] I don't know how I will ever repay his kindnesses. It seems that fate has taken amusement in bestowing qualities upon me that doom me to a misfortune that then falls upon everyone whom I love and who loves me.

Do not fret about the letter.[75] The cause of my misfortune has been an error, but an error common to generous souls throughout the ages, and which was suffered by Demosthenes, Cato and Washington. If justice is done me, I will go to live in a quiet corner, as I did in Havana, in the same innocence which was upset by the iniquitous, the envious and the cowardly, who know very well that no one was planning to do anything, and who in order to satiate their contemptible passions have condemned so many families to sorrow. I forgive them, because I am incapable of hatred, but now I know the depths to which human perversity can descend.

If iniquity triumphs, I pride myself on having too much perseverance to lie down and die. I need little to live, and with any small sum that Ignacio might advance me, I will be able to establish some small business here, whose products will be sufficient to meet my needs, which for someone free of vices like myself (it isn't arrogant to say so) are few.

In sum, do not worry, and have faith that I am going to get by very well here from now on, with the cold weather behind me. I am going to have a look at Philadelphia, and then perhaps spend some time in the country.[76]

My regards to Franco, Doña Pepilla and Don Antonio, and remembrances to all those at home.[77] Tell me if Silvestre and Pancho have been to see you. If you do see them, give them my regards, and also to Domingo. Be serene, and take good care until such time as you may be embraced by your most loving son

José Mª

I am also writing Blas,[78] but am not including the letter so that this one, which is going in the care of a friend, will not be too bulky. Please tell him so.

To María de la Merced Heredia y Campuzano [BNJM; Augier no. 39]

New York, March 19, 1824

Dearest Mother:
With the greatest pleasure I have received your second letter of February 19, which I herewith answer.

I have written to you repeatedly not to worry about my situation here, since the worst months of winter have passed, and it is not nearly as cold now as when I arrived and in the two months that followed.

The only motive that could have uprooted me from here was the necessity of asking the sun for some hints of life in a more benign climate, to combat my body's afflictions. But that is done with now, and nothing will remove me from the United States. Only if things do not sort themselves out by next winter, and if you and Ignacio are in agreement, will I be happy to go to Italy, where it will not cost me any more to live than it does here. But if you are not so disposed, I will haul off for Charleston or New Orleans. What in the world could impel me to go to Mexico or Colombia, except the overriding necessity of my own preservation! Ambition? I have never had any, and God knows that as regards the cause of my misfortune, or rather in the pretext thereof occasioned by the fury of my persecutors, I had my sights on the welfare of my country and of the human race, rather than on my own. At least I don't have reason to recriminate myself for self-interested emotions, unworthy of a generous soul.

So please do not worry, and let me have the pleasure of knowing that you are awaiting the decision regarding my fate as calmly as I am. We must let time and events run their course.

I see in your letter what you have said about my having gone to Matanzas to work. But my staying in Havana would not have impeded the effects of my persecution. I am grateful nonetheless for Franco's good sentiments, and I have never doubted his friendship.

If time permits I also will write to Ignacio on this occasion, in care of Franco. I am not enclosing his letter, so as not to make this one too bulky, which the son of Don Agustín Hernández has offered to take in his charge.[79] I will write to Blas Osés as well.

There is no need for me to tell you how grateful I am for Ignacio's kindnesses.

Please tell Antonio Angulo to write me and let me know the state and prospects of the hearing, so that he can explain everything to me and satisfy my desires in that regard. And let me know who the judges are in Havana who will be involved in the matter.

Toward the end of this month or beginning of the next I will take a trip to Philadelphia, and then perhaps I will go spend the summer in the countryside, but please write me here, and I will make arrangements so that your letters reach me wherever I am.

Remembrances to all those who remember me, my love to my sisters, regards to Aunt Francisca and children, to Doña Ángela and hers, to Franco, Doña Pepa Gómez, Antonio and Father Márquez,[80] and please do not forget to write me.

Yesterday I learned that the day before a ship left for Havana, and I was much vexed not to be able to take advantage of the occasion to write you. But for the past five or six days it has been snowing heavily and I haven't been able to go out.

I have dispatched Aunt Francisca's letters for Santo Domingo.

Good-bye, be well and as happy as your most loving son desires.

José Mª

Do let me know what is going on with Silvestre and Pancho García,[81] and Domingo del Monte, and if they have gone to see her.

To María de la Merced Heredia y Campuzano [BNJM: Augier no. 40]

New York, March 27, 1824

Dearest Mother:

The last letter that I have received from you is that of February 19, even though many ships from Havana have arrived here since then. This has me worried; please don't let any opportunity to write me go by, since this is the greatest consolation that I can have in my exile. In the *Noticioso* you will find what ships are loading bound for New York and the merchants who dispatch them, in whose offices you can send me letters; if you rely on the mails, the letters will get lost without fail. Don Agustín Hernández can also let you know when he writes his son; tell him in my name to do so, as I know he will not deny me that small favor.

I have written you two or three letters since receiving your last. Please don't fail to write me about the state of the hearings; you can ask Franco about them—he will know. Or better yet, ask Antonio Angulo, who since he is in the law profession will be better able to explain what is going on, so as to relieve me of my doubts, which is the cruelest state that I know.

As for things here, the cold weather has mostly passed, and the grass is beginning to get green. I am planning to go to Philadelphia in six or eight days, but you should continue to write me here. After that trip, I am thinking of retiring to some small town, where I can live more comfortably and cheaply. With each day that passes I feel my old love for solitude increase, and I am fatigued and bothered by the bustle of this immense city. Rather than living with people who profit from my privations, I will look for a modest and virtuous family who will treat me with affection and will try to sweeten my sorrows with their solicitous attentions.

On this occasion I am also writing to Blas and to Ignacio. Let me know what is going on with Uncle Xavier.[82]

Tell Ignacio to write me and let me know what is happening with the Matanzas prisoners, and with the girls. I am told that both Rita and Dolores Junco are going to get married. Is that true? Good-bye for now; since I have no news to tell you, and can only speak of myself, in telling you that I am fine I am saying all there is to be said. My affectionate regards to my sisters and other female relatives, and to Franco and family, Antonio de Castro and his sister. Do not fail to write and do not forget your most loving son

José Mª

March 29: I am enclosing the letter to Ignacio. Please place on it the necessary postage and send it along to him. Let me know if Pancho García, Domingo and Silvestre have gone to see her.[83] If you see them, give them my remembrances.

March 30: I am not sending Ignacio's letter, because I will send it to him directly. Today I am feeling very well. Good-bye.

To Ignacio Heredia Campuzano [BNJM; *Moda*; Augier no. 41]

Philadelphia, April 15, 1824

Much loved Ignacio:

A few days ago I wrote to Mother, but not to you since I didn't want to make the letter, which I was sending with a friend, too bulky. But now I want to write you with some news, which I will send to you when the occasion permits.

For the past ten days I have been in this celebrated city of Philadelphia. It is in a very advantageous location, set between the Delaware and Schuylkill Rivers, the first of which serves as its port, and the second of which supplies its inhabitants with water. Countless times you will have heard that Philadelphia is one of the most regularly designed cities in the world, and that is true. All of its streets are traced in straight lines and intersect at right angles. Those that run parallel with the rivers are called First, Second, etc., up to Thirteenth, and end at a magnificent plaza called Central Square, because in fact at some point it will be the center of the city. From there the streets are counted in the same way, the only difference being that they are called First, Second, etc. of the Schuylkill—those that are between Central Square and that river—and the same with those between Central Square and the Delaware, while those right next to the rivers are called Front Street. The two main streets, which are wider than the others, cross at Central Square and are called Broad Street or High or Market Street. The numbered streets, which run parallel to Broad, are called South First, South Second, South Third, etc. (those that are to the south of High Street), or North (those to the north). The other streets that run parallel to High, and that cross the numbered streets, bear the names of the trees that adorn them. With this summary I think you would be able to draw a map of Philadelphia.

The market is very extensive, and is supported by more than 300 columns, I believe, but I prefer the one called Fulton in New York, which, although smaller, is cleaner and enables the buyer to examine everything in it with a short stroll, while here it would be necessary to walk five or six very long blocks.

The street of fashion, and therefore the busiest, is Chestnut, where pretty girls can be found strolling in greater abundance than in any other part of the United States. How I have recalled, watching them go by, your laments regarding the lack of pretty girls in Matanzas!

The public buildings and establishments most worthy of attention are the Bank of the United States and those of Pennsylvania, Girard, and Philadelphia, the Masonic Hall, the Prison, the Museum, the churches, the Mint, the Public Library, the State House, the Quaker Hospital, which is admirable, and the waterworks.

The Bank of the United States is all of white marble, and in the most simple and pure Greek style.[84] It has only one floor, and is separated from the street by a great iron railing, presenting two equal and sublimely beautiful façades to Chestnut and the parallel street. Each façade has a portico of eight grand columns, reached by eighteen steps also of white marble, a single door with two flanking false doors, and three windows with splendid marble casings. Light enters the building through windows along the side walls. It is without a doubt the most beautiful building that I have ever seen anywhere, and I take great pleasure in strolling along its portico, where it is always delightfully cool. I believe that the model for this edifice was the Parthenon of Athens, but I doubt that the latter, even in its time of greatest splendor, could equal the simple elegance and beauty of this American building. One of the façades is not yet completed, and when it is and they publish engravings of it, I will send you a copy. But no picture will be able to capture the purity and transparency of its marble, nor represent to the astonished eye that tremendous mass crowned with laurels high in the air by the triumph of human ingenuity. The main hall, where business is conducted and payments are made, is sumptuous, although without any extraneous decoration; but perchance do those six columns that support such a vast and resplendent dome need any?

The Girard and Pennsylvania banks are in the same style, although they do not attain the beauty and sumptuousness of that of the United States. The Bank of Philadelphia, the Masonic Hall, and a church near Central Square are all in the Gothic style, and are also worthy of note. The most handsome church is the First Presbyterian, which is on Washington Square, and its portico and colonnade give it the appearance of an ancient Greek temple. Also worthy of a look is the Philadelphia School for the Deaf, which is on High Street. The State House is not nearly as sumptuous and beautiful as that of New York.

The Museum is worthy of attention, especially because it contains the skeleton of a mammoth.[85] All my prior notions disappeared when I first saw it. Never before has an object made such a vivid impression in my mind, nor given rise to such deep reflections. The presence of the enormous remains of a monstrous animal that has disappeared from the earth, besides astonishing with its immense size, which almost exceeds the limits of what seems possible, can only induce in the spectator the most profound musings, cast him into the unfathomable depths of time, and persuade him to seek some light amid the darkness with the formation of some systematic explanation.

It would be absurd to suppose that such a perfectly organized thing is just a caprice of Nature, and even though some, with affected skepticism, have so claimed, the enormous quantity of remains that have been found in different parts of the globe would be sufficient to demonstrate that they belong to a fearsome subspecies of animal that did, in fact, once exist; and which, animated with the breath of life, like us, once made this earth that we inhabit tremble with its enormous weight. To the astonishment of men, its bones have been found in the fields of America and the Siberian wilderness. But to what era can its existence be attributed? Does some memory of these monstrous beings remain among any of the peoples of the globe? No: not even those inhabitants of the regions in which their remains have been found have any knowledge of them in their historical traditions. Only a fable of the North American savages might apply to them: "Some ten thousand moons ago," they say, "a race of invincible and evil beings covered the earth: they were as big as mountains; they were as furious as the eagle who dives for its prey from the clouds; and as swift as a bolt of lightning . . . the lakes dried up when they quenched their thirst in them . . . arrows could not pierce their impenetrable skins . . . pale with fear, men could foresee their total annihilation . . . their cries of affliction were carried on the four winds, and reached the ears of the Great Spirit, who cast his thunderbolts against these oppressors of the earth. They all were felled, and only one, defying the fury of heaven, raised up its haughty brow with a horrendous roar, and tumbled at last into the waves of the Ocean."

I am not sure if my memory has faithfully retained these lines which I have seen I don't remember where, but I could not help but recall them when I saw the *mammoth*.[86] If in fact this animal was herbivorous, as the form of its teeth would suggest, the destruction of this terrible species was necessary so that the fragile human family could extend across the earth. In sum, I would never finish if I tried to tell you all the thoughts aroused in me by these shapeless remains of a primitive, buried world that was destroyed with all its animate creatures in some cataclysm of nature. After untold centuries these bones have appeared to point us to that world, like the naked mast of a ship which, dragged to shore by the waves, gives vague notice of an unknown shipwreck. And we, we too will suffer an equal fate someday, when a wrathful page is turned in the eternal book of destiny, and the beings who succeed us will search, perhaps, for our traces, as futilely as we seek to penetrate the darkness that separates us from the unfathomable era in which that immense skeleton lived upon the earth. Realms of conjecture in which human understanding becomes lost, and imagination itself strives in vain and halts in terror . . . What is man, then, unless he raises his eyes to Heaven, and seeks there his immortal abode?[87]

The *Water Works*, as they are called, are about two miles from the city.[88] A waterfall on the Schuylkill River turns an immense wooden water wheel, which in turn moves two pistons, by which water is pumped from the river to storage ponds atop an adjacent hill, 36 feet higher, I believe, than the level of the river. From there water is distributed throughout the city by subterranean conduits, so that on each block there is a pump and everyone has water available nearby. It is the same in New York. The cost of these waterworks is estimated to have been $400,000; and the quantity of water obtained is some three million gallons every 24 hours. The river forms there an artificial waterfall of no great height, but the view is delightful. Imagine a crystalline sheet of water a thousand feet long, sparkling beneath the sun's rays. Add to that the idyllic view of the nearby crags, the covered bridge that crosses the Schuylkill, and the surrounding highlands, which they call Fair Mount, covered with groves of trees and country houses, and you will have an idea of the beauty of the scene.

The façade of the theater on Chestnut Street is of marble, very elegant and beautiful, with three doors on the ground floor, and a small colonnade on the second.[89] There are two statues, one on either side, that represent Comedy and Tragedy. The theater's interior has only three tiers of seats, and in beauty and decoration is inferior to that of Havana.

Philadelphia is the foremost city of the United States. Its population exceeds 100,000 souls, and some say it has as many as

130,000. It is very beautiful, and must be even more so when the trees that adorn its streets and squares are in full leaf. However, the very regularity of its layout and the almost complete uniformity of its buildings induce in those who view it some vague feeling of fatigue. I felt as if worn out by the accumulation of repeated and equal effort that went into the construction of those rows of immense and uniform houses. You may say, if you wish, that I am so *reguiberry*,[90] but so it is, and for the same reason I find the brilliant irregularity of New York much more to my liking. When I surveyed Philadelphia from the reservoir that overlooks the city, I felt that something was lacking, and then observed that only two church spires arose from that immense mass of human habitations. Those same towers, which I first saw from the river when I arrived on a misty day, seemed like two phantoms suspended in the air above the city, because of their height and isolation.

In Philadelphia, as in New York, I have witnessed several fires, and I think you may enjoy hearing about how they are dealt with here. When the homeowner or the *watchman* stationed on the corner gives the cry of alarm, if it is in the middle of the night, the young men pour out into the streets yelling *fire*; and as if by magic the pumpers appear at once with men who are paid to work them, called *firemen*; once I saw 32 such pumpers. Without any fuss or confusion a hose is attached to a hydrant in the street, and a stream of water is directed to the burning house by the *firemen* via a sort of tube. No soldiers or agents of public administration are anywhere to be seen. Only the insurers give signs of being upset, and for the rest it is a big party. The inhabitant of the house comes out and with the most remarkable indifference sits in the doorway of the house across the street to watch the shindig, with no need to worry about his furniture, since it will be paid for if he is insured, as almost everyone is. The chief of the first pumper that arrives (who will earn five dollars courtesy of the homeowner) grabs the megaphone and directs the operation. Soon lots of people congregate, but no one is obligated to pitch in, and the young fellows man the pumpers. If the doorway is blocked by the fire, ladders are raised to the windows, and the *firemen* enter through them to drag things out and direct the water to the blaze. The fire is put out, and everyone goes home with the same impassive seriousness.

Now when this letter reaches you, you won't be able to complain as you have before that my letters are too short. It amuses me to think that reading it will keep you entertained in the coffee grove, with our good friend Don Pedro in attendance, spectacles perched on his nose. I hope it gives you the same pleasure that it has given me to write it, with the sensation that I am speaking with you despite the waves of the ocean that separate us.

Good-bye: I will give you more news on another occasion, and I hope that from now on you won't have any complaints for me. An embrace for Chea, and regards to Don Pedro, the great and intimate secretary, and other friends, not excepting Señor de la Riva, and Abus. And do not forget me or fail to write at length to your most loving nephew and friend

José Mª

To María de la Merced Heredia y Campuzano [BNJM; Augier no. 42]

New York, April 23, 1824

My dearest Mother:

I wrote you from Philadelphia in answer to yours of March 8th, and upon arrival here found three letters from Ignacio, but none from you until yesterday, when I received two dated March 14 and 28, which have given me much pleasure.

Now I am taking advantage of Agustín Hernández's trip to write you, and to send to Ignacio the picture cards that I had promised. I am adding some verses, and two more little picture cards, the larger one showing the falls on the Connecticut River in the state of Massachusetts, and the other one a view of Broadway, near the house in which Agustín and I used to live.

Your advice concerning brandy is unnecessary, since as you know I never have been inclined to such low and shameful vices. I did drink it in winter, because it was essential, but now I only drink water or a bit of cider or beer as a substitute for wine, which is terribly expensive.

I also am sending one of the portraits in profile that was done of me in the Philadelphia Museum. You should place it against a black background.[91]

As regards your other pieces of advice, let me assure you that I never fail to attend mass on feast days, and I went to confession before

Holy Week, with a priest from Guatemala who was here. So please stop your useless worrying, and think only of living tranquilly and restfully. Let me tell you, your letter of the 8th gave me a very bad time.

Tell Osés that I have written him two or three letters since the one I received from him, and show him the verses that I am sending. Ask him if the Meléndez edition in 4 volumes can be found in Havana, since I would be very happy to have it, and if it is, then Captain Hazard, who is a good friend of Agustín and of mine, can bring it to me.[92]

Agustín is a living letter, and he will tell you at length about me, this city and its inhabitants.

In Ignacio's letter you will see that I am thinking of going to spend time in some smaller towns in order to make progress in my English, but you should still write me here, noting on the envelope:

> J. M. Heredia, Esq.
> Care of Messrs. G. Y. and S. Howland
> New York

These Howlands are the merchants to whom I have been recommended and who will forward me letters, wherever I may be.

Pía's and Felipa's complaint is unfounded, as is their accusation of ingratitude. If in every letter I had to mention the name of every single friend and relative, I would never finish writing. So tell them to cease with such foolishness.

I believe that Luciano will give you a lengthy account of me; let me know if he is already in Matanzas. Pancho García hasn't bothered to answer the letter that I sent along with Luciano, which I never thought he would fail to do.

Good-bye and be well. Give my sisters my love, and regards to Aunt Francisca, Magdalena, and Aunt Ángela and Aunt Concha Barba and families, special regards to my comrade Antonio and to Dolores and Félix; tell Franco, Doña Pepa and Antonio that I do not forget them for an instant, and tell the Fernándezes not to get cross if I don't always send them regards. Good-bye, and be as happy as your most loving son prays to God for you to be.

José Mª

When someone goes to Matanzas, send along to Ignacio the enclosed picture cards and verses.

I am not writing at greater length, since I only could repeat what I have already written to Ignacio, and since you will see my enclosed letters to him, there is no point in wearing myself out more.

Tell Aunt Francisca that the last two letters I have received for Santiago will leave for Santo Domingo straightaway, within eight to ten days. And that the others have already been sent.

Ignacio's letter is open at one end, so that you can take it out and read it, and seal it again without ripping the envelope, and thus save the trouble of addressing a new one.

To Ignacio Heredia Campuzano [Escoto; Augier no. 43]

New York, April 23, 1824

Much loved Ignacio:

Upon arriving from Philadelphia I found your long-awaited letters of February 22 and March 14 and 21. They have been especially welcome because for almost two months I had no word from you, and I was beginning to fear that you might be ill or that you were beginning to forget about me, and both possibilities were extremely distressing. Now as I read again your letter which, you tell me, you composed in the coffee grove, in my mind's eye I see you there, in shirt sleeves, writing at the same little mahogany table upon which Jaureguiberry kept his provisions.

With regard to the letter authorizing a payment to me of $50 each month, I already have written you that I received and presented it, and thanks to it I have secured the monthly payments for March and April.

I am sure that you had a wonderful time during your trip to Havana with Abreu, and the truth is that I would have loved to be a member of that little party. But how can that be? During these last days I have walked the streets of the City of Brotherly Love, admiring its beautiful sights, and speaking a great deal of English with its "navy officers" (that is what the Quakers look like to Juan de Acosta).[93]

The trip from here to Philadelphia is very comfortable and pleasant. One leaves New York at six in the morning and crosses the bay to Amboy, continuing up a river that flows into it not far from its entrance, to New Brunswick. From there one travels overland to Trenton, a distance of 25 miles, and from there boards another steamship that descends the Delaware River to Philadelphia and arrives at sunset. The price of passage is four dollars, plus one dollar for lunch and dinner, for a total of five, to cover a distance of almost one hundred miles.

The towns of Burlington, Bristol and Bordentown are delightfully situated along the banks of the Delaware. The last of these, although less handsome than the other two, was the one that most attracted my attention, because there resides Joseph Bonaparte.[94] On my way to Philadelphia I could not see his palace because of the thick fog that enshrouded the banks of the river; but today in order to see it better I disembarked and took a coach along a newly opened road that passes in front of his gate. As we went by, I saw Bonaparte from a distance; he was coming to meet a young woman who had accompanied us in the steamboat from Philadelphia. An admirable, patriarchal down-to-earth-ness! The young lady who had won the attentions of a monarch had made the trip alone, amid forty men, perfectly protected by the sublime force of custom and the safeguard of laws.[95]

Joseph's palace is not yet finished, after a fire consumed one that he had built before. It is worth noting that when that happened, all the inhabitants of Bordentown ran to help, even though it was the middle of the night. Joseph later published a letter in the newspapers, in which he thanked the townspeople in a tone more suitable for a monarch than a fellow citizen. In it, he said that he had never doubted that the inhabitants of Bordentown would know how to show proper gratitude to him for having chosen to locate his residence in their midst. The proud Americans took that very badly; and at least one of them told him so, adding that the serious mien with which they received his gracious smiles on the night of the fire should have made evident how little those smiles mattered to them; and that they had come to his aid only out of a sentiment of common kindness and humanity. That was just punishment for the indiscreet arrogance of the Count of Survilliers.[96]

What thoughts were stimulated in my mind by the sight of that palace! How mutable human affairs are! How the resident of that estate must meditate upon that when from its windows he surveys the immense perspective that the banks of the Delaware offer him!

Naples! Madrid! Bordentown! As he watches that splendid river flow by at his feet, how he must review the various events of a life fraught with misadventures! Does he ever thank Heaven that after such a tempestuous life he has come to reside in peace among these fierce and generous republicans?[97] I suspect not, because the anecdote that I have just recounted, and the fact that he still demands to be called *the king* by his servants, clearly indicate that his soul does not possess the mettle to enjoy his present lucky state, and that he imagines himself still surrounded by the usurped splendor that the crown at one time earned him . . .[98]

Despite the seriousness of such reflections, I couldn't help but laugh when I remembered that vile ruse by which Lucas was able to get a bit of money out of him, and went off chuckling at his credulousness. Do you remember how he threw himself at Joseph's feet, exclaiming "Oh my King! Oh my Lord!" etc.?[99]

But the most agreeable emotion that I felt during the whole trip was when I disembarked once more along the bay, and saw, on a crystalline April afternoon, at a distance of some six to eight miles, beautiful New York rising from the ocean. Two centuries ago upon the island on which it was founded only some miserable savages could be found, gazing dully at a sun to which they were exposed in all their naked misery. Today a city, the mistress of the seas, looks on as the sons and the products of every region of the earth flock to it; and happy with its one hundred thousand enlightened and fortunate inhabitants, it towers above the sea, crowned with spires and the masts of ships. Countless steamboats speed continuously along its bay and the rivers that embrace it, scorning their currents as well as the ocean winds. It is a grandiose sight, which would make any person proud of his humanity, were it not that the human mind that has produced such a city finds itself degraded by errors and crimes at every turn.

Within the next two weeks, I plan to go to New Haven or some other small city, where, isolated from the company of other Spanish speakers, I can make more rapid progress in my English. Perhaps Navarro or Caraballo will go as well, but since each of us will live in a separate house, our goal will be achieved. At the same time we will be able to keep an eye on each other, and help each other out in any predicament we may find ourselves in; otherwise it would be irksome to be alone amongst all these "Greeks." However, you should continue to send your letters to me via New York, placing the letters in care of

Latting who will forward them to Mr. Howland, who will know my whereabouts and forward them to me.

I am very sorry about the business of A . . .'s letter, because I would have been very happy to receive one from him; but you did the right thing, and my sense of friendship and gratitude oblige me to approve of your prudence. Tell him that I don't write him because it isn't safe to do so, and I don't want to expose him to any unpleasant consequences should a letter from me fall into the wrong hands, since the mere fact that I write him might discredit him with certain people. That way he will not attribute my silence to having forgotten him or to ingratitude, of which I am incapable.[100] Do you think you may be able to get me a copy of my letter to Pancho Hernández along with the commentary that, according to my mother, that friend made? I very much would like to see it, and I will be very grateful if you send it.

There is no need to tell you how pained I am about Rueda's death. You know the esteem in which I held him, and how obliged I was to him for his recent kindnesses and demonstrations of friendship.

I very much enjoyed the paragraph that you devoted in your letter to giving me the news from town. Please continue to do so, and in your Sunday letters from the coffee grove, tell me all about the most noteworthy events that have occurred during the week. It shouldn't be hard for you to devote a half hour, which otherwise you would spend sprawled out sleeping like a caiman (to quote Chea), to giving me that great consolation in my ill-fated "old age."

I had a silhouette done in the Philadelphia Museum, and I am sending along one of the copies. If you put it against a black background, you will have a sort of portrait of me.

I already have written you that Betancourt has relocated to Baltimore, which I am extremely happy about.[101] In Philadelphia I ran into the famous Caraso, to whom, it seems, they gave a good scare in Cuba.

Good-bye for now, brother. Remember me to all the girls, give Chea an embrace for me and tell her to have some pity on the carpenters, and not to forget that poor knock-kneed one. My regards to Don Joaquín, to Don Pedro Hernández, Veguilla, Corneta and one-eyed Alfonso; my very best regards to Dalcour and Borthiribort.[102] Do not fail to write me, always let me know how the legal proceedings are coming along, and tell me about all my friends, and be as happy as your most loving nephew wishes you to be.

José Mª

My good man, you have told me nothing about Señor Don Juan de la Riva y Vértiz, and you know how much I care for him.

I am sending my mother some lines of verse and some picture cards, with the request that she send them along to you, for you to amuse yourself in the coffee grove.

New York, 3

As I am including with this letter the one that I wrote you about Philadelphia, to avoid confusion I have written "New York" above and will number my letters. I think it behooves us to number all our letters, as I will be doing from now on; that way we will know if some of our letters get lost.

April 24

Today I received your overdue letter of March 7. With regard to what you tell me about the Bank of the United States, I can tell you that it has $35 million in assets, divided in shares of $100 each. It pays its shareholders 5% per year, and even though it is in Philadelphia, it has offices for deposits and withdrawals in all cities of any importance. But there are many other banks that pay higher interest than it does, because with less assets they are able to transfer and employ them usefully with greater ease. In New York alone you have the Bank of America, the City Bank, the Union Bank, the Phoenix Bank, the businessmen's bank, the merchants' bank, the mechanics' bank, the North River Bank, the East River Bank, Bank of New York, the Franklin Bank, the Manhattan Bank, and others that I can't recall. The one that pays the most interest is the Bank of New York, which pays 8%. Its $100 shares are at 135–137, and those of the United States Bank are at 109–111. Those of other banks, like the Bank of America, the Union Bank and the City Bank, which with their great assets only pay 5%, are at 95–97.

Beyond that, I wouldn't venture to tell you much, since, even though I now speak some English, my command is not such that I would attempt to enter into conversations about political economy with these people. So you must have a bit of patience.

The profits of the banks proceed from the loss of bills placed in circulation, and from the earnings of 4% per month that they make by advancing money on promissory notes to be paid back in installments.

I think you will enjoy hearing about an incident that demonstrates the character of these people better than any description. The state legislature relieved DeWitt Clinton of his position as director of canal construction. Last Monday on every corner and in every public place and newspaper the following notice appeared: "An expression of public sentiment. The citizens of the city of New York who disapprove of the removal of DeWitt Clinton, who for fourteen years has served without any salary or compensation, from the position of director of canals, will meet at five o'clock this afternoon in the park, to adopt the resolutions that justice and the honor of the state of New York demand." I trembled when I saw this announcement, fearing social upheaval. At the appointed hour, the vast space of the park, which is the principal square where City Hall is located, filled with people. No measures were taken to prevent the gathering. A table was brought and placed in the midst of the crowd, but scarcely had the speaker climbed upon it, when others of the opposing party upset the table and knocked him to the ground but without laying a hand on him . . . He got up and dusted off his dress coat with the gravest demeanor; and while some of his friends came to help clean him off, others shoved the troublemakers away from the table and surrounded it. The speaker got up on it again, and continued his harangue unperturbed. The result was an agreement to name a delegation that would go to express to citizen Clinton the displeasure with which the people of New York regarded his removal; their satisfaction with his conduct; their indignation regarding the injustice committed by the legislature; and their hope that after the next elections justice would be done him. Upon which all present went on their way without the authorities saying a word to anybody.[103] There was some minor scuffling among those who were most worked up, but no one else got involved, because as you know, here one can kill a man with his fists[104] without the law getting involved, but they invariably hang a man who takes a sharp knife in hand to go after someone. That is why all the table knives have rounded ends, to avoid trouble.

I am not sure if I will be able to send you something to read in the coffee grove, even though with these two letters you already have enough to occupy a whole morning. If there is time I will send you something that I have written about the state prison. Now you can't complain that I haven't written you at length, since these seven sheets of paper are the equivalent of all the letters you have written me. Good-bye for now. Give Doña María an embrace for me, remember me to all those mentioned above, and do not forget your most loving

José Mª

I am going to try to copy a sort of diary that I have been writing, so that I can send it to you in the care of some acquaintance. Let me know if my letters sent directly are costing you anything, and how much, and I will send it in pieces, so that you are not charged additional postage.

To María de la Merced Heredia y Campuzano [Augier no. 44]

New York, May 1, 1824

My dearest Mother:

I already have written you a long letter that will go on the same ship as this one, but since the ship has been delayed until today, I am writing you a few lines to let you know I am fine.

It has been some days since I have had a letter from you, but I am reassured by one that I have received from Ignacio dated April 4, in which he tells me that all is well with you and the family.

I am very sorry about the death of my good friend Dr. Hernández.[105] May God punish his cowardly assassins. Are those men not capable of remorse? Or do they suppose that death does not await them as well, and that upon departing this life they will not hear, from the thundering mouth of the accusing angel, the long litany of evils that they have caused with their vile vengeance? May I never be condemned to the torment of seeing those men before me constantly; I would rather remain here. If I return to Cuba, I will go to live in Havana and only return to Matanzas infrequently, and that way avoid the presence of our iniquitous persecutors. My heart—too generous—does not wish them ill, but I don't know if my blood could remain calm in the presence of the vile Hernández[106] and a few others.

I also have learned of the death of Sterling. Let me know what the family is planning to do.[107]

Good-bye, be well. Give the delinquents a thousand embraces;[108] tell Ignacia that this letter is for her too, and that she should write me; regards to Aunt Francisca and Magdalena, whose letters are on their way by ship to Santo Domingo; to Franco, Doña Pepa, Antonio, Doña Ángela, Antonio Angulo and family, the Fernández girls,[109] and you be as happy as your loving son desires.

José M^a

Do not be surprised if there is a lapse in my letters, for in eight days or so I am leaving on a trip of 400 miles to see the falls at Niagara, and will be away for some days.

Let me know the number of the house in which you are living.

To María de la Merced Heredia y Campuzano [Augier no. 45]

Brooklyn, May 8, 1824

My Dearest Mother:

It has been many days since I have had the pleasure of receiving a letter from you, and the last that I received from Ignacio was only through April 4, which has me uneasy. I hope, however, that this is due to the lack of a ship coming this way, or of your awareness of one.

Tomorrow I will leave for Albany, capital of this state, and from there I will travel on to see the famous falls at Niagara. Perhaps once there I will be inspired to continue on to Canada, and from there come down through Boston. So it is likely that you won't receive a letter from me for some days, and with this warning you shouldn't have reason to worry. But the lapse will not be long, since I will write you from Quebec and Boston on the way back.[110]

A few days ago I wrote you at length and sent the letter along with Agustín Hernández, and I have nothing to add now, except that I am well.

The last two letters that I have received for Santiago are on their way via the offices of a merchant who dispatches a ship directly to Santo Domingo. I will write him as well.

I wrote Ignacio two days ago, and I plan to do so again from Albany, if I learn of a ship ready to sail from New York.

Tell Ignacia to read the description of Niagara Falls, which I am going to see, in *Atala*.[111]

Good-bye, dear Mother. My regards to Osés, Franco and family, the Fernández girls, Doña Ángela and husband and children, Aunt Francisca and Magdalena, and a thousand embraces for my sisters. Give me your blessing and do not forget to write to your most loving son

José Mª

15th

The 9th dawned very cold, and I didn't depart on my trip. I have decided to wait for some days, until the weather stabilizes and this blasted cold weather finally ends. I will leave during the first days of June. You should always address your letters like this:

J. M. Heredia, Esq.
Care of Messrs. Goodhue & Co.
New York

If you don't, with my change of houses the letters may get lost. Good-bye.

To María de la Merced Heredia y Campuzano [Augier no. 47]

New York, May 25, 1824

My dearest Mother:

I have received two letters from you, dated April 24 and May 11, via Silvestre Alfonso and Pancho Ruiz,[112] and as always with great pleasure.

With regard to the letter I wrote before fleeing, I must say that I find no substance in your statement that the letter is damaging to me. No one forced me to write it; it was the result of prudence and reflection, not recklessness. My imprisonment had been decreed and my fate was inevitable. Why should I give any credit, with a silent escape, to the malicious rumors that our enemies were spreading? Even if I had denied everything in writing, what would that have been worth, when hundreds of cowards had run to the feet of the dictator of Matanzas, to say not only the truth, but whatever the rancor and perversity of our prosecutors dictated? There was something solemn and grand in my confession of the simple truth at that moment, coming as it did from a man who did not do it out of fear, nor to win some despicable pardon, which at any rate he renounced by fleeing the country. My letter did not implicate me in any crime; the only thing to fear was the imprisonment that might result from the indictment which, in its obscurity, might implicate me. When the harm was already done, my confession could only serve to make them see that I was not as they supposed, and that there was someone with sufficient energy to tell the truth, and undeceive those gullible ones who, thinking they were at the edge of the abyss, saw the vile Hernández as their savior, and frenetically testified against us. I also was afraid that these crude and fanatical Spaniards might go too far and do harm to my family, and I tried to abate their fury in some way. Perhaps I am fooling myself, but I believe that that letter opened the eyes of many, and was a fitting conclusion to the indictment. At any rate, I have harmed no one, but rather the letter will prevent them from slandering me. Anyone who says that my letter is what is preventing me from returning to Havana should read the testimony of Don Antonio Betancourt, Don Juan G. Aranguren, Don Manuel Andux, Don Manuel del Portillo and Don Francisco Mihoura,[113] and then look for the pages I wrote on the 5th and 6th of November; there they will see how wrong they are. And let them rip out the aforesaid testimony and replace it, if they want, with a hundred copies of my letter. If they do that, I will embark for Havana the next day. Please show Franco this paragraph, and tell him for me that while I am profoundly grateful for his kindness, I am sorry that they have deceived him.[114]

    As for your recommendation that I save out of my monthly allowance, that is not so easy, since everything here is very expensive. What I intend to do is travel, since passage on steamships and canal boats is so inexpensive that travel amounts to no more than changing lodgings. I had planned to depart very soon, but have been detained by some comrades who have arrived on the *Fulton*. But I will leave within a week or so.

By now, Agustín Hernández will have had time to rest up from his trip to Havana, and he will have given you a long account of my life here. I estimate that it will cost between $250 and $300 to print the *Historia de Venezuela*.[115] I had thought that if it were to be published I would write an appendix, but subsequent events prevent me from doing that. They would accuse a fugitive like me of being biased. If you have someone there who can copy it, it would be a good thing to do, and then send it to me with someone who can be trusted. I think that these days there is more opportunity for making money in publishing than ever, since people are less caught up in weighty matters and their attention is freer. In addition, from here I can send copies for sale in Mexico and Colombia, which would be more difficult from Havana. So have a copy made as soon as you can. Does José Miguel Angulo have good handwriting? Perhaps some of the Dominicans with free time can do it. It would have taken me about two weeks to do. Why shouldn't someone else be able to do it in that time?

With regard to money, there is no need for you to worry. I have secured enough to live on for two years, should some unfortunate occurrence so require, and during that time it is impossible that in this fortunate country I wouldn't be able to find some honorable and independent occupation, once I learn its language well.

As for the fears that you express about a hasty marriage, I could only laugh at first and then nearly weep. This is hardly the time for affairs of the heart for me![116] What could I offer a girl but a heart that has been dried up by its own ardor and by misfortune? A fugitive, with neither home nor homeland, would I dare to subject a girl that I loved to the turmoil of my perilous life? I would have to be mad to do so, and thank God I am still far from that.

I am sending the little chair via Matanzas, in the care of an acquaintance who will be leaving in a few days.

I will write to Ignacio on that same occasion. Take good care, give my regards to the Fernández girls, to Franco and family, the Castros (tell Antonio to come and see me), my love to my sisters, to Rafaela, to Coqui and son, and to Aunt Ángela's family, Aunt Francisca and Nena.[117] Do not forget, and give your blessing to your most beloved and obedient son

José M^a

Let me know how much it costs you to receive my letters by mail, so that I can adjust accordingly.

To Ignacio Heredia Campuzano [BNJM: *Moda*; Augier no. 48]

New York, June 2, 1824

Much loved Ignacio:

With great pleasure I received your two letters dated May 6th and 9th, and I am taking advantage of this occasion to write you at length.

None of your letters are missing; I believe I have received them all, because checking the dates I see that you have written me every Sunday since you left for Havana, and I have received all the others as already acknowledged. But when I left for Philadelphia, the last one I had received was that of February 13, and when I returned I received the others almost at the same time. So keep writing me via Howland, or tell Latting to send your letters to Goodhue & Co. Cristóbal Madan works in their offices, and he brings them to me right away.

I have already mentioned, and you will know that the great Teurbillo[118] is here, having escaped from prison in Havana, and I ran into him when I was called by his landlady to serve as interpreter when she was working out an agreement with him. I was much surprised to see him, and I am so glad that he has been able to save himself from some unfortunate outcome. Mariano Tarrero and the most praiseworthy Dr. Miguel Antonio de la Madruga have not appeared, and I fear that they will be caught.[119] They had gotten separated from Teurbillo and were not able to board ship. How they must have regretted that!

Now let us speak of my trip to Niagara. I will begin it in three or four days, since the honorable Don Juan de Acosta has asked me to wait so that he can join me. I am very happy about that, not only because I appreciate his excellent character, but also because to venture into such godforsaken places alone is not a pleasant prospect. If the ship by which I send this letter is detained, as is always the case, then the bearer of this letter will inform you of my departure.

This trip will offer me the opportunity to write you about my adventures. I don't know that I will send you, for now, the observations that I promised you, because as I make progress in my English, I correct some of my previous errors, and I am afraid there will be more, and I don't want to inflict those upon you. As long as God gives me life, there will be time for everything.

I am enclosing another poem by Ossian; I say "another" because I believe you have already received "The Battle of Lora," which I sent to Mother, with the request that she send it on to you.[120] I already mentioned to you that in English it is in prose, and I have tried to return to poetry the treasures of which ignorance has deprived it. It is not up to me to decide if my attempt has been felicitous or disastrous, but what I can say is that the genius of the blind bard of Albion should have risen on occasions to the level of that of Homer, if men of letters, who can be fanatics at times, had not placed limits on human ingenuity, declaring that nothing can equal the Greek poet. But in my favor I have the vote of an extraordinary genius who is worth more than all the academies of Europe: Napoleon read Ossian constantly, as Achilles did Homer.

It seems to me that the approval of the immortal Quintana authorizes me to send you a few poems that you have not yet seen.[121] Along with the poem "Imistona" I am sending an ode to the night and two sonnets, which I believe are the best I have done. After you have read the notebook, send it on to Pepilla with the understanding that it is to be returned, so that you can send it to Mother.[122]

Let us speak a little of beautiful New York. The weather now is lovely, although until the end of last month the cold still remembered that this is its domain. All of the trees along the walkways and streets are in leaf, and offer their modest shade to those who are bothered by the sun. In addition, all the shopkeepers, booksellers, etc. put out their awnings along the sidewalks in front of their stores; and since Broadway is full of these, one can almost walk along without ever being in the sun. The gardens have opened, and one can find ice cream and refreshments there. Don't imagine that they are anything grand: these gardens are no more than a courtyard with a few spindly bushes and thirty or forty alcoves,[123] with a little table and two benches where one can sit to have refreshments. The gardens in Brooklyn are better because they are more spacious. The Military Garden is worthy of attention. The only thing I didn't like was to see a bust of Napoleon alongside one of Washington. When will men cease to be unjust, and admire true glory, which is to do what is right and good?

The garden called Vauxhall, at the end of Broadway, is the best that I have seen here. It is large, it has lots of beautiful flowers and there are proper gazebos, not just alcoves. At its center there is an equestrian statue of Washington, quite second-rate, and along the paths there are various plaster busts representing heroes of antiquity. I was very happy to see there one of father Homer. Upon each of the gazebos can be found the name of a distinguished American patriot. But so that you will see that here no one passes up the chance to make a profit, let me tell you that they charge a *real* at the entrance, and then, if you want, they give you wine or ice cream. The important thing is to get rid of the idlers, and make the visitors spend some money. On some evenings the garden is completely illuminated and there are fireworks; then admission costs four *reales*.

I don't know if you know that Vicente Rocafuerte has been appointed secretary to the Mexican plenipotentiary in London. He has left for his destination, and I believe that they did not give him native plenipotentiary status.[124]

The United States Congress has ended its session, and all thoughts now are on the next presidential election. There are many candidates, but the most noteworthy ones are: John Quincy Adams, son of former President Adams, current Secretary of State, and the author of that beautiful speech translated by Rocafuerte;[125] General Jackson; and Mr. Crawford, Secretary of the Treasury. It is generally believed that Adams will be elected, and I hope that it is so.

Tell me what Domingo del Monte is doing in Matanzas, what has become of Veguilla, and if he is still so in love as when he would become enraged upon hearing the name of that poor ethicist. Tell me about the Delmonte girls, the Rueda girls, Nicola, etc., and don't forget the great Govín[126] and the others of the noble profession of the pen. I never get news about the town, which so interests and amuses me. Does Don Norberto de Norris still hold the high position that he had? Is Sotico as vile and stupid as always? Speaking of him, do you know that I forgot to mention to you his audacity in telling you that I shared part of my legal fees with him? It is such a lie; a few days after I took on a few cases he told me that he should be given the fourth or third part of the fees. I told him he was much mistaken, and to persuade me, he cited the glorious names of Fue and Diatifas.[127] Finally I told him to stop driving me crazy, and if he wanted he could take his papers, since I didn't need them at all. What a scoundrel and swindler that one is. Don't give him any portion of my fees, but give the commission to poor Corneta, so that he will have that little income, and won't have to squeeze so hard on the appraisals.[128]

Please send on the enclosed letters to Domingo and Veguilla, and the one for Pancho García you should give to his brother José, so that he can send it on either to the sugar mill or to Havana.

Silvestre Alfonso is now here, along with Pepe, Cirilo Ponce, Pancho Ruiz, Saco[129] and others from Havana, who arrived on the *Robert Fulton*.[130] They are very determined and confident about learning English in four months, but time will tell. It is too bad that Dr. Lanas is not here, since he knew how to work such miracles.

I miss you more with each day that passes, and I constantly imagine myself with you in the coffee grove when it is in flower, the two of us sitting and conversing under the awning, and breathing that aromatic air that only can be found on the island of Cuba. Oh well, we must be patient, and wait to see how all this turns out.

Don't forget to fill me in on the conspiracy hearings.

And you must not complain that my letters are too brief. Good-bye for now. Be well, give Chea an embrace for me, my regards to Abus, Don Pedro Borthiribort and my other deserving friends, without forgetting that one,[131] and count always on your most loving

José Mª

I am enclosing an article on theater; I thought that half a page would be enough, but it did not turn out that way.

Be advised that this letter should be delivered to you in person, and you can do as you wish with the first page of the article.

To Ignacio Heredia Campuzano [BNJM; *Moda*; Augier no. 49]

Albany, June 7, 1824

My dear Ignacio:

Since the shores of the Hudson are so celebrated for their sublime beauty, I think that you will not mind reading the following lines whose intent is to sketch them as they have appeared to me in the trip that I have just made from New York to this city.

The steamships that run this route are very beautiful. It was on the Hudson that these were first established after the discovery and successful application of steam power, and that alone would be sufficient to draw the attention of the traveler to this river. Some of these ships, like the *Chancellor Livingston* and the *James Kent*, have more than a hundred permanent bunks in separate cabins for men and women. Their cleanliness and beauty cannot be praised enough. The cost of passage is $6 including meals.[132]

I embarked at six in the morning, and soon we began our journey. On the far shore of the Hudson, facing New York, is Jersey City, more commonly known as Powles Hook, in the state of New Jersey. The handsome town of Hoboken is about three miles upriver, along the same shore. That is where New Yorkers go to duel, and a little farther along can be found a small white obelisk that marks the spot where the illustrious General Hamilton died at the hands of Coronel Burr, sacrificing to a false sense of honor a life that was precious to his family and his nation. His killer lives in New York, and has never been prosecuted since the duel occurred in New Jersey, and by crossing the river he eluded the retribution of the law.

Across from Hoboken is Greenwich, which is the refuge for New Yorkers when yellow fever strikes in summer months. It has a sprinkling of new and elegant buildings.

After Greenwich, the New York shoreline inclines gently toward the water, and in contrast the New Jersey shoreline is rough and craggy until the point where the small river that connects the Hudson with Long Island Sound forms the island of Manhattan.

From there on, the New Jersey shoreline becomes higher and higher, until it forms a very lofty and steep cliff, which with the name of the Palisades continues for many miles, and gives the river a unique appearance. This immense wall of granite rises perpendicularly 200 to 300 feet above the surface of the river, in which it reflects its grand and melancholy countenance. Its ridge is crowned with pine trees, and here and there some vegetation sprouts from the cracks in that immense cliff, whose end point, enshrouded in the river mist, is invisible to the eye of the traveler. Its massiveness was never so apparent to me as when I spotted some men who were gazing at the river from its summit. I was astonished by their apparent tininess, and at the same time I felt an involuntary shudder of terror to see them at the very edge of that immense precipice.

The New York shoreline forms an admirable contrast. All along it one sees cheerful hamlets and cultivated fields adorned with the luxuriant green of spring. From the river, one has the sense of being between the smile of Nature at its most benign and beautiful on one side, and the austere frown of Nature at its most wild and sublime on the other.

At intervals one sees waterfalls tumbling noisily from the Palisades to the Hudson. The river broadens considerably until it reaches a width of five miles in a spot they call the Tappan Zee. This is a sort of lake, ten miles or more long. At its end a point juts out that seems to block passage, but once around it, one obtains an immediate view of the Highlands, through which the river passes.

The Palisades end at the Tappan Zee, and with them the state of New Jersey, and both banks present an equally cheerful picture which extends to the Highlands, which one can see in the distance. All along one sees country houses, meadows, and long rows of poplar and fruit trees, which seem to stretch out before the traveler as he advances.

Upon arriving at Peekskill, the nearby Highlands seem to close in upon the river. Its channel becomes very narrow and deep, and the Highlands seem to grow visibly as the ship swiftly advances, and the traveler casts a farewell look at the cheerful fields of Peekskill as the ship rounds the point where the river takes a sudden turn and is enclosed by mountains.

The scene changes here, and takes on a more severe character, and incomparably majestic and sublime. Farewell, cheerful plains! Wherever one looks, one sees only craggy mountains 1200 to 1500 feet high, which rise up almost perpendicularly from the river that laps at their base and reflects their long shadows upon its still waters, and which change in appearance according to the greater or lesser force of the sun's rays and the atmospheric conditions. In some parts one sees immense cliffs devoid of any vegetation, while other parts are covered with pine trees, within whose uniform and gloomy verdure one can see the long, stark outline of plunging waterfalls. The military academy of West Point, with its 250 cadets, is located along the right bank.[133] Many interesting events of the Revolutionary War are associated with this spot.

Immediately following is the Sugarloaf, whose conical shape has given it its name.[134]

In stretches the part of the mountains facing the river is cut perpendicularly by the Palisades, and from a distance they seem to be the wall of some old fortress. What most surprised me was to see some letters perfectly carved in the face of the cliff, which could be distinguished from a distance among the mosses. Who was the reckless man who, on some ridiculous whim, lowered himself on ropes into that abyss? Truth can indeed seem stranger than fiction, and if it had not been for the number and the perfection of these carved letters, I would have thought that they were but a caprice of nature.

After passing West Point, the traveler sees the beautiful countryside of New Windsor and Newburgh open before him, and as he approaches them, he passes the last hills of the Highlands, which rise up like giants to guard the rich plains that follow. The passage of the river through the Highlands is of some 16 to 18 miles. These Highlands are a branch of the great Appalachian or Allegheny chain.

Upon leaving the Highlands behind, one sees in the distance the Catskill Mountains, another branch of the Appalachians, extending to the north. These are the highest mountains in the state of New York. Their highest peaks rise more than 3000 feet above sea level.[135]

At sundown we reached Poughkeepsie, a town situated on the east bank of the river, which because of the unevenness of the terrain and the unusual aspect of its surroundings, presents a most novelesque appearance. Its houses seemed to me to be well built, especially one that displayed to the river a beautiful portico in the Greek style.

We continued our journey, and as the sun set I cast a glance at the scene that surrounded me. The sun's last rays illumined the transparent vapors that gathered around the Catskill Mountains, and made them appear to be floating in a long cloud of gold. Behind the trees rose the steeples of Poughkeepsie, and in the distance the imposing Highlands. On both sides rich fields opened before the eye, and their beauty was enhanced by the soft and melancholy shades of twilight. Some becalmed sloops could be seen in the distance, and their motionless sails were reflected in the waters, along with the shadows of the mountains. The surface of the river was as smooth as polished silver, and only was stirred by the movement of our floating Leviathan. Meanwhile the sun disappeared in a sky adorned with all the brilliance and purity of that of Cuba, and the friendly Moon began to admire her reflection in the bosom of the waters.[136]

We then passed along the Catskill Mountains, and the steamship made a stop to take on and let off passengers in Hudson, a city situated on the east shore of the river, 28 miles below Albany. The town of Athens is on the other shore. The countless people I saw strolling in the moonlight, enjoying the cool air along the banks of the river, made a very pleasant picture. I cannot give an account of any more than this, because as we departed from Hudson I went to bed, and next morning upon waking I found that we were at the wharf in Albany. The river is navigable for larger ships as far as Hudson.

I should say something about the steamships and their service. On this trip there were some 60 passengers on board, not counting women. The food was quite good, although I wasn't able to enjoy it fully because of the excessive voracity of my companions. The distance from New York to Albany is about 160 miles, which the steamships cover in 21 hours. I have seen the *James Kent* make the trip in less than 15.

I will not mention the many towns along the banks of the Hudson, since that would only amount to a litany of outlandish names, and anyone wishing to know these only has to examine a large-scale map of the state of New York. My purpose here is not to write a geography book, but to communicate my impressions to a dear friend. So suffice it to say that what I most enjoyed and admired was to see, moored at the wharf of every one of these little towns, some boats that were loading and unloading cargo and that were, in sum, full of activity and life.

Generally, the boats employed on the Hudson are sloops, which have a shallow draught, can accommodate a great deal of cargo because of their width, are swift and stout, and have a section with six to eight very clean cabins, equipped with everything for passengers. I had thought that the calculation that there are two thousand sloops in service on the Hudson was an exaggeration, but now I do not doubt its accuracy.[137]

To Ignacio Heredia Campuzano [BNJM; *Moda*; Augier no 50]

Troy, June 8, 1824

In my last letter, I told you about my trip along the Hudson and my arrival in Albany. Now I must give you an idea of what the capital of New York is like. The appearance of Albany is disagreeable, because its streets are generally narrow and dirty. It would be hard to find another place with such a confused mix of clean and tasteful modern buildings, and dark, run-down older ones.

Market Street, which runs parallel to the river, has some good buildings, among them the Mechanics and Farmers Bank, which is of white marble and has an elegant glass dome. Next to it is the Bank of Albany, whose handsome façade of white marble is disfigured by the unsuitable roof that dominates it.

Across from these banks, State Street runs into Market at right angles. The view that it presents at that juncture is quite pleasing: its breadth offers a pleasant contrast to the narrow crookedness of the other streets, and it is adorned with the State Bank, fine houses, some trees, and above all the Capitol building, which forms the opposite terminus of State Street from Market. This is a handsome stone building, which presents to State Street a portico supported by four handsome columns of white marble, and it is crowned by an elegant dome atop which majestically arises a statue representing Justice. The Capitol is at the top of a hill, and from its portico one enjoys a handsome view of the city, the Hudson River, the rich fields and nearby hamlets, and the distant mountains that complete the picture. On the same hill, to the north of the Capitol, there is an Academy built of stone with two wings, which is quite a fine and beautiful building.[138]

I went into the Capitol building. All of its corridors were deserted and its chambers closed; the function of each was indicated in yellow lettering on tin plaques. I looked for someone who might take me up to the dome, but I didn't find a living soul to speak with. That open, abandoned building seems more like a solitary, intact temple in the midst of a ruined city, rather than the meeting place for representatives and lawmakers of a great and powerful people.

There are many churches in Albany, but since I did not spend a Sunday there, I cannot give an account of their interiors. But judging by its exterior, one on Hudson Street, which looks like an ancient Greek temple, is worthy of attention for the purity and simplicity of its architecture.

Albany has lots of people from out of town, and so it has some very good inns. Above all, one marvels at the great number of highway coaches, which everywhere can be seen entering and departing the city.

Albany is now the center of the immense commerce that derives from the Western and Northern canals. Its wharves are always crowded with the great covered boats that navigate the canals, whose products are carried to New York by the Hudson River sloops. Despite this fact, and the advantages that it enjoys as state capital, it has a population of only 12,000–13,000 inhabitants.

This morning I left Albany for this city. The distance is 6 miles, and the price of the coach just 6 *reales*. We came along the west bank of the Hudson River, and when we arrived at Gibbonsville,[139] where there is a United States arsenal, we crossed the river in a flat boat like our *andariveles*,[140] impelled by wheels turned by two horses, and we arrived here after a one-hour trip. Along the way I got my first look at the great Western canal.

Troy is a handsome town, much more attractive than Albany. Its streets are drawn in a straight line, are lined with poplars and other trees, and are wide and clean. The houses in general are very well kept; and few strolls could be more pleasant than the one I took up a nearby hill, from which one can enjoy a varied and expansive view of the river, the canal, Albany in one direction and in the other Lansingburgh and Waterford with their delightful countryside.

Troy has two banks, very fine inns, cotton, wool and paper factories, several flour mills, a firearms factory, and a number of other establishments. It has between 5,000 and 6,000 inhabitants, and is said to be the fourth city of the state in terms of commerce and wealth.

To Ignacio Heredia Campuzano [BNJM; *Moda*; Augier no. 51]

Utica, June 11, 1824

My dear Ignacio:

Yesterday at seven in the morning, I left Troy for Schenectady in a handsome stagecoach. The distance is thirteen miles, and the price is 5 *reales*. We crossed the river again in the cable ferry, and arrived at Schenectady without incident.

Schenectady is located along the banks of the Mohawk River, and has a bank and several churches. Union College is there, with more than two hundred students, and is located in a beautiful spot. The Great Western Canal passes through the streets of the town, whose population is close to 4,000 inhabitants.

I went to see the canal and get information about the departure of the packet boats. With that object I entered a covered boat, which

I found to be full of books, all of them new and many in deluxe editions, and there was a lottery office as well. The books are perfectly arranged on shelves; and in a compartment of the boat I saw the bookseller's family which, comfortably settled in its floating home, was going about its everyday business. This bookstore operates along the canal to accommodate the lovers of reading in all the towns it serves. That same afternoon I saw it leave for Utica.

I continued on, and came across a museum . . . Yes, a covered boat full of wax figures, portraits, paintings and natural curiosities, which sails along to the sound of a creaky organ that summons all the local yokels, played by a ragged rascal who, in the advertisements, gives himself the pompous title of "Superintendent." The boat is called the *Canal Museum*. Don't these seem like fairy tales?

The time has come, I think, for me to tell you about this great canal which, although not yet complete, is already transforming the face of this country for the better, drawing to it the blessings of abundance and the admiration of other nations.

"In this admirable enterprise," reads *The North American Review*, New York has displayed an enterprising and exemplary spirit, beyond all praise. The canal of the Great Lakes is an undertaking that the most powerful government could boast of . . ."[141] "The canal of Languedoc is no less the admiration of Europe, than the glory of the reign of Louis XIV; yet . . . it cannot enter into a comparison with the great western canal."[142]

This canal was begun on July 4, 1817, and is now navigable for a distance of some 300 miles. When it is finished, it will be 360 miles or so long; its width at the surface is 40 feet, at the bottom 28, and it is 4 feet deep. It begins near Albany at the Hudson river, running along its west bank until the place where it empties into the Mohawk; from there it follows the banks of that river until Rome, where it heads to the southwest, crosses the Oneida River, and turns again west, passing through Onondaga County, about a mile and a half from Salina, at the southern end of Onondaga Lake. It crosses the Seneca River in Montezuma, and passing through Lyons and Palmyra, crosses the Genesee River in Rochester. To the west of the Genesee it continues in the same direction for 60 miles; from there it turns south, and joins the Tonnewanta,[143] 11 miles before it joins the Niagara River; it continues along the channel of the Tonnewanta for those 11 miles and after reaching the Niagara it runs parallel to the east bank of that river until Buffalo on Lake Erie, where it ends. There is a difference of more than 550 feet between the level of Lake Erie and that of the Hudson. Upon leaving the former, the canal climbs 48 feet through locks and then descends another 600 feet to the Hudson. Along its entire route it will have some 80 locks, each one 90 feet long and 14 feet wide.

One only has to glance at a map of the United States to understand, with amazement, how this splendid work of engineering makes New York the center of a vast network of transportation and commerce. The western part of the state, which is very fertile, will be settled rapidly, and perhaps without this great artificial river it would have remained woefully uncultivated for many centuries. What colonist would not be discouraged in view of the hundreds and hundreds of miles that separate him from the sea, and the costs of transportation through that vast wilderness which would absorb all the profits from his products, leaving him, like another Tantalus, in the bosom of misery, despite the unavailing fertility of the land that he cultivates?

But the Erie Canal has leveled that terrible obstacle, putting the inhabitants of western New York in contact with the ocean. It has been calculated that one horse can haul via the canal what it would take 60 horses to haul overland. What an enormous advance!

Who the initiator of this great project was has been the subject of much debate. It seems most likely that two or three people proposed water connections between some points in the interior, and these proposals gave birth to the magnificent idea of the great canal. DeWitt Clinton, then governor of the state, has been without a doubt the most active promoter of the undertaking. However, to show you that man is unjust and ungrateful even in the most fortunate countries that are admired as temples of enlightenment and virtue, I must tell you that the state legislature has removed him from the canal commission on which he has served, to his great glory and to the great good of his nation, for many years, without salary or any other compensation. The most scandalous thing of all is that there has been no effort to justify this ruling; in another letter I told you about the results that this had in New York City.[144] A general cry of indignation has been raised everywhere against his cowardly enemies. This and the view of the splendid fruits of his labors are enough to satisfy his generous soul.

The anticipated cost of the canal was $5,000,000 and in an outcome that could only happen here, it has been determined that it will end up costing some $200,000 less.

During the week that ended on the sixth of this month, 273 boats arrived at and departed from Utica. More than 1500 tons of merchandise were shipped west on the canal, and more than 20,000 bushels[145] of wheat and more than 12,000 barrels of flour were shipped east. (That is, they passed through Utica, which is more than 100 miles from Albany.) It was calculated at that time that canal tolls had produced more than $70,000 this year, and mind you, the canal was opened to traffic on the 5th of May.

The effects that the completion of the canal will have are incalculable, as is the enthusiasm for similar enterprises which has spread throughout the United States thanks to this brilliant example.

According to *The North American Review*, "by an artificial navigation of sixteen miles, the voyage between Buffalo and Pittsburgh would be uninterrupted. The communications between the Ohio and Lake Erie are numerous and not difficult. A shortcut would join the Muskingum, which discharges itself a hundred and seventy miles below Pittsburgh with the Cayahoga [sic]. The junction of the Scioto with the Sandusky, the Miami of the Lake with the Miami of the Ohio[146] is practicable. Michigan and Erie may unite their waters by means of the river Raisin, while by the Chicago river [sic] which runs into the former, and a branch of the river Plein [sic], a passage might be secured into the Illinois, and thence to the river Mississippi."[147] "The time must soon arrive, when that extensive territory from the Ohio to the great lakes, and from the Missouri to the borders of Pennsylvania, a country fertile and healthful, inhabited by a race of hardy and vigorous men, capable of supporting a population of enormous magnitude, a country, in comparison with which the fairest kingdom in Europe is almost sterile, will hereafter receive all which may supply its wants or add to its luxuries through New York, and will in return transmit, by the same channel, the rich fruits of an exuberant soil, owned and cultivated by a free population."[148] "The imagination is startled by its own reveries, as it surveys the coasts of Erie, Huron and Michigan, and traverses the rich prairies of Indiana, or the gloomy forests of Ohio."[149]

On another occasion I will tell you about the northern canal, which joins the waters of Lake Champlain with those of the Hudson, and extends for 61 miles from Whitehall to Waterford.

But now to return to the narration of my trip, almost forgotten in my description of the canal. Since I do not much like the clattering of carriages, and I desired to see the great artificial river of the west, I booked passage on a packet boat in Schenectady, bound for Utica.[150]

This mode of canal transportation is at once inexpensive, comfortable and safe. The packet boats enjoy all the conveniences of steamboats without their dangers, nor the discomfort of excessive heat in this season. They are 75 to 80 feet long and 12 to 13 feet wide. Thus they form a handsome cabin with eight to ten windows on each side, equipped with glass panes and blinds to protect the passengers from the sun and rain. This cabin is divided into two separate chambers for men and women; in the latter there are permanent berths and in the former the berths are set up at night. These packet boats are pulled by three horses, one behind the other, and travel about 4 miles per hour (which is the maximum speed permitted by law on the canal) without stopping until they arrive at their destination, except for a few minutes to take on or let off passengers along the way. The change of horses is accomplished imperceptibly.

Fresh horses are made ready alongside some lock, and before the boat has passed through the latter, the operation of unhitching and hitching the horses is complete. The price is four cents per mile with meals, and three without.

We departed Schenectady at seven in the afternoon to the sound of a strident trumpet, which summoned forgetful passengers even after the boat was in motion, and continued to shatter our eardrums as long as there were houses in sight.

Upon going up on deck in the morning, I experienced the most agreeable sensation. The banks of the canal were covered with flowers, and the neighboring fields displayed in their vegetation all the luxuriance of June. At the same time that I admired them with pleasure, I felt free of the iron hand that pressed my heart in the fields of Cuba when I remembered that their bounty was born of the sweat, at times of the blood, of so many miserable slaves.

That morning I enjoyed a pleasure that I had not sampled in more than seven months: the singing of birds in the morning. Why must the bloody hand of misfortune embitter even the most automatic responses of pleasure, which beautiful Nature allows the unfortunate to feel from time to time? I was able to enjoy that delightful birdsong only for a moment, and then at once it reminded me of solitary walks at night along the avenue of mango trees, the sweet ecstasy with which I listened there to the birds, our afternoon rambles, our plans to improve the coffee grove, the old armchairs, the little table sullied by Jaureguiberry,[151] and where you and I sat so many days; in sum, all our simple pleasures, all our innocent hopes . . .

As we went along, the countryside took on a wilder and gloomier character, much like my own thoughts, until we arrived at a place they call Little Falls. There the Mohawk River, whose banks the canal follows, winds around a steep, craggy peak that blocks its path. Skirting the base of that peak, the river dashes through the rocks with a mighty crash, and runs for quite a distance in the wildest confusion. The scene is ornamented with the rather distant view of the town, a proud aqueduct by which the canal crosses the river, and the high cliffs that channel the torrent. Those cliffs, undermined at their base, jut out over the traveler's head, and seem as if they are about to tumble down upon him, an effect which is made even more frightening by the enormous boulders at the foot of the ravine, which have fallen from on high. I have never seen such craggy terrain. Even the great beds of rock below, lying in inclined planes, break through the thin crust of soil and reveal the very skeleton of the earth. This cannot have been so always: such confusion does not correspond to the normal order of Nature. Without pretending to be a geologist, I am sure that at Little Falls I have seen the imprint of some terrible convulsion of our planet.

On the crest of the cliffs on one side towered some enormous pine trees, which seemed to sway among the clouds and defy the lightning bolts of the heavens. On the opposite side, there were barely a few scrubs of vegetation. In contrast to the life and movement that one had noted before along the banks of the canal, here all was desolation and solitude. Only up above, on one of the high precipices, could be seen an old man, leaning motionless against the trunk of a pine tree. He contemplated the raging torrent below, and seemed to be the very genius of solitude and meditation, contemplating sadly the agitation of men and the tempests of life.

But upon arriving before the town, the scene changes greatly. The river continues on its furious course, but man has not let it tumble away in solitude. They oblige it to turn the wheels of some mills and other factories. The town is situated in the most picturesque spot, upon some hills, and must command a varied and extensive view of the surrounding countryside.

We ate upon table service which had been ordered in Utica from Liverpool, and arrived by ship from one port to the other, even though Utica is some hundred leagues from the ocean. All the plates and other dishes were illustrated with scenes from the canal, with inscriptions that allude to the advancement that this great work is giving and will give to the state of New York.

As the weather was fine, now and then I would spring ashore and follow the packet boat on foot along the canal bank. On one of these walks, a traveling companion pointed out to me a tree called *maple* in which they make an incision at a certain time of year, and distill an excellent, pure sugar. Cubans would not much like to see the proliferation of this tree.[152]

We continually found ourselves surrounded by plains covered with grain, which, swaying in the breeze, resembled the gentle rolling of the ocean, and reminded me of the lovely verses of a modern poet, not sufficiently appreciated by his contemporaries:

> When in the East
> The sun reigns gloriously, and the sprigs of wheat
> Undulate before the soft breath
> Of the morning breeze, the entire valley
> Seems like a golden sea.[153]

Some of the canal boats that we came across were enormous covered barges, laden with merchandise or produce from the interior. On some of them one sees entire families, who are relocating from regions to the north in search of more fertile soil or a more benign climate in the western part of New York, or Ohio or Michigan. Far from regaling themselves in the luxury of the packet boats, they pile onto covered cargo boats, with all their furniture and farm implements, and for a modest price, and without the slightest fatigue, glide slowly for hundreds of miles upon those beneficent waters.

At seven in the evening we arrived at Utica, having traveled the eighty miles from Schenectady in 24 hours.

Thirty years ago Utica was an impenetrable forest, and now it aspires to be the state capital. Its progress is truly astonishing. It has two banks, some churches, factories of various sorts, and a population of three thousand souls.

The inns all along the way would do honor to our Havana. The ordinary prices are three *reales* per meal, and one or two for a bed. In Albany they are more expensive than in New York.

I have arrived in Utica on a beautiful moonlit night, and I have decided to stay so as to walk around the town, and take the packet boat to Rochester in the morning. The packets leave from Utica for the west and east at seven in the morning and seven in the evening, every day, so that without stopping one can travel the entire navigable length of the canal, which is some 300 miles, from Albany to Brockport.

I have been very satisfied by my walk around town. All these new settlements are of admirable cleanliness and regularity. They all have very wide and straight streets and are lined with trees on both sides, so that at midday one can walk along them enjoying their delightful shade. Their buildings and in particular their churches, while not having an appearance of luxury and aged grandeur like those in Boston, New York, Philadelphia and Albany, are extremely pleasing to the eye because of their tidiness and their elegant and noble simplicity.

Utica has many advantages in addition to these. It is the center of interior commerce in the state, its warehouses are full of products from all over the globe, and its Genesee Street is full of shops and stores. Rather than a town in the interior it seems like a large maritime city. Near Utica there is a great bridge over the Mohawk.

So far I am very pleased with my trip. The banks of the canal delight the eye with the inexhaustible richness and variety of their scenes, and the soul cannot but be filled with admiration and a noble pride, upon seeing that artificial river which, violating the eternal order of Nature, has climbed the peaks of hills, compelled by the triumphant force of human ingenuity, and which pours prosperity and life wherever it flows. The mind gets lost in joyful contemplation of the incalculable benefits that will result, and is elevated to God Himself.

I feel very much recovered from my melancholy, and I am sure that "he who finds himself oppressed by the demon of sadness, like that malignant spirit that upset the soul of Saul, will find, in a trip along the Western Canal, the same consolation which the music of David's harp gave to the unhappy king of Israel."[154]

To Ignacio Heredia Campuzano [BNJM; *Moda*; Augier no. 52]

Lewiston, June 15, 1824

My dear Ignacio:

The same day I wrote my last letter, I left Utica for Rochester in a packet boat. The distance is 160 miles, which can be traversed in 48 hours, and passage including food costs 6 dollars and 40 cents.

On board I encountered a girl of 12 or 13 years, as lovely and pure as an angel, who served us lunch, and then sat down to do a handwriting exercise. The captain told me that she was his only daughter, and that he was having her taught to read, so that she could keep the books and take exclusive charge of the management of their floating home.

Since the land along this part of the canal is less populated, it does not present such varied scenes, and thus we spent the whole second day floating through lonely forests.

The most striking scenes are the canal's crossing of the Seneca River and the view of Onondaga Lake.[155] The vast expanse of calm water is very agreeable to the eye, and is in harmony with the land that stretches away, perfectly level, to the foot of the hills that complete the scene in the distance.

Along the lake is the town of Salina, and the noteworthy salt factory near its springs. This product is exported to Albany and New York by canal. It is truly remarkable that, from this desolate interior region, salt is sent to the very shores of the ocean.[156]

One can only smile upon hearing the names that have been given to the towns along the canal: from Utica to Rochester, one passes through Rome, Syracuse, Palmyra, Manlius and Montezuma.[157]

I have noticed another thing: I have passed through towns that are not even mentioned in geography books published in this state in 1823. Wherever there is a bit of clearing, one sees houses being roofed, churches under construction. It is as if the banks of the canal were being populated by magic, and the sound of its beneficent waters, like the harp of the ancient Theban, were gathering around it the habitations of men.

Early on the third day we arrived at Rochester, where the canal crosses the Genesee River on a stately aqueduct constructed right over the furious rapids that tumble over the nearby falls; a more sublime and admirable sight than the celebrated hanging gardens of Babylon.

The first house in Rochester was erected in 1812, and today the town boasts more than 3,000 inhabitants and excellent buildings, among them the courthouse, several churches, presses, mills and other factories. This town is situated on the banks of the Genesee River, which empties into Lake Ontario a few miles away. Because the river flows across a vast rock mesa that extends from Ohio along the shore of Lake Erie and into the western part of New York, it plunges to Lake Ontario over two waterfalls, one in Rochester, 96 feet high, and another three miles below, 75 feet high. The mist that rises from the first of these looks from a distance like the smoke of a fire, and prismatic colors float within it in wild splendor.

At the edges of the town there are piles of wood debris[158] like in our haciendas, and there are still stretches of road in which they have not cut the tree stumps. In material form one can see man wresting a dwelling place from the wilderness.

After lunch, we took another packet boat for Brockport, twenty miles beyond, where for now canal navigation ends.[159] Before embarking we had a tremendous quarrel with the owner of another boat, who insisted that he could offer us a cheaper fare. In our boat, we paid six *reales* with food included.

Just before arriving at our destination, we enjoyed a truly original scene. The cheaper boat was coming along behind us, and to prove how fast it was by beating us to our destination, its owner was trying to pass us, wearing out the poor horses mercilessly. Our captain vowed that he would not let that happen and, jumping to shore, ran alongside our boat, with all the burning sun of June beating down upon him, and began to whip his horses just as gallantly as his rival. We passed a bend that hid, for the moment, the other boat, and in that interval, our captain began to beg anyone passing by to jump on board, in order to further impress and show up the other by pretending to have even more passengers. We passed under a bridge where about twelve men were idling, who, at the invitation of our brave commodore, precipitously jumped on board; but unfortunately they had not calculated that the boat carried a strong forward momentum, and, just as if the deck had slid out from under their feet, they all fell flat on their backs, to the great consternation of the ladies below deck, who, knowing nothing of our captain's scheme, thought that the sky had fallen. Before the men could get up, the other boat appeared, and its passengers celebrated the mishap with heartless laughter. That was the last straw for our poor captain. Exhausted from his labors, he began to curse furiously, while our new passengers got to their feet and calmly and gravely dusted each other off.

When we got to town, we found that there were no carriages available until the next day, and we were obliged to wait things out in a shabby inn, where we were free to be bored to our hearts' content.

The hour finally arrived for our departure, and we piled into a great stagecoach with nine seats, pulled by four horses. Two Englishmen with their wives, or so they claimed, plus another woman, two Americans, Don Juan and I occupied the interior of the carriage, and another passenger rode on the coachman's seat.

We traveled for thirty miles and the Englishmen did not say a single word. The only voices to be heard were mine and that of the extra woman, whom I immediately engaged in a long conversation in French, until the Englishman with whom she was traveling, who must not care for foreign languages, broke his silence to suggest to me that, since I desired to learn English, I would do well to practice it.

We followed the route of the so-called Ridge Road, which is itself something of a curiosity. It is a kind of mesa or alluvial ridge, which extends some 80 miles from the Genesee River to Niagara, along the southern shore of Lake Ontario. It is raised in the middle, and in general is from 4 to 8 *varas*[160] wide. In some stretches it is 120 to 130 feet higher than the lake, from which it is 6 to 10 miles distant. The first forty miles of this natural road are amazingly flat and pass through cultivated lands. The rest of the way until Lewiston it is uneven, cut by ravines and streams, and surrounded by thick forests within which there is the odd open field, created by the new settlers as they clear the land.

To cross the swamps, in the afternoon we found ourselves on a long and unusual causeway, which consisted of tree trunks laid horizontally one next to the other, for a stretch of some two miles. You can imagine how delightfully the coach rode over such a surface! I stood it for a while, even though the jouncing kept impelling my head directly toward the Englishman seated across from me; the idea of his kisses did not exactly appeal to me. Seeing that this entertainment was not going to end any time soon, I decided to get out and travel this stretch of the road on foot, and so I did. Now, do you think that the Englishmen cursed and swore? No Sir: they remained unperturbed; just one said with a forced smile that the road did not much resemble the one between Liverpool and London.

I had gone on ahead of the coach, and when I saw a certain bridge crossing a stream, I began to despair of greeting the great Waterfall the next day. The bridge consisted of some loose pieces of board, thrown over beams suspended on posts on either bank; I paused, and when I saw that the coachman was prepared to follow me, I began to fill in gaps, pushing one piece of board against another, all the while holding my breath in terrified suspense. The heavy carriage rolled onto the bridge, the pieces of board bounced under the wheels, the horses' hooves slipped and they almost fell through the cracks, but the whip kept them going, and against all odds they got to the other side.

We arrived in Lewiston after having traveled more than 60 miles for $2½. We dined and I went to bed. What a night, almost on the shores of sublime Ontario, under a moon that was rising gloriously behind the Queenston highlands, and hearing the vague and distant sound of the great cataract, wafted to my eyes on the southern breeze! You might imagine that sleeping amid such surroundings I would have strange and marvelous dreams. But no. I dreamed of Cuba and the San Juan River, here on the banks of the Niagara and among the most sublime scenes of North America.

To Ignacio Heredia Campuzano [BNJM; *Moda*; Augier no. 53]

Manchester, June 17, 1824

My eyes have feasted contemplating the marvel of creation, the most sublime spectacle that untamed nature offers on this earth.

At six in the morning on the 15th of this month I departed Lewiston. From the highlands one can enjoy an extensive view toward the Niagara River, which narrowly runs along a high-walled ravine; of Newark and Fort Niagara at the river's mouth, some seven or eight miles away; of Lake Ontario and its far shoreline outlined as a light zone of blue and which at times seems like a transparent little cloud extended over the waters.

The sky was absolutely clear; only toward the south one could see two clouds that constantly changed shape, sometimes dissolving into thin air, but reappearing a few seconds later in the same place. I asked about the cause of that phenomenon, and was told that it was the vapor or spray from the falls. I had heard about that, but hardly could believe that it would be visible at a distance of more than two leagues.

We continued along, following the banks of the Niagara River at some distance, and upon rounding a steep slope, caught our first sight of the great falls, at a distance of some two miles.

We arrived at Manchester, I alighted at the Eagle Hotel,[161] and without waiting another moment, ran to satisfy my eager curiosity, which very much had been spurred by the fleeting glimpse that I had enjoyed of the magnificent scene.

I headed along a path that took me to the end of the bridge that connects Goat Island with the American side, and the furious rapids led me to the edge of the precipice. As I advanced along the shore, the English or Horseshoe falls came into view behind Goat Island, and when I was able to view them completely, I found myself at the edge of the American falls, and shuddered when I realized that, unaware, I had come to within a few steps of the tremendous abyss.

I stopped, and for a few minutes I was unable to distinguish my own sensations in the midst of the confusion that the sublime spectacle caused in me. The immense, roaring river swept by in front of me, and almost at my feet it hurled itself down from a prodigious height. The waters, dissolved into fine mist upon violent impact, swirled up again in tremendous columns, which at times extended over the whole abyss and concealed part of the scene. The profound thunder of the falls was deafening, and the rainbow, arched over the precipice, was all that one could see clearly in that frightful confusion.

The Niagara River is actually a channel by which Lake Erie discharges its waters into Lake Ontario. The difference in elevation between one and the other is about 400 feet. The river is about 35 miles long and its width varies according to the terrain, from 6 to 7½ miles. It has a number of islands, but the largest is Grand Island, which was ceded to the State of New York by the Seneca Indians. It is 12 miles long and 2 to 7 miles wide. The height of the shoreline of the river from Lake Erie to the falls varies from 4 to 100 feet; but from the falls to Lewiston and Queenston,[162] 7 miles more or less, the shoreline is invariably 200 or more feet high, and the banks sharply and precipitously box in the river for the whole distance. At Lewiston the precipice on both banks abruptly ends, the river widens, and the terrain continues almost at water level the rest of the way to Lake Ontario, about 7 miles more.

Some geologists have inferred from this that the cataracts first existed near Queenston and Lewiston, and the force of their torrent has gradually worn away the river bed, opened up that long precipice, and made the falls retreat to the place where they are now, and which they are slowly leaving behind.

Based on the slowness with which the present-day edge of the falls is being worn away, they have calculated the long span of time necessary to execute this operation for a distance of 7 miles upon a base of the same material.

After Grand Island, one finds New Island,[163] and after that, about two miles from the falls, all navigation of the upper part of the Niagara River comes to an end, because from there on the current is so violent that no boat would be safe if it were to venture beyond.

However, at first one does not see any sign of the river's acceleration. There is no sound, and when the atmosphere is calm no movement can be detected. On the contrary, the river seems as smooth as a mirror, and one would be tempted to bathe in its perfidious, crystalline waters, if not warned of the danger by the tree branches that speed by, swept away by that torrent, as irresistible and imperturbable as the eternal order of destiny.

But Goat Island is in the middle of the river, and divides it into two arms. Here the river bed becomes uneven and rough, and the waters are hurled roaring among rocks cut like steps, and cover them with foam with a violent din beyond description. These rapids continue for about half a mile, and it is calculated that along them the river descends some 80 feet; but what most amazed me was that, as the waters near the precipice, they take a direction opposite to the slope, and crash into each other as if they wished to avoid the irresistible destiny that impels them, until, finally defeated, they are dispersed into the abyss, thundering deeply and hurling immense columns of vapor into the air, among which the rainbow gleams with the most vivid colors.

The rough sketch that accompanies this letter will give you a better idea than the most minute description could of the shape of the falls and their surroundings. The perpendicular height of the western or English waterfall is 150 feet, and that of the eastern or American waterfall is 162 feet, although others say 196 feet. The English falls are about 2000[164] feet wide, and the American 1,100, which, with the 980-foot width of Goat Island, make the total width occupied by the falls more than 4,000 feet. In the American falls, and along the edges of the English falls, the water that is dissolved by the force of its fall descends in long threads of foam. But in the circular section in the center of the English falls, an immense vault of greenish crystal seems to be suspended, whose base blurs with the cloud of mist that is raised by the impact at the bottom of the precipice. What most amazed me was to see that in this part, instead of the waters hurling themselves violently, they descended with a majestic slowness, as if the accumulated torrents supported each other as they fell from the edge to the bottom of the abyss.

Whenever there is sun, prismatic colors can be seen dispersed here and there upon the falls; but when the air is calm and the sun in certain positions, the entire rainbow can be seen, as I have witnessed now on two mornings, beginning at the bottom of the English cataract and ending at my feet at the edge of the American, encompassing the entire magnificent scene beneath it.

There is much disagreement about which is the best view of the falls. I prefer that of Table Rock, on the Canadian side. One finds oneself more isolated at the foot of either of the falls, and can better appreciate the tremendous volume of water that is hurled down, and feels the force of its thunder incomparably more. But the agitation of the spray is such that only part of the scene is visible.[165] At the foot of the American falls, I could not distinguish anything of the English falls, even though the sun was shining in a cloudless sky and made the tumbling waters glitter like a shower of diamonds; only from time to time could I hazily see the trees swaying on the crest of Goat Island.

The rapids are perhaps as worthy of admiration as the falls. The fury of ocean waves whipped up by storms scarcely could give you an idea of the tremendous turbulence of the Niagara rapids. Nonetheless, General Porter has thrown a bridge over them, between Goat Island and the American shore. Bath Island,[166] which has an establishment with baths, refreshments and billiards, divides the bridge in two. More than once I have paused on the bridge, and looked below at the fury of the waves; the sight has made my head spin, and I hardly have been able to comprehend how the bridge survives. Among the rapids there are some little islands, never trod by humans, undermined by the constant impulse of the current. It would not be surprising if some day, unmoored at last, they are swept away with their trees into the depths of the abyss.

I crossed to Goat Island and walked its circuit to obtain different views of the falls and the rapids. In other times the eagles made their nests there, thinking they were absolutely safe; but they have gone away since the daring hand of man has opened passage to the island, which would seem impossible if one did not see it. I did find a number of wood pigeons, which made me miss the famous shotgun that terrorized the parrots at Jesús María.[167]

After wandering through the untamed woods of Goat Island, I sat at the edge of the English falls and, fixing my gaze on the plunging waters and the rising mist, I abandoned myself freely to my meditations. I don't know what congruence that lonely and wild spectacle had with my own feelings. In that torrent, I seemed to see the image of my passions and the storms of my life. Just like the Niagara rapids, my heart churns in search of that ideal perfection that, in vain, I seek upon the earth. If, as I am beginning to fear, my ideas are no more than shimmering illusions, born of the vehemence of my good and sensitive soul, why can I not wake up from my dream? Oh, when will the novel of my life end so that its reality can begin?

There I composed hurriedly the lines of verse that I am enclosing, and that but feebly express some of my sensations.

How many sublime and profound musings can surroundings such as these inspire in a serene and tranquil soul! What free rein they give to the fiery imagination of religious enthusiasm! Despite all that physics has demonstrated, who would not believe that the divine hand that for so many centuries has fed the source of that frightful mass of fresh water, once raised the oceans to the peaks of the Andes, when a universal flood engulfed the earth? The same God whose visage is reflected in the sea and who speaks in the midst of the tempests, placed His hand upon the North American wilderness, and in Niagara, great and sublime like the thunder of the ocean, left a profound trace of His omnipotence. Do you see those columns of mist that, rising in an impetuous rotating movement, mingle with the brilliant clouds of summer that slowly float over this marvelous expanse? That is how the prayers of the just rise to the Lord, and with His favor unite the earth with Heaven. Do you see how the rainbow gloriously gleams above this unfathomable and tenebrous abyss? That is how the light of immortality shines, which hope and religion kindle above the gloom of the grave.

The next day I continued my perambulations. On the perpendicular cliff of the American side there is a stairway of wooden boards by which one can descend to the base of the falls. I started down them, and I can assure you that at the halfway point I looked up and then down and was struck with the most profound terror. In addition, the spray that arose furiously from the cataract came down upon me like a strong drizzle, and was exceedingly uncomfortable.

I crossed in a boat to the Canadian side, and ascended another stairway to the spot called Table Rock, which you will see marked on the accompanying sketch. This is a great shelf of rock that extends horizontally some forty or fifty feet over the precipice. From there I was able to appreciate the width of the American falls; the quantity and massiveness of the slabs of rock piled up in a row at its base, like trophies of its fury; the height of the precipitous face of Goat Island which, cut perpendicularly like a wall, divides the waters; the extent and the fury of the rapids; and finally, all the grandeur of the English falls. Chateaubriand's image is as true as it is beautiful: "it does not seem like a river, but rather like a sea, whose torrents rush toward the gaping mouth of an abyss."[168]

A few years ago, a piece of the precipice was swept away next to Table Rock, and the latter, judging by its shape and the wide cracks that the filtration of the waters has opened in it, is soon to suffer the same fate. It takes no little nerve to approach its edge and from there look down at the pounding of the plunging falls. I did so, if with some apprehension, and could only see confusion and a frightful obscurity.

I continued along the shoreline of the river, up to a magnificent hotel called The Pavilion,[169] from whose balconies there is an extensive view of the falls, the rapids, and the upper part of the river as far as Navy Island, along with the surrounding countryside. But the view from Table Rock is to be preferred by those who enjoy more powerful and sublime sensations.

Upon returning along the bank of the river, I happened to see a boat that had set out from Navy Island and was heading toward the Canadian shore. I set my spyglass upon it, and I saw a single man in it, who was struggling with the current which was carrying him along toward the rapids with terrifying speed. If he were to falter even for a moment, he surely would be doomed. I followed his movements with extreme anxiety, and I doubt that he suffered half the anguish that he put me through, until he finally reached the shore, a little above the rapids.

I have been told about an Indian who fell asleep in his canoe, which was tied to a tree along the upper reaches of the river. Some villain who happened by untied the canoe. But the Indian awoke only upon hearing the roar of the rapids. Horrified, he made an attempt to paddle to shore; but seeing the futility of it, he let the paddle go, covered his head with his blanket, and abandoned himself to his awful fate.[170] Oh! What poet could express that unfortunate man's emotions during the fleeting moments that preceded his annihilation?

I returned to Table Rock and descended the stairway that leads to the river's edge. From there I went on ahead toward the foot of the great cataract, determined to reach it. But the thunder of the falls, the spray that soaked me, the rocks that slid from beneath my feet, the realization that no one else was following me, and the sort of tremor that Niagara imparts to everything that surrounds it, compelled me to give up my plan. I stopped and cast an attentive glance upon the terrible and magnificent scene, which doubtlessly I will never forget. That ocean of water, dissolving into dense, crystalline foam, plummeted down a few steps from me, deafening me with its roar. The edge of the cataract extends horizontally like Table Rock, of which it is a continuation, and the vast sheet of water extended before it leaves room to enter into a sort of gallery, which is the true palace of Niagara. Many have entered and have told marvelous tales of the experience; but I had no wish to imitate them. Whatever they may say, there can be no safety where a false step, which is very easy in that darkness, or a slip upon a moss-covered rock, would lead the curious to an instant, inevitable death.

The impression that the din of the cataract resonating in the hollow of those shapeless crags had upon me is indescribable. Those who have heard it from above have only a vague idea. Its admirers have tried in vain to express it. Cannon shots and thunder are only a momentary crash compared with that tremendous, unchanging, eternal roar, which he who has not descended to the foot of the falls can only strive in vain to imagine.

Before casting a last glance upon the marvels before me, I broke off a piece of stone covered with beautiful crystals, and crossed the river again.

From the middle of the river, there must be a splendid view of the falls on clear days; but I had the misfortune to be given a dark and stormy one. Here is the description of the traveler Howison, who visited Niagara and the Thousand Islands[171] with all the enthusiasm of a poet:

> [In] the middle of the river . . . I was now within the area of a semicircle of cataracts, more than three thousand feet in extent, and floated on the surface of a gulf, raging, fathomless, and interminable. Majestic cliffs, splendid rainbows, lofty trees, and columns of spray were the gorgeous decorations of this theatre of wonders, while a dazzling sun shed refulgent glories upon every part of the scene. Surrounded with clouds of vapour, and stunned into a state of confusion and terror by the hideous noise, I looked upwards to the height of one hundred and fifty feet, and saw vast floods, dense, awful and stupendous, vehemently bursting over the precipice, and rolling down, as if the windows of heaven were opened to pour another deluge upon the earth. Loud sounds, resembling discharges of artillery or volcanic explosions, were now distinguishable amidst the watery tumult, and added terrors to the abyss from which they issued. The sun, looking majestically through the ascending spray, was encircled by a radiant halo; whilst fragments of rainbows floated on every side, and momentarily vanished only to give place to a succession of others more brilliant. Looking backwards, I saw the Niagara river, again become calm and tranquil, rolling magnificently between the towering cliffs that rose on either side, and receiving showers of orient dew-drops from the trees that gracefully over-arched its transparent bosom. A gentle breeze ruffled the waters, and beautiful birds fluttered around, as if to welcome its egress from those clouds of spray, accompanied by thunders and rainbows, which were the heralds of its precipitation into the abyss of the cataract.[172]

So writes Howison. I was not able to enjoy the brilliance of this scene because, as I said, I crossed the river on a dark, stormy day. The sky was completely covered with clouds that were so thick that one could not tell where the sun was in the sky. The wind from the storm, roaring among those caverns, whipped the spray from the cataract around me with such fury that in its whirlwind one hardly could see the lofty precipices and the great masses of water tumbling down from the heights. However, that very same confusion and the lugubrious darkness of the sky gave the spectacle a peculiar sublimity. From time to time the wind abated a little, and one could see the black clouds that were sailing over the precipice, and from below they seemed to touch the torrents of water and unleash them from their tenebrous bosoms. It seemed to me that I was seeing an indignant God, opening the cataracts of Heaven once more upon a wicked world.

For a long distance beyond the falls, the surface of the river is covered with foam, which with its extraordinary consistency, gives it the appearance of an open field of snow, agitated by constant storms, rather than that of a river.

It was hard for me to leave that place behind, and before I did I returned to the edge of the American falls. I stood contemplating them for a while, and as I turned to leave, scarcely had I moved away from the rock upon which I had been standing, when I saw it break off and tumble into the abyss with just the light pressure from my feet as I stepped away. That rock, upon which I had thought I was safe a few seconds before, had fallen where no human feet would ever tread upon it again.[173] I shuddered: my insatiable curiosity was rather dampened; I ascended the stairway with extra care and retired to rest from the day's exertions.

To María de la Merced Heredia y Campuzano [BNJM; Augier no. 54]

New York, July 5, 1824

My dearest Mother:

You must be surprised by the channels by which you have received this letter. I believe that sending it this way, you will not find it has been opened as has happened with the others, even though it bears the same seal, since it is not about that but about something else that is not in my power to remedy, nor in yours.[174]

Regarding what you write in your last letter about the money from my Uncle Domingo,[175] I can only respond that from here it is difficult for me to judge the current state of Cuba and thus calculate how safe it would be to invest the money there. If you would like to avoid worry, send it to me as a money order, and I will deposit it in a bank here, where it will be safer than if it were buried yards underground. The banks give from 5 to 8 percent interest, and the insurance companies up to 12 percent if you invest in shares. I don't see that this has any bearing on your widow's pension, and don't know if anyone can send one's money, as one wishes, to a friendly country. Above all, consult Franco on this, and then make your decision. I think that even though the money won't earn a great deal here, it will be safe, and since there will be no need to touch the returns, these will gradually and imperceptibly grow, and will yield earnings upon earnings. So I am inclined toward your sending it, since in addition everything can be handled by having a money order sent for payment to me through a third party.

The weather has become terribly hot, and since every summer there is yellow fever here, I have resolved to move for a while to New Haven, the capital of the neighboring state, which is free of that disease. I will leave tomorrow. New Haven is about 20 leagues from here, but there is a steamboat that goes there almost every day, and the mail coach goes there daily.

So continue writing to me in New York and I will receive the letters without any interruption, and I will continue to write you via the same channels.

My affectionate regards to Osés, Franco and family, the Fernández girls, Aunt Ángela and Aunt Francisca, all the children, Ignacia and the little delinquents. Be well, and give thanks to God for the good health of your most loving son

José M^a

I forgot to mention the verses that you refer to in your letter. It is a terrible falsehood that I have written a single line about Independence or about any other public matter. Please so inform anyone who should tell you anything different. What does Coronel Carrerá say about me? The things he must say! Please let me know what he thinks of this whole mess.

To Cristóbal Madan[176] [Augier no. 56]

New Haven, July 10, 1824

My dear Sir Don Cristóbal Madan:

My dear Consul:[177] I am here in New Haven now. I very much regret that I was not able to visit Your Lordship before my trip, as we had agreed, but I overslept.

Please tell Mr. Perit that I have accommodations in Mr. Hower's house, and how much I like this city. My only regret is that I have not come earlier, and have lost so much time.

I have left the following books for Caraballo, in two small packages:

Oeuvres de Racine	4 vol.	12 fr.
Pensées de Pascal	2	6
Lettres provinciales	2	5
Fables de La Fontaine	2	6
Poésies de Malherbe	1	3
	11	32fr.

These belong to Don Leonardo Santos Suárez, and are part of the collection of French classics that he has ordered. When he arrives, please do me the favor of delivering them to him, and of asking him to be so kind as to make the payment of 32 fr. to Mr. Colomb, the clerk of Mr. Bongera [torn] whose business is at 45 Wall St.

Since some very thick letters may be coming to me from Havana and Matanzas, and even some published matter that I have ordered, I beg you to send them to me via the packet boat, since thrift, as you know, is always a good thing for a student to carry in his pocket. To that effect, please pick up any that they send me via Howland's office.

I think, my friend, that at some point you will find yourself obliged to quit this laborious and sterile post that the republic has assigned you, and which you execute to everyone's great satisfaction. However, you have only your own kindness to blame, which forces you to suffer the impertinence of fugitives and vagrants.

Farewell, my dear Cónsul. I hope you will forgive me for the trouble I give you and dispose as you please of your affectionate friend

W.K.Y.H.[178]
J. M. Heredia

Please excuse my makeshift English, and let me know about any boat being provisioned for Havana and Matanzas, when it is leaving, and any other news that you have.

To Ignacio Heredia Campuzano [BNJM; *Moda*; Augier no. 57]

New Haven, July 17, 1824

Much loved Ignacio:
    I have written you two letters since my return from my trip to the west, and in the last of these I mentioned to you, upon the eve of my departure, my decision to come here to spend a few months in the cool air, isolated among Americans to see if I might make some progress in their most horrid language.
    The date of this present letter will be sufficient for you to know that my plan has been accomplished. On the 8th of this month I embarked on a packet boat since the steam ship had gone out of service because of mechanical difficulties the preceding day. [Torn] We set sail at 12 in the morning. You know what a good sailor I always have been, and between that and the good weather, the trip was very pleasant. Nothing makes a more delightful and lasting impression upon me than sailing on a fast ship with a good wind, and to place myself forward to watch the water break over the bow. Anyone who takes a sea voyage with me will find me there in fine weather, and in the stern in foul.
    The trip here is also very safe, since the whole route is via the sound that separates Long Island from the New York and Connecticut coasts. We arrived in New Haven the next day at sunrise, and we disembarked in the best mood in the world.
    New Haven might be called the garden of New England. Its streets are very wide and drawn straight, intersecting at right angles. The houses are generally of wood or brick, but all are painted and provided with resplendent green shutters. In most of the city, the houses are not attached but separated by small yards. All the streets are shaded by rows of trees, planted at short intervals, which always provide a delightful coolness, and since their crowns touch and even become intertwined in spots, they form long, deep green archways, and thus one might say that the oppressive heat of summer is unknown in New Haven. But how ferociously cold it was when I passed through here in December!

Upon seeing this handsome town, I cannot help but wonder why we in Cuba, beneath that terrible, devouring sun that beats down upon our heads all year long, have not taken measures to defend ourselves from it, the way these Yankees have done so industriously, with their heat here that lasts but a few days and even at this time of year is rarely as intense as our heat in the tropics. Shall I tell you why? I believe the reason is the apathy of Spaniards with regard to everything except money, and also a certain aversion to shade which I cannot explain. Wherever you look you will see that their first thought is to mow down the trees, and they don't bother to plant more. In our torrid cities one can hardly spot a tree under which to rest, not even in the outskirts! So it is that the Tenochtitlán Valley, destined by nature to be the Eden of North America, has been condemned to denuded sterility, by destroying its trees and entirely desiccating its soil. I believe that the only reason they have not destroyed its lakes is because they have not been able to.

But to return to the topic of New Haven: in the center of the town there is a handsome green, covered with grass and ringed with trees, where there are several churches, and among them a building for the legislative sessions. New Haven is the co-capital of Connecticut, and the legislature meets one year here and the other in Hartford. Yale College, which is a university, borders the green. It is reputed to be the foremost institution of its kind in the United States, and currently has 372 students. I came bearing letters of introduction to present to some of the professors, but so far they have only served for me to be shown the mineralogy collection, which is quite extensive and interesting.

To the east and west of New Haven, the ranges of mountains that stretch from the interior end in nearly perpendicular cliffs, which are called East and West Rock. In the latter, two of the judges of Charles I of England, Goffe and Whalley, took refuge. They fled from England to the colonies, where they lived hunted, anguished and in peril, without a moment of peace until they found eternal peace in the grave. Their fantastic adventures made a profound impression upon the colonists, whose descendants still marvel over them, and are quick to show foreign visitors the old cemetery where the two regicides are buried. I have seen these graves, marked by very old stones, upon which their names are roughly carved. On another occasion I will write you at greater length about this interesting topic.

Although New Haven is a seaport, it has little maritime commerce, and what is most notable in this regard is its pier, which extends some half mile into the bay, which is shallow. In this it reminds me of Matanzas. Its population: more than 7,000 inhabitants.

Yesterday I received your three kind letters of the 13th, 20th and 27th of June, and with the first the judicial decree of Vives.[179] Now I only have to await that of the Audiencia. If the case is not dismissed and measures are taken to continue the prosecution, I know that I will never be found innocent, although that has already been more than clear to me, and I am only awaiting the results from those bodies finally to calm my spirit. If the prosecution continues, as you know it will be a long time before I can return. With that in mind, why don't you let me go to Caracas for two or three months in the winter, rather than Charleston, just to see how it is there, what prospects there may be for me, and then return here in April? I don't believe that they would think ill of that in Cuba, and anyway since they have an open jail cell waiting for me should I reach port there, it is only right that I be able to go search for some sources of life in the sun of the tropics, and take a stand against my sorrows. And that can happen only in the lands that have rebelled against Spain. As for staying here or going to Charleston, it is six of one and half a dozen of the other, since the difference in climate amounts to a few inches more or less of snow. I know that I should not speak to you in this way, and that someone else might think that this was disdain or ingratitude for your favors, and that I continue to pester you when I owe you so much. But I know your heart too well to believe that you will take offense, all the more so when I repeat to you that I will not leave the United States without your consent, even if it tears my heart apart. Anyway, give it some thought, and see if you might give me permission, knowing that if I were to go to Caracas, it would be as if Dirichity or Abus[180] were going; I would not get mixed up in anything, any more than a Swedish or Russian traveler.

As I have told you before, the idea of being licensed to practice law in the United States is untenable. All I would achieve would be for them to think I am a madman. Any other option is more feasible.

Nonetheless, I assure you that my soul feels oppressed, and I almost want to die when I envision that my only hope consists of living among these people for the rest of my life, listening to their horrid language. Would you believe that after seven months of continued study, I hardly have managed to learn to speak a little and incorrectly, and am virtually at a loss when I am spoken to? But there you have it. The language is nothing but anomalies, and I cannot understand how such a great nation is satisfied to use such execrable gibberish.

Anyway, do not be offended by this assessment of things, which is born only of the fraternal trust that exists between us. Do answer me regarding the permission I seek to go to Caracas, knowing that you will be blindly obeyed, whatever you decide.

As I have told you before, continue to send your letters to me to New York. I am enclosing my third letter from my trip west, two and a half sheets of paper written in crowded handwriting, which along with this letter of a sheet and a half, should make for a good dose of reading, enough to occupy an hour in the coffee grove, along with the commentaries that it will inspire in you and our friend Don Pedro. I am imagining him with his eyeglasses perched on his nose, listening to you read, as you sprawl comfortably, in shirtsleeves, in your armchair between the two doors.

I have no news from New York about the sweets and sugar that Chea has sent, to whom thanks are owed. I will inquire about them.

At the beginning of September I am planning to take a trip to the east, to Middletown, New London, Providence (the capital of Rhode Island) and to my hospitable and beloved Boston; I will be there for a week, and will return here via Worcester, Springfield and Hartford, and then on to New York, to decide in council, presided over by Juan de Acosta or Pancho García, where we will go to flee the cold, be it Charleston, Savannah, Saint Augustine, Camden or Augusta. As soon as this is decided, I will send you notice immediately so that you will know where to direct your letters, and I will depart during the first days of October, with the first frosts, which are glorious to see and not so glorious to shiver through.

Do not treat me like Jaureguiberry. Good-bye, my remembrances to my friends and to the girls I know, in particular to Josefita, Isabelita and the lovely Luz, whom you must ask to accept a long message for the divine Lola, whose innocent memory has cheered some of my moments in exile.

An embrace for Chea, my best regards to Abus and my much esteemed Borthiribort. And know that at your disposal, I remain your loving

José M^a

To María de la Merced Heredia y Campuzano [Augier no. 58]

New Haven, July 18, 1824

My dearest Mother:
 The day I left New York, I wrote to tell you that I was relocating to this city to enjoy the cooler climate, and remove myself from the danger of the yellow fever which afflicts New York in summer months, and also to be alone and make some headway in my English, by not hearing or speaking anything else. I attribute my scarce progress thus far to the fact that in New York I have been speaking Spanish continuously with other émigrés, or French or Italian with foreigners, without being able to adapt to English, which here I will be forced to use.
 This is the most beautiful city in all New England, and the people here retain an admirable purity of custom, which one always misses in the great commercial cities. The truth is that if it were not for the winters and this confounded language, I would not be in any hurry to look for someplace else to reside, and I would advise you to come here to live, free from the anxieties and dangers that always will be simmering in our poor Cuba. But everything has its downside.
 In the aforementioned letter, I wrote you that my opinion is that you should send Uncle Domingo's money to me, since it will not be safer in anyone else's hands.
 I have not received any letters from you after the one that Pancho brought, but I know through Ignacio that at least up to the 27th of June all was well at home.
 So they are finally going to try us? Oh, if you only knew how painful it is for me to be absent from Cuba now! Isn't it a strange twist of fate that I am denied the opportunity to employ, in my own defense, all the vehemence and fury with which my heart opposes all injustice and which I have employed to the benefit of others? It boils my blood to think that my defense, in which I would be able to thunder and confound the evildoers, will perhaps be entrusted to the stupidity and venality of the innumerable harpies that infect our courts, and only know how to devour avidly the subsistence of the unfortunate. But in the end it doesn't matter. What good can a sterile eloquence do against execrable political calculations?
 Enough of that—I am raving. Aunt Francisca's letters have been sent on to Santo Domingo, and I left the last two in New York with instructions to forward.

I am planning to return there toward the end of September, and make preparations to move on to one of the southern states where the cold will not affect me so much. I will let you know which city I choose as my winter quarters. Most likely it will be Charleston or Savannah; there I will be closer to you, and our letters will arrive sooner.

My health, thank God, is excellent. I hope for the same for all of you at home.

Good-bye, and be well. Give my regards to Franco, to the most kind Doña Pepa whom I remember always, to Antonio, Osés, Aunt Francisca, Aunt Ángela, Magdalena and Antonio Angulo and the Fernández girls. My love to Ignacia and the three delinquents, especially the little person, and you take good care, and don't forget your loving son

José M^a

Having written and sealed this letter, I had the pleasure of receiving yours of the 2nd of this month. I am glad to hear that the hearings are moving forward. As for what you ask me regarding the letter I wrote upon my departure from Cuba, I already have responded to you at length in the letter I sent you by the steam frigate, and if they have intercepted that letter, I have no wish to repeat it all. Suffice it to say that I wrote the letter because it seemed to me then, as it does now, that it was the right thing to do. No one forced me to write it, because there is nothing in the world that can force me to do what I do not want to do. If Ignacio has spoken with you about this, then you must know what is what. Whoever has told you that the letter is the only thing working against me now has deceived you. Let them ask Betancourt, Juan Aranguren, Andux, Portillo and Mihoura. When I wrote that letter it was clear to me that in the accusations against me much more had been alleged than what was true and I had said, and the order of imprisonment had already been issued. So the letter only served to undo some erroneous ideas. I am glad that it has been published, since I never have done anything to be ashamed of. So please, do not pay attention to idle chatter, and let us wait to see how the matter is decided.

To María de la Merced Heredia y Campuzano [BNJM; Augier no. 60]

Norwich, August 12, 1824

My dearest Mother:

    I have received your letter of the 16th of July, and by it and previous letters I see that you have not received any from me since May. I hope that by now you have received the repeated letters that I have sent you from New York and New Haven since I returned from Niagara. It is not surprising that you did not receive any from me during the month of June, because I could hardly write overseas from Canada and the western hinterlands where I was traveling. I hope as well that even though some of my letters may have gone astray, thanks to the ones I have sent to Ignacio, which have gone by a safer route, you will know that all is well with me.

    I am very happy to hear about the progress being made by Rafaela and Dolores,[181] and that you find yourself settled in Havana and content. I would be very happy to see you all as soon as possible, although I am less hopeful of that than you. But I am prepared for anything, and above all what I want is for the affair to get sorted out, and not lose any more time. I am making provisions so that even here I will not be without the means to live. But if it is decided that I cannot return to the island of Cuba, it is unthinkable that I should live forever in this horrible climate, and we'll have to see where I end up. Ignacio tells me that I should go to Europe next year, but I am rather lazy and I think I will let things be for now. What is more, in Europe I would have to deal with the same enemy that I fear here: the confounded cold. In any case, let us see what their lordships of the Audiencia have to say, and then we will discuss it further.

    Some days ago I received two letters from Santiago, which contained two for Aunt Francisca, and I sent them on in the care of Señores Machado and Calvo, and by now she will have received them. Santiago has invited me to spend the winter with him, and the truth is that if upon my return to New York I come across a good ship headed toward Santo Domingo, the temptation will be powerful, because winter here is horrible. Do you remember Pensacola?[182] Some have advised me to go there to spend the months of December and January, because, they say, the climate is the same as in Havana.

Good-bye, be as well as I wish you to be, give my regards to my aunts and cousins, to Antonio, Franco and family, the Fernández girls and Agustín Hernández if you should see him, my love to my sisters, and special regards to Osés. Do not forget your most loving son.

The inkwell is so bad that I am not sure if you will be able to decipher this letter. Continue to write me in New York.

José M^a

To María de la Merced Heredia y Campuzano [BNJM; Augier no. 61]

New York, August 27, 1824

My dearest Mother:

Yesterday I received your letter of the 10th of this month, which Señora de Argaiz delivered, and I see by it that you have not received any of the letters that I have written you since my return from Canada. I do not know what to attribute this to, except that certain riffraff find it amusing to intercept them, as before they opened them. Anyway, if by other channels you are able to get news about me, then the harm they do us is not so great.

I have returned here to New York, because I no longer could suffer the rigor with which the *Yankees* treated me with regard to meals, which often amounted to no more than cucumbers, potatoes, and salted meat or fish.[183] When winter approaches, I will go perhaps to Charleston, so as not to have to deal with as much cold as here, although really I would like to go someplace where there isn't any cold at all.

I am glad to hear that the *Historia de Venezuela* is being copied. Also to be copied are all the documents regarding Father's negotiations with the Marqués del Toro and the Caracas *junta*, which are in a folio-sized notebook, all in my handwriting.[184] If the copy is complete before I go to Charleston, send it to me here with someone you trust, addressing it like this: *for Messrs. Goodhue and to be remitted in person to Don José Ma. Heredia*. These gentlemen are very respectable merchants and good friends of mine. Directing the package to them will preclude all risk of it going astray, in case I am not here, and it always is easier to find well-known merchants than an obscure émigré. I am anxious to get news about the exact state of things, and of the probability that the conspiracy hearings will turn out well. Oh human misery!

There is no point in writing at greater length, since my letters are getting lost. My regards to Doña María if she is still in Havana causing commotion, and to my other aunts and uncles and cousins. Do not forget Franco and family, a thousand endearments to my sisters, and you be as well as your most loving son wishes you to be.

José M^a

I am taking advantage of this opportunity to write to Osés as well.

To María de la Merced Heredia y Campuzano [Augier no. 63]

New York, September 4, 1824

My Dearest Mother:

I have just received your letter of August 18, which has confirmed my suspicion that someone is taking villainous amusement in intercepting my letters. May God give him his due and may I have occasion to reciprocate in kind.[185]

I am sorry to hear that it is so hot there, especially for poor Osés, to whom I am writing.

Ignacio has *Las leyes de Indias*, in Matanzas, since I thought it was useless for it to be sent here.[186]

It is vexing for me to hear that the copying of the *Historia de Venezuela* is going so badly. Do not worry about the documents in the appendix, since I can obtain them here easily. I had thought that I would write an appendix, and even had begun some notes, but my persecution prevents me from continuing, since it will be believed that my depiction of things has been colored by the bitter gall of resentment.

As for that individual's manuscript, I will not elaborate because it is almost sure that this letter will be lost, but I will say here that nothing can be gotten with negativity; only with sweetness can something be achieved.[187] The work is of great merit, although I do not know for sure of its state of completion, since I only saw the first notebooks. Father consulted with me, as a man of letters, about the style of the *Historia de Venezuela*, but I considered myself very much a novice jurist to attempt to assess his writings on law.

If Franco loves me, that is good, since I also love and revere him as one of the most sincerely virtuous men on earth.

This letter is going to be sent to you through him, and perhaps that way will escape being burned.

It is not surprising that the *patrona* is avoiding your visits. When did you ever have dealings with her? Don't you see that that would awaken suspicions that are not to her advantage, because it would compromise her reputation and that of the *patrón* among our enemies? Don't keep insisting, just keep your gratitude, which they are well aware of, to yourself, and be nonchalant about the whole matter.[188]

Please write to Ignacio, tell him that there has not been any ship for Matanzas for some days, and that I don't dare write him via Havana.

Good-bye, my love to my sisters, regards to all our relatives, to Franco, Doña Pepa, Don Antonio and Osés, and do not forget your most loving son

José Mª

To María de la Merced Heredia y Campuzano [BNJM; Augier no. 65]

New York, September 18, 1824

My dearest Mother:

Yesterday I had the pleasure of receiving your letters of August 26 and the 4th of this month, and of seeing from the latter that, upon receiving four letters from me that perhaps had gone astray, you will have been reassured that I had not forgotten you, nor by the mercy of God was I ill or in the next world.

With regard to the money, I must tell you that whoever has told you that it would not be safe in the Bank of the United States is greatly mistaken. If thirty-five million dollars, spread out over 24 states, a capital in which the most firmly established government on earth has a great part of its treasury invested, cannot guarantee the security of two thousand dollars, then one must conclude that that money would not be safe on the moon, entrusted to a celestial intelligence. One will be able to have access to that money anywhere, and the worst that could happen is that they would retain my profits, without paying me the interest accrued, if I don't go to collect them on time. If it is invested in shares, and you want to withdraw it again in cash, the worst that could happen is that you would lose a half percent in their sale, which can be realized in 24 hours, because there are countless speculators in those purchases and sales.

As for the merchant who would be safest, from where you are you will be able to determine that better than I. Franco can tell you.

I already have told you that once the copy of the *Historia de Venezuela* is complete, you should send it to me addressed as follows: *To Messrs. Goodhue & Co., to be remitted to Don José Ma. Heredia, New York.*

There is no need to tell you that it should be sent with someone you trust. Don't worry about the Spaniard, for in two months I will have him come here.[189] They should also copy the documents relating to Father's commission which are in a large notebook in my handwriting. Have Blas compare the copy with the original to assure its correctness.

I see what you write about my going to Jamaica, and I think I would do better to go to Santo Domingo. Remember how cruel it is to go somewhere where you do not know anyone, and the slightest indisposition can fill one with anguish and alarm. Besides, Pancho García has told me that Jamaica is an unhealthy place, and as expensive as Havana if not more. In Santo Domingo I would find myself among family and with my grandmother and uncles and aunts, and Santiago, and since there is not a state of war between that country and Spain, no one could look askance on my going there to spend two or three months with my relatives. All is at peace there, and it is surprising how much commerce there is with the United States, and they won't be able to say anything without clashing with those people, since with my certification of residence in New York, they will not consider me anything but an American. So, should a ship be available in November, I don't think you will mind if I go there straightaway, until March or April. And do not think that this is part of a plan to head from there to Colombia or some other port in insurrection. I have made a commitment not to do that, and will stand by it. If I had wanted to renounce the island of Cuba, without leaving New York I would have found employment with the Guatemala legation.[190] I have not written Ignacio for some time because there has not been the opportunity. Now I am planning to write him, even if just a few lines, and send them through Franco.

I returned the money order from Galicia to Pía or Felipa, after one of my unsuccessful attempts to cash it.[191]

I have nothing more to add. My regards to my aunts and uncles and cousins, my love to my sisters and my affectionate remembrances to Franco, Doña Pepilla and Antonio, without forgetting the Fernández girls, who must be in their glory with the change of government. Do not forget your most loving son

José Mª

My dear Ignacia: I do not know why you complain that I do not write you, when I have so little to tell you. You who have things to tell me should never miss an opportunity. So do so, knowing that your chitchat will give infinite pleasure to your most loving brother

José Mª

To María de la Merced Heredia y Campuzano [BNJM; Augier no. 67]

New York, September 29, 1824

My Dearest Mother:

Although I have not received any letters from you after that of the 4th of this month, and I have answered it with two or three letters that are on their way, I do not want to put off telling you that I am well, thank God, so that you will not worry.

I have not decided yet whether I will go to spend the winter in Charleston, since it seems to me to be foolish to undertake a journey along a dangerous seacoast at this time of year, only to encounter freezing weather and snow in Charleston. I am thinking that if the cold weather gets to me and I have the opportunity, I will go to spend two or three months in Santo Domingo, instead of Jamaica as you have proposed. I know no one in Jamaica, it is an unhealthy country, and it costs a fortune. I elaborated on this in my last letter.

I hope that if I do go, you will not think badly of it, since there is no need to, when my only motive is the primary necessity of man, which is self-preservation. What is more, that country is not at war with Spain.

Even though Machado has done such a good job with the letters, since he is now here in future I will send them in care of Franco, who, I believe, has a post office box, and thus I trust they will arrive safely.

I have not received a letter from Ignacio for some days, but then again no ship from Matanzas has arrived here in the last month. The last time I wrote him via Havana.

Please extend my best wishes to Osés, Franco and family, our relatives, especially Aunt Francisca and Aunt Magdalena, and my love to my sisters. And do not forget your most loving son

José Mª

My dearest Ignacia: I am going to send you some verses with a friend who will leave here for Havana in a few days (José G. Pinzón), and I will see if I can obtain for you a copy of *Telémaco* in French, like the one Pepilla has.[192] It would make me very happy to hear you play the piano, whose harmony would dissipate the darkness in my soul, as David's harp eased the sorrows of Saul. But how can that be? Some day we will be together again, as your most loving brother desires.

José Mª

To María de la Merced Heredia y Campuzano [BNJM; Augier no. 68]

New York, October 6, 1824

My dearest Mother:

Although I have already answered the last letter that I received from you, which was that of September 4, I do not want to miss this opportunity to tell you that I am well, thank God.

In my last letters I told you that that I had resolved to spend the winter in Santo Domingo; but afterwards I have thought it best to wait for your answer, and that of Ignacio, about that. I will put my family's wishes before my own, even if I must make a very painful sacrifice by spending another winter in this horrible climate, and even more when I have the sweet satisfaction of seeing things in my poor homeland going from bad to worse, with constant imprisonments and disturbances. A fine country to forget, if nature did not prevent me from living in these frozen climes, and if I could transport my loved ones here.

I think that you should send me Uncle Domingo's money without further delay. If you don't invest it, what will you do with it, exposed as it is to the danger of thieves large and small? To invest it there seems to me to be foolish in these bleak times in which we live, and I am glad that you are of the same opinion. Send it to me, then, and you won't need to worry any more about it.

That is all for now. My regards to my aunts and uncles and cousins, especially to Magdalena. Tell her that yesterday I sent via Puerto Príncipe the last letters I received for Santiago. My affectionate remembrances to Franco and family, to Osés and the Fernández girls, and the same to my sisters, especially Ignacia and the person.

Good-bye. May God keep us and make you as happy as your most loving son prays.

José M^a

My dearest Ignacia: Pinzón is not going to Havana, as I had thought, but to Matanzas. I have a copy of *Telémaco* here for you, in the same edition that Pepilla has, but it is in paperback and I don't know if there will be time to have it bound. If possible, I will send it to you.

Good-bye: have fun, and do not forget your brother

José M^a

Mamá: After I had written but not yet sealed this letter, I received yours of the 14th of last month. I never miss an opportunity to write you, but letters from the North get lost in the mail, and what is more there are ships that I do not know about until they have already sailed because their cargo is all loaded, and they do not put it in the papers.

As for the money, I already have told you that you can obtain the bill of exchange through Mitchell. If Mitchell cannot, Franco can tell you who else might be good.

I will send on the fat letter for Santiago at the first opportunity.

Please tell Ignacia that today I took *Telémaco* to be bound, and I will give it to Cirilo Ponce who will be leaving for Havana in some 12 to 15 days, and via Cirilo I will write her at length. He is a good fellow, and I will be happy if you get to know him.[193] His father is the husband of that pretty woman with all the children in Matanzas. I also will send some little present for Antonio.

Nothing more for now. Keep well, for the consolation of your most loving son

José M^a

To Ignacio Heredia Campuzano [BNJM; Augier no. 69]

New York, October 8, 1824

Much loved Ignacio:

Two or three days ago, I received your most welcome letters no. 12, 13 and 14, which have given me great pleasure as your letters always do.

In the last of these I see what you say regarding a trip to Colombia, and in answer let me tell you that I already had given careful consideration to the qualms that you express, and I never would have considered defying such considerations had I not given up all hope of ever being done justice.

However, let me reiterate what I wrote you regarding my absolute deference to your wishes. I shall set aside, then, my cherished plan to enjoy the climate along the banks of the Guaire.[194]

I also wrote you that should that plan not come to fruition, I was planning to go to Santo Domingo, a country that is not at war with Spain, and where I have relatives and friends. But I fear you may have some objection, and I will await your response, since, I repeat, under no circumstances do I want to do anything against your wishes. Perhaps you will think that this is all foolishness on my part, but if so, it must be because you have no idea what winter is like in these parts. You should hear how the Americans say that Spain is an Eden, because there is no winter there . . .

I shall not go to Charleston, because, besides the risks involved in sailing along the coast at this time of year, I have little to gain, the only difference being that it may snow a bit less there than here. And as you know, once the temperature falls to zero, one hardly notices one or two degrees below the freezing point. And I must take into account that I would be isolated there, and without the comforts that I enjoy here. I only would decide to go there, perhaps, if Silvestre and Pancho were to urge me to do so; but they are of the same opinion as I.

I make my rounds of the offices, and will find one where I can sign on as an assistant, even though I think I am too much of a dunderhead for the clamor of the world of business.

I already have mentioned to you that Mariano Tarrero and Melitón Lamar[195] have arrived here, the latter as a page to San Juan de Dios. They have taken rooms in the house where I used to live, which had turned into a barracks of émigrés. In order to find some peace I have moved to another house, along with that good fellow Don Juan de Acosta.

You are a strange one: you tell me as if it were a fresh bit of news that Rita has not married José Gertrudis Pinzón, when he is going to be the bearer of this letter.

The poor political boss! Is it possible that that awful San Roberto could cost our famous friend Señor Don Juan de la Riva y Vértiz[196] such a drubbing? How the fanciful conjecture that we made during our siesta reading time has come true, regarding Riva's face if he ever had to wear a prisoner's vest! I declare that a canvas sack isn't far behind the lowliest garb that the Arabs impose upon those who fall into their clutches.

I regret that I do not know any owners of gardens so as to be able send you the seeds that you want, and I would just buy them and send them if you had not told me repeatedly that you do not want them that way, because they will be old and useless.

Via Pinzón I am going to send you the cape that I brought with me and that I used last winter. It is in terrible shape, and since now there are those who know me here, I need to buy a more decent one for eight to ten dollars, so as not to appear ridiculous. The one I am sending will only be a nuisance here, and there it might be of use for you for the coffee grove, or so that silly old Alejo doesn't get wet when it rains.

I am sending along with this the last two letters from my trip west. It is quite a portfolio, and tomorrow you will have your reading with the good Don Pedro. I wish I could tell it to you in person rather than write it, seated between the two of you, while Doña María la Goicochea, seated across from us under the awning in the coffee grove, would take a rest from her usual commotion with the less noisy one of praying the rosary.

I have the displeasure of announcing to Doña María that, according to what Pancho has told me, the sugar and the sweets arrived while I was in Connecticut, and Tolón[197] and the other good-for-nothings dispatched them without my having seen a bit of them.

As a prudent man, you will decide if it is better to keep this from her, or if you tell her, prepare her well beforehand. There is no need to make too much of it, nor to want to take bloody vengeance upon Tolón and the other gluttons.

What I do ask is that you not send me anything, since, after infinite pacing and swearing at the customs house in order to clear some trifle, it is as if you sent nothing at all, with all these ne'er-do-wells around here on the hunt for sweets. I am charging José Gertrudis with the task of paying you a visit and giving you a full account of my glorious achievements; he is well able to do so, since he lived with me for some time.

Via the schooner *Betsy* I have shipped a barrel of apples to you, with the mark Y.H.[198] It is going in care of Noriega, the son-in-law of Acosta, and that way you won't have the disaster that it costs here to get any little trinket through customs. I will be very happy if they arrive in good shape, and that when you and our friend Don Pedro eat them in the coffee grove, I will be your topic of conversation.

I am enclosing a letter for Mamá, since there won't be any ships leaving for Havana from here for six to eight days, and I do not want her to worry.

If you see Captain Western, don't forget to give him my most affectionate regards.

What has become of Veguilla? Give him my respects, and also to Pancho Abreu and Don Joaquín and *Licenciado* Nicolás, who by now must have offspring.

Good-bye. My best to those who have not forgotten me, many fond regards to Doña María, and know that I am at your service always. Your most loving

José M^a

If some acquaintance goes to Havana, send along the travel letter to Mamá.

To María de la Merced Heredia y Campuzano [Augier no. 71]

New York, November 6, 1824

My dearest Mother:

I have received recently your most welcome letter of September 28, and I see by it that the many letters that I have sent you since July either have been intercepted or have gone astray. I am grateful for the advice that you give me, born as it is of the tenderness with which you have always regarded me, and I will not fail to follow it.

Notice the date of this letter. One year ago today a prison cell was opened for me, which now would still enclose me, or have seen my corpse exit from it, if the most generous and unselfish friends had not extended a hand to me to escape from that sewer of evils, whose air is fatal for anyone who has not banished the slightest sentiment of sensitivity and virtue from his heart. The most horrible injustice dictated my imprisonment. A year has passed, and what measures have been taken to clarify the truth and execute justice? We have seen nothing but entanglements and repeated schemes to make the obscurity that surrounds that infamous indictment even more impenetrable. A year has gone by, and perhaps another century will pass in the same way, unless God takes a hand in the matter. In the meantime, exposed to the rigors of a destructive climate, I spent four months of agony here, between the suffering of my body and the agitation of my spirit. Spring brought me some strength and hope, and now another terrible winter approaches, perhaps to finish the job that last winter took pretty far. You yourself have told me that there is no hope that the conspiracy hearings will be concluded before next year. Why then should I wait here, in imminent danger? I would go to Charleston or

Savannah, but those places are even farther north than Pensacola, whose climate you well know, and thus I have little to gain, and it would be a futile attempt to head off misfortune. It is not in my interest to go to Jamaica, since to find oneself sick and abandoned as happened to Pancho is a very sad thing [illegible] . . . Santiago the enclosed letter, and Caminero the one I am copying (I had not written to him). A ship bound for Santo Domingo is available to me, and I plan to take advantage of it. The climate there will have the same salutary effect as that of Veracruz and Havana when we were returning from Mexico. It is absurd that I should completely ruin my health out of fear of what my enemies might say. You cannot rationally disapprove of my fleeing a climate that is disastrous for me, to a country where I have such close relatives and resources, and which is not at war with Spain.

If the government of Cuba wishes to enter into an honest reconciliation, it will not fail to realize the unshakeable strength of that decision. But if it continues along the same path as up to now and, filled with unworthy suspicion, always has its hand raised above its subjects, I would be the most foolish of men, and I would be unworthy of the precious gift that Heaven gave me in my liberty, if I were to put myself once more beneath the knife, even if it were with the promise of amnesty. You know how well such promises are kept. Having made the terrible sacrifice of breaking the ties that bound me with Cuba, I have resolved not to lose the fruits of that sacrifice; I would rather perish in exile than live agonizing amid suspicions and fears.

Ignacio himself, when he expressly forbids me from going to Colombia or Mexico, only says regarding Santo Domingo that it is a sad place and within a few days I would be bored. But that is not true: all I desire is a gentle climate in which to spend this winter.

I will be there until March or April, and then I will return to the United States to see how things are looking and what I shall do with myself.

I have promised Ignacio and you that I will not go to Mexico or Colombia, and I will be true to that promise. I wrote you more than two months ago about traveling to Santo Domingo, and I have had no answer; I would continue to wait, but already there are two inches of ice here at daybreak, and the opportunities to sail for Santo Domingo are not frequent; were I to miss this ship it is very probable that I would not have another chance through the whole winter. I think that you will be swayed by these convincing arguments, and, loving me as you do, your foremost thought is for my life and health, without which a pardon or any other resolution of the hearings will be in vain. So in light of all this, I am going, because I believe that you will not look ill on it, and I would rather lose my life than cause you to shed a single tear.

Continue to write me here, since I will make provisions for my letters to be sent to me via Puerto Príncipe, for which as many ships leave from here as for Havana.

If the money order has been issued for me, I have made arrangements for it not to go astray and to be cashed. If it has not, wait, or if the circumstances become more urgent, send the bill of exchange to Silvestre, putting his name second and mine first. Try to send it through Drake and Mitchell. I will be happy to have the money here, since, given the way things are going, I foresee, with great sorrow, that within two years the torrent of war is going to sweep across the island of Cuba, even though its people do not wish it.

With regard to the piano, it seems best to me that, should you wish to buy it, you do so there. You will be able to obtain it there at a good price, since the merchants buy at a cheaper price and then smuggle them in. Remember the armoire that you ordered from Forbes, and it cost you ninety-some dollars when in the shops they could be had for $75. Add to that the risk that something so delicate could be damaged during the voyage, and that they might crate up for me some piece of junk, since I know as much about pianos as I do about witchcraft, and the *Muslim* I might go to buy from would hand me off to some crony of his, to bamboozle me. So it seems to me better that you buy it there at your leisure, since you will know what you are dealing with.[199]

As for the work in Cristo's hands, I will tell you again as before: it was about the legislation of the Indies, and if anything can be gotten from Cristo it is by asking nicely; any other way, you will only end up disappointed.

I am sending along two letters from Santiago for Aunt Francisca, and one from grandmother to be sent on to Uncle Domingo.

There is no need for you to advertise the fact that I am going to Santo Domingo, if you don't think it advisable.

Good-bye. Give my fondest regards to Aunt Francisca, to Ángela, Magdalena and all my cousins, to Franco and family, and to Osés, to whom I am not writing because I am fearful of implicating him unnecessarily. A thousand embraces for my sisters, and be confident that God, in accordance with the purity of my intentions, will not fail to protect your most loving son

José Mª

Much loved Ignacia: The *Telémaco* is on its way with Cirilo Ponce, along with some sonnets and other poems of mine, since I believe that right now you don't have anything of mine, and it should be pleasing for you to have, in those effusions of my soul, some part of me. Show them to Osés. And you, be as well as your brother wishes.

José Mª

To María de la Merced Heredia y Campuzano [BNJM; Augier no. 73]

New York, November 21, 1824

My dearest Mother:

I wrote you and Osés at considerable length two or three days ago, via Matanzas, so here I will write just a few lines to tell you that I remain very well, thank God, and that I received yours of October 16 and 17. The letters that I had here for Santiago are now on their way to Santo Domingo on the same ship that would have carried me. I have had letters from Santiago until the beginning of October, and I suppose that one for Aunt Francisca that I sent via Ignacio, which I sent on the same occasion mentioned above, will have the same date. I hope that he has good news for her. He has told me only that he was awaiting me, and that all the family was well.

I very much would like to have letters from Havana, since your last has left me eagerly anticipating the outcome of the hearings and has revived my hope which, in truth, I had almost lost. May God grant that the doors of my homeland be opened for me, and then we will see to the rest. However, if the hearings drag on and you can send me the money, it would not be a bad thing for it to be here earning its steady 6%, free from all risk and care, and for you to have that anchor of hope in case things should go to rack and ruin, which should never be thought impossible in this tempestuous century in which we live.

My best regards to Franco and family, Osés, Aunt Francisca, Magdalena, Abus the philosopher, Antonio Angulo, his parents and other relatives, without forgetting the Barbas, especially Dolores and Antonio. All my love to my sisters, and may you enjoy the peace that your most loving son desires for you.

José Mª

José Alfonso y García[200] (alias Pepé) sends you most cordial greetings.

If there is any important news regarding the hearings, please write me, addressing your letter to me in New York, and send the letter on the first ship leaving for any port in the United States; I will receive it promptly, even if it costs me a bit more.

To María de la Merced Heredia y Campuzano [Augier no. 74]

New York, December 11, 1824

My dearest Mother:

Yesterday I had the great satisfaction of receiving your letter of November 4, and of reading in it that all is well at home. My last letter from Ignacio is dated the 7th, and so I have been left wishing for another ship to arrive so as to know the final result of the hearings which cannot be far off now. I have seen a copy of the prosecutor's statement, and I have almost regretted not being among the prisoners, so as to be able to raise my voice in defense of the unfortunate ones against whom is applied, erroneously and horribly, the principle with which it concludes.[201] Perhaps I will be one of them. However things turn out, I will apply to myself the words that I put into the mouth of Saul, "Misfortune / is less cruel when suffered than when feared,"[202] and my spirit will recover its tranquility the day that I know whether I can return to my homeland, or if they will banish me from it forever.

So as to get a taste of earning a living in these parts, I have taken a job teaching Spanish in a school, and they are paying me 500 dollars a year, with room and board.[203] So far, in the month that I have been on the job, it is going quite well; if it were not for this infernal climate, I would be quite well set up. I am busy for only three and a half hours a day, and I could make even more money, since they have proposed to me that I give private lessons, but I have declined because of the cold weather. They came to me to offer this arrangement, without my having made any overtures myself, since I did not even know about such teaching. In Boston they also have offered to establish an academy for me. So you see, as I told you, with God's favor I will not be lacking a means to make a living, even among these Jews.[204] Needless to say, even more so in other places where my language is spoken and I can practice law. You would have a good laugh if you could see the gravity with which I set myself to speaking English for hours on end.

As for my health, so far it has been better than I could have expected. It is true that winter has been moderate so far, and hardly any snow has fallen.

I sent Ignacio a splendid book with Madan's son,[205] who left for Matanzas a few days ago; it contains all the good English poets, and it is to be sent on to Blas.[206] I have sent it via that conduit because of the difficulty in finding acquaintances to deliver things. Tell him that he should accept it as a token of our friendship, and that I do not write him because I do not even know if this letter will reach its destination.

I believe that the *Historia de la América* was published in Spain at the time of the Constitution.[207] Blas in Havana may know better than I here. Please ask him to find out, and let me know where it is, since it would be nothing for me to continue it; a year of dealing with these people has given me a better command of English than Father ever could have had.

You will have seen already what I have told you regarding the piano: that it would be better to buy it there if you want one, since here they would deceive me, and if not it would be a miracle.

Good-bye: my fond remembrances to Aunt Francisca and Aunt Ángela, to Magdalena, Franco and family, Osés, and all my love to my sisters. Do not forget in your prayers nor fail to bless your most loving son

José Mª

To relieve her anxiety, tell Aunt Francisca that it is known that the French are not going to Santo Domingo, and that that country is so tranquil that six ships have left from here with more than 500 emigrants who are going to settle there.

To María de la Merced Heredia y Campuzano [BNJM; Augier no. 75]

New York, December 28, 1824

My dearest Mother:

The last letter I have from you is from November 18, and I have answered it more than once. Today I am sending you these lines which I will leave with Goodhue & Co. for them to send along on the first ship, since perhaps it will be dispatched on a day of such bad weather that I won't be able to go outside, especially since the school in which I live is at the other end of the city. I will leave a letter for Aunt Francisca as well, which I am including with this, since I see that mine are getting lost.

The letter from Santiago with which Aunt Francisca's letter came is from November 4, and all was well with him.

I am eager to receive a letter, since I am worried about Blas's illness, and anxious to know the resolution of the hearings. Even if I am not included among those to be exiled, the conditions that accompany an absolution might be such that it won't be in my interest to go and accept it, but in any case my fate will be decided and I will feel at peace.

If Mitchell issues the order of payment for Philadelphia, it will be the same as if for New York, since within 48 hours I will be able to claim it. So do not let that hold you back.

Even though you erased it, how could you have thought that the name of the illustrious gentleman from Coro would not be obvious to me—he who, in imitation of the most praiseworthy gentleman of La Mancha, has not learned his lesson despite the infinite troubles he has undergone in his horrible insistence on laying waste to his poor homeland? I always thought that man a fool, but I thought that bullet wounds would have cured him of his simplemindedness. But how could that be![208]

Good-bye! Do not be surprised by the bad handwriting, since it is colder than the devil. My regards to all my friends and relatives, without forgetting Perico del Ángel, all my love to my sisters, and do not fail to write to and do not forget your most loving son

José Mª

As I have told you before, if there is any interesting news, you can write me via any United States port.

To María de la Merced Heredia y Campuzano [BNJM; Augier no. 76]

New York, January 20, 1825

My dearest Mother:
Via the frigate *Reaper* which left yesterday, a quite long letter should be on its way to you, which I wrote you upon receiving one from José Miguel Angulo which disclosed to me the outcome of the hearings, and that they have exiled me to Spain (a fate for me more horrible than torture, had I not been saved by an act of friendship). Following that, there arrived news that, although previous to the aforementioned letter, attempts to deny its veracity. But I will not be beguiled by false hopes. I am resigned to my fate, and I will be able to bear it.
Yesterday I received your letter of December 12, and I will not forget the request regarding Antonio, as soon as there is some acquaintance who can take it.
How infinitely happy I am that Uncle Manuel has gone off to Spain. May he never return from a country so worthy of him!
Pepé and Pancho return your greetings, and Silvestre sends them to you as well, even if you do not remember him.
I am greatly desirous of knowing what Ignacio thinks about these things, and that you are reconciled, as you must be, to our fate.
I have nothing else to tell. I continue in good health, and the winter, thank God, remains mild.
My regards to all my acquaintances, and may they not forget me, especially Osés, Franco and family, all my love to my sisters and the others at home, and do not forget to write to your most loving son

José Mª

The letters for Santo Domingo only cost me half a *real*, whether the packages be large or small, as long as they come directly to New York.

To María de la Merced Heredia y Campuzano [BNJM; Augier no. 77]

New York, January 28, 1825

My dearest Mother:

I have received your letters of December 31 and the 2nd of this month, which have given me much pleasure, since I see that you have received the news of the iniquitous sentence of expatriation with the same equanimity of spirit as I.

As regards what you say about not going to any of the independent countries, I already have told you that for now I have no plans to leave here, although that sacrifice is perhaps more painful than that of my life. I would like to erase from mine each and every day of winter; despite the short time that the sun is above the horizon, the day seems more tiresomely long than all the days of my tiresome existence. If one goes out, one catches cold; if one stays inside for many days by the fire, the body aches and circulation becomes sluggish, and the blood scorches and burns. Oh! Is this living?

If truly you are thinking of coming here in spring, then don't do so until May, and wait for me to give you the word, since we are at very serious risk of there being a war, because of the pirates.[209] Do not fail to bring a very compelling letter of recommendation from Osés for Señora Argaiz, so that (in exchange for money) you may live in her home, since any other way you will be most uncomfortable, living among people whose language you cannot understand.

I see what you say regarding Franco and his proposal. I am grateful to him from the bottom of my heart, but even if it could be arranged, I refuse to return and live in Cuba under the present circumstances. How could I go there and have them look at me as a convict—that is to say a pardoned convict—and have the families of so many poor devils curse me, believing that I had bought such a favor with some great and secret act of infamy. No. I would go perhaps to spend some days with my family, and nothing more. All I want is for them to let me live in some gentle climate that will restore my constitution which has been weakened in this horrible one. There I will practice law or make a living by teaching schoolboys, as I do here. I have no desire for glory, just pure water and air instead of liquid ice and coal vapors.

Good-bye. My fondest regards to my sisters and all our relatives, and to Osés and Franco and family. Do not forget your most loving

José Mª

To María de la Merced Heredia y Campuzano [BNJM; Augier, continuation of no. 77]

New York, January 31, 1825

My dearest Mother:

I have received your letters of December 31 and January 3,[210] which have given me great pleasure, since I see that you have accepted with fortitude the iniquitous sentence which closes for me the door to my homeland, without my having committed any crime other than having perhaps prevented its ruin.

Be that as it may, upon reflection I think that it is best that you not come here. Why should you double your sorrows with another separation, when time will have mitigated the bitterness of the first? Why should you spend money, which you do not have in abundance, for such a trip? Besides the fact that I cannot help you right now, I don't want you to fall farther behind, nor suffer the discomforts and risks of a sea voyage. I do not doubt that, with the favor of God, within a year I will be able to send for you, when I am better established. But for now, I beg you not to undertake such a thing. I remain well, thank God. May He give me health and life, so that, despite all the tyrants in the world, you soon may be reunited with your most loving son

José Mª

As I already have said, I do not want a pardon. Ask Ignacio; I will abide by his decision. My regards to Pepé.

To María de la Merced Heredia y Campuzano [Escoto; BNJM; Augier no. 78]

New York, February 8, 1825

My dearest Mother:

Even though I have answered your letters of December 31 and January 3 more than once, I do not want to miss the opportunity to send you a few lines.

On this same occasion I am writing to Franco, explaining my reasons for not wanting to accept a pardon. He will tell you these, and when you reflect upon them I have no doubt that you will be convinced that it is not in my best interest to return now to Cuba. I will not repeat these reasons here, because I am still weak from an ailment that I have suffered, like the ones in Mexico. But the spring is approaching, and I hope that you will not be so cruel, now that there is no hope for a happy outcome to the hearings, as to wish me to agonize through another winter here.

What you should do is send me my diploma, and give me your blessing to go and work in peace in Jalapa, since it is your wish that it not be in Colombia; I have no doubt that God will help me, and reward my fondest desire, and will allow us to be reunited there and never be separated again, since there are no tyrants there to persecute good men. Mexico is in the most profound state of peace and order since the death of Iturbide.[211] May all villains like him meet the same fate, so that the world may enjoy the advantages of Mexico and the United States. Therefore you should not have doubts nor condemn me to live any longer among foreigners. The fat one[212] has written me that I can have my monthly allowance wherever I want.

I already have told you that I do not think it advisable to come here, only to encounter troubles and increase your sorrows. I repeat that I have hope in God that we will see each other again, and never more be separated.

I also have told you that if you are not going to use the money in Cuba, send it to me so that I may deposit it in the bank of the United States, where it can be safe earning its five percent. It doesn't matter if the order of payment is made for Philadelphia.

Good-bye. My love to my sisters, regards to Osés, Franco and family, Aunt Francisca and Magdalena (whose letters are on their way to Santo Domingo). Do not fail to heed the pleas of your most loving son

José Mª

To María de la Merced Heredia y Campuzano [BNJM; Augier no. 79]

New York, February 14, 1825

My dearest Mother:
    Although the last letter I have from you is your note of January 4, which I have answered several times, I do not want to let this opportunity pass to write you, even if just a few lines.
    This letter will go with Machado, who is sailing on the *Brown*, and he will be able to tell you more than I can write. If he should leave during the next few days, I will buy some little thing for Antonino,[213] so that that same friend can take it. I also have given him a letter from Santiago for Aunt Francisca, which I received yesterday. It must be recent, since the one he wrote me was of January 10, and I will be happy if it is a more pleasant letter than those I have received for the past month. None has given me greater sorrow than Ignacio's last, in which he advises me to go to Europe in the spring. Why does he insist upon tormenting me and doing me greater harm even than my sentence? The latter only has deprived me of an agitated and wretched homeland, while my friends, because of an ill-fated error, wish to take my very life, since that is what spending another winter away from the tropics would mean. May God liberate me from this winter, and from the next I will extricate myself. My only desire is that you recognize that that is not the only option open to me, and stop deceiving yourself into thinking that I would not have suffered what I have suffered if I had given the prosecutor's hypocritical clemency the credit it deserved. I beg you to send me my diploma as soon as possible, keeping a sworn copy, and let me pursue the fate that has been given me, in the knowledge that, even if I should spend the next four years in Europe, I will still end up doing the same. The bearer of this letter can fill you in on the current state of things in Mexico, and in any case, even if that country were in the most

frightful state of revolution, it would be better for me to face that than to run the risk of dying here.

 I am convalescing very slowly from my illness, although I imagine I won't be fully recovered until May or June. But if I have a relapse, I am going to convalesce in La Guaira or Veracruz, that is to say, in Alvarado, which is where commerce is now.

 I want to settle in Jalapa, as I have explained to you at length in a letter that I wrote seven days ago. In sum, you are my mother, you saw me suffer in Mexico, and surely you do not want to condemn me to a slow and horrible death. I have no doubt that in your next letter you will give me permission; I do not want a pardon, since it will do me no good if it means that they regard me as a bad and harmful man, and who knows if the same might not happen here, since it would not be the first time that in America they hang someone who trusted in the certificate of pardon that he wore on his chest. Have you yourself not said that my sentence is a blessing from heaven, for my safety? Then how can you deceive yourself, or wish to deceive me, with the business about a pardon?

 I am going to seal and dispatch this letter; I don't want to run out of time and not be able to send it. Give my regards to my aunts and cousins, Franco (whom I have written about the pardon) and family, and Blas. All my love to my sisters, and do not fail to heed the pleas of your most loving son

José M^a

To María de la Merced Heredia y Campuzano [Escoto]

New York, March 4, 1825

Dearest Mother:

 Yesterday I had the pleasure of receiving your letter of this past January 26th, which has filled me with the satisfaction of knowing that everyone at home is enjoying good health. However, your letter also has left me saddened to know that you continue to insist that I stay in this destructive climate. You say that *I am fine here*. Fine! How can you think that when you saw how I suffered in Mexico, and you know that that does not begin to compare to this! No, I am not fine. Last month I had two bouts of illness that were so severe that I thought they would end my cares once and for all. You think that I can go on living here because I have managed to get by for a year without dying; but every day I become weaker, and this winter I have been much worse than last.

You say that you do not regret so much the sentence that has been handed down to me, because if I had been found innocent, I would have departed from here, and you would suffer endless anxieties regarding my safety. What lamentable blindness! You would have hoped then that we might be safely reunited, as you do now (when I have been declared incompatible with peace on the island) if they pardon me? Ferdinand VII never has seen fit to pardon anyone, but even if he were a Titus[214] I hereby and forever renounce his mercy. Do not be fooled. Only one thing—the triumph of my principles—will ever allow me to return to Cuba with honor and in safety.

When you suffered such pain to give me life, do not now attempt to deprive me of it little by little. Send me my diploma so that I may go and work as a lawyer in Jalapa. What are you afraid of? Don't you see that the ease with which Iturbide was punished gives evidence of the firmness and stability of the Mexican government? There is not a single Spanish soldier remaining on the whole American continent; it is a known fact here that on December 9, Bolívar dispatched the Viceroy of Peru and his entire army of 10,000 men.[215] England and these United States have recognized Spanish American Independence. So what do you fear? Even if there were some remote danger—which there is not—would it not be better for me to be exposed to it than to fall victim to pulmonary consumption? That, without a doubt, will be my fate if I spend another winter here—and this current one is not yet over. For heaven's sake, do not reduce me to despair, something to which my spirit, embittered by my misfortunes and suffering, is already too inclined. The only hope that sustains me is that I may be reunited with my family; that hope will be in vain if I end up in the grave here. Once again I beg you urgently, for the sake of my sisters, for your own sake and for that of my father's memory (he would have thought this useless sacrifice to be criminal) that you not leave me in despair and that you let me go where my destiny may take me. I know that you will not deny me that, and that if you do, it is only because you are being harangued by some fanatic.

If my way of expressing myself in this letter strikes you as harsh, please forgive me and attribute it to my piteous state. I already have written you that I am not in favor of your coming here, since that would only cause you distress and anguish.

    Good-bye for now. Remember that during the time when I honorably waited and hoped to be able to return to the bosom of my family, I never said a word about leaving the United States. But now I am compelled to do so by the necessity of self-preservation. There isn't a single person here who doesn't tell me that to spend another winter here would be tantamount to suicide.

    Please give my love to my sisters, and my regards to Osés, and Franco and family. And please take pity on me, close your ears to political and religious fanatics, and don't leave in despair your most loving son

José M^a

    Please consult with Franco. Since I haven't gone outdoors for close to a month, I haven't been able to buy anything for Antonino.

To Domingo del Monte [Augier no. 81[216]]

New York, March 15, 1825

My dearest Domingo:

    I begin this letter with the most painful emotions. Our former, intimate correspondence in happier times cannot but bring to mind a thousand memories of love and happiness, which have vanished like a dream. Your letter of January 11 has revived in my spirit all the sensations that I communicated to you so openly and frankly as soon as I felt them. You complain of my silence, and I see that you have not received the letter I sent you in response to your previous one. Not to repeat what I wrote you then would be a failure of frankness and candor, which are inseparable from friendship. News from Havana, and the harsh reception that you had in Guane,[217] led me to believe, painfully, that my friend had been in league with the most execrable tyrants, and had abandoned all virtue. The hurricane that swept me from Cuba soon thereafter, found me plagued with such gloomy ideas. Judge for yourself if indignation and self-respect could allow the victim to address a person whom he judged to be in collusion with his executioners. However, your recollection of our tender and long-standing friendship has convinced me of your innocence. Let us renew, then, our correspondence, since it seems you are not afraid of engaging in it with a fugitive like me. But if you think that this might compromise you in the slightest degree, let me know, and I will be silent, since the worst misfortune of all would be to entangle a friend in my sad fate.

I will say nothing of the bitter days of my persecution. Their fury must be evident to you, Domingo, who know me so well. Afterwards has come the atrocious decree which bars me forever from my homeland, and which has not had half the impact upon me as the painful act of tearing myself from it, when such well-founded and promising hopes of peace and happiness lay before me. I will not say, like Graco,

> Ho tale un cor nel petto
> che ne' disastri esulta: un cor che gode
> lottar col fato, e superarlo . . .[218]

but the villains who have exiled me will not succeed in making me lose my life to sorrow. The new American nations offer me a homeland. In them I will be able to live in peace, without terror disturbing my nights' rest. I will live far from my family, but that will not be forever.

I only wish I had made that decision fifteen months ago, and had not ruined my constitution during two winters in this horrid climate, awaiting with inconceivable blindness the outcome of my legal case. But the human heart has sentiments capable of dominating and silencing all others, and which even stifle the voice of reason, whose severity can intimidate us. My desire to return to the bosom of my family and breathe the air of my homeland, while I was not yet denied the chance to be counted among its sons, deluded me regarding the cruel designs of the reigning aristocracy.

You can imagine how I have suffered through so many months of almost constant illness, between the afflictions of my body and the perpetual agitation of my spirit. These two winters have destroyed not only my body, but also my intellectual faculties. When once I wrote, complaining of an unrequited love,

> ¡Cuánto es horrible
> el desierto de un alma desolada,
> sin flores de esperanzas ni frescura![219]

I was far from believing that these lines of verse, whose expression seems exaggerated, would soon become the truest portrait of my situation.

    Good-bye, Domingo: I have tired you enough with this unhappy elegy. But what else can you expect of me? Those auspicious notions that in other times offered themselves to my feverish imagination, even in the midst of its affliction, have fled so far into the distance that I cannot comprehend how once I could believe them. I have bid farewell to my homeland, to my mother and sisters, to love, to my friends, to all pleasures and hopes. Only my heart remains, and you will have a place in it as long as I live.

José Mª

> A me Romano,
> Roman tu pure, orrido dubbio or muovi;
> Ma non mi offende: in te il sospetto vile
> Nascer, no, mai non può . . .[220]

To María de la Merced Heredia y Campuzano [Augier no. 82]

New York, March 18, 1825

My dearest Mother:

    The bearer of this letter is an acquaintance of mine, and soon he will return here. So there will be no better occasion for you to send me my law diploma. I have written you so many letters about my need to leave here, that I do not want to tire you any more, since you must have received at least one of those letters. I feel that I can no longer live in these frozen climes. This winter I thought I would die, even though it has been such a mild one that there is no longer ice in the rivers, when other years there is ice until May. I am better now, thanks to God and to spring, whose first signs are beginning to appear. But I remain very weak, and I have no doubt that if I wait until autumn, I will be done for. Do you wish to sacrifice me? If I must go to Mexico, it will be better that I take my diploma with me so as to be able to work, and they will hold me in some consideration, because without it, if I tell them that I am an attorney they will laugh when they see my face, since I cannot seem to grow a beard. Have a sworn copy made and send it to me. Osés can take care of it, or Antonio Angulo.

The bearer of this letter is going to be in Havana only for a few days, so do not procrastinate. It would cause me the greatest sorrow were he to return without my diploma, since that would prove to me that you persist in wishing me to stay here, and it would leave me with the terrible choice of either disobeying you or condemning myself to the most horrible of deaths—that of succumbing by degrees to the slow rigor of pulmonary consumption. Remember how I was in Mexico, and you can imagine how much worse I am in this horrible climate, whose cold is unlike anything I have experienced on this earth.

I have sent Doña María Pepa's letter on to Caracas. This year, the mayor there is Don Esteban Ponte y Cordero. Camacho is *regidor*, and the Marqués del Toro has been governor until recently.

With the same bearer you may send me the copy of the *Historia de Venezuela*, well wrapped. He doesn't have to know what it is.

I have nothing more to tell you; with what I have written, those who open our letters have enough to amuse themselves. My most affectionate regards to Osés, Franco and family, my Aunt Francisca, for whom I am enclosing a letter from Santiago, Magdalena and Abus, and the rest of our relatives. A thousand embraces for my sisters, and do not forget your most loving son

José M^a

Don't forget the business with Mitchell, since with every moment that goes by things get more complicated. Be sure to have that anchor set, since we do not know what the outcome of these threatening storms will be.

To María de la Merced Heredia y Campuzano [BNJM; Augier no. 84]

New York, April 12, 1825

My dearest Mother:

Yesterday I had the great satisfaction of receiving your letter of March 19, in which you answer mine of January 28 and February 8 and 14, and in which you express your agreement that I go to Mexico.

How wrong you are in believing that winter has passed! There is still snow and ice, and the only difference is that when the sun comes out, it warms things a bit. In September it will all begin again, but I trust in God that it will not find me here. I really don't know how it is that I haven't perished. I have been ill three times, and thought I would never get better, but I am improving now with the slight change in the weather.

Do not fail to send me my diploma at the first opportunity. Machado is my friend and he will send it safely. The *Historia de Venezuela* can be sent via the same channel, although I really do not know if in the present circumstances its publication is in my best interest. I will think about this; I do not want the only doors remaining to me, through which I might be able to live in peace in a country that will not kill me like this one, to be closed.

I find José Miguel Angulo's complaint to be very strange. How can he fail to see my motives for not answering him? I have resolved never to write to anyone in Cuba besides you, Ignacio, and once in a while to Blas. I do not want anyone to be able to say that I have caused him the slightest trouble. Please tell Antonio that,[221] and assure him that even though I have chosen not to follow his advice, I am extremely grateful for the concern he has shown me and that I beg him to continue to show toward my loved ones.

I am awaiting a letter and money order from Ignacio so that I may set out, since my monthly stipend has been suspended with the bankruptcy of Adanis. With that document and my diploma I will depart at the first opportunity, since I trust that the order of payment from Mitchell will arrive without delay, and investing that money in the bank shares can be accomplished in one day.

I believe that I will have the pleasure of Pancho García's company during my trip to Mexico.

I am sorry to hear that there is illness at home, but as you say, we can only resign ourselves to the will of God.

I will be very happy to be able to leave in June, since later in the year the weather for sailing is not very good. Therefore I hope that, if you still have not sent the diploma and order of payment, you do so without delay.

Before leaving I will arrange for a way for you to direct your letters, both to me and to Santo Domingo.

I have nothing else to tell. Many regards to Franco and family, Osés, Antonio and José Miguel and especially to Aunt Francisca, Magdalena and Miguel. All my love to my sisters, and do not forget your most loving son

José M^a

Dearest Ignacia: I have received your note, which has given me great pleasure, and I beg you to keep writing to me.

You must believe that, although the iniquitous decision that has barred me from my homeland has deprived me for now of the pleasure of living with my family, it has also removed me from a situation that is too bitter and dangerous for someone of my proud nature. What pained me most was Mamá's insistence that I remain in this horrid climate, but now that she has given me permission to go to Mexico, I am more content with my fate, and ready to face with the same resolve both the mutability of fortune and the injustices of men.

I will not write you more now since they are waiting for this letter. Before departing I will send you my poems published in a little volume.[222] Good-bye: do not forget your most loving brother

José M^a

To María de la Merced Heredia y Campuzano [BNJM; Augier no. 85]

New York, April 17, 1825

My dearest Mother:

It is nine o'clock at night and I have just learned that Ignacio Zequeira[223] is about to leave for Havana, and although I don't know if this letter will get to him in time for him to take it, I do not want to fail to write you.

Having just answered your letter of March 19, I received yours of the 25th. If we continue in this fashion—with question after question, and advice upon advice, until the end of time—I won't ever be able to leave for Mexico. So I am thinking of booking passage on a very handsome armed brigantine that is leaving for Alvarado within 18–20 days, after I make arrangements here for my friend Don Tomás Gener to collect and secure the money. I have resolved to do this because if I wait for an answer to my last letter, it will arrive in July or August, and I will have to sail for the Veracruz coast at the worst time of year, not only because of disease but also because it is the rainy season and the roads become impassable. Whereas now I will be going at the best time of year, and I can expect to be in Mexico, God willing, by the end of June.

Tell Aunt Francisca that the letters for Santo Domingo should be addressed as follows: *To Don José Ma. Heredia, to be forwarded to Don Santiago Garay*, since if they are not addressed this way they may end up in Mexico. I have written Santiago to do the same.

Turning to other things. My health is not as bad since spring has begun to make an appearance, and the best way for me to keep improving is not to wait for another autumn to catch me here in this accursed climate.

If by the time the ship leaves I haven't received my diploma, nor a letter of credit that I expect to receive any time now from Matanzas, I will have to wait, which I would regret very much, and should July find me still here, I may not be able to depart until October, which is not a very good time of year, but in any case there is no danger comparable to that of another winter in New York, which I would be incapable of enduring.

If you have not sent the money by the time you receive this letter, and you wish to send it, then do so to Don Tomás Gener, who will take care of it just as well as I could do.

I have told you that it doesn't seem to me to be a good idea to sell the house, since that money cannot be invested in any better way. Do not be so afraid, since things in Cuba will sort themselves out better than you think, and things will either continue in their present state or will change in such a fashion that they won't be able to steal from anyone. But as regards those two thousand dollars, it would be better to have them here, if you do not plan to use them. However, if they are going to take half of that in fees, I think that you will do better to use that money to buy some little house, or something else that will bring you some income, since here with all certainty it will only yield 4 percent.

I will write you from Alvarado and Mexico City, via New York, and you should do the same. Address the letters to New York and I will not fail to write before my departure, and I will indicate to you another address according to the arrangements that I make.

This afternoon a brigantine from Matanzas arrived, and I hope it has brought me a letter from Ignacio.

I have nothing else to tell you. My most affectionate regards to Franco and family, Osés and his father, the Fernández girls, and do not forget Aunt Francisca and Magdalena (whose letters are on their way today to Santo Domingo), nor Abus and José Miguel. All my love to my sisters and do not forget your most loving son

José Mª

I am not writing Dr. Angulo because I feel it is useless.

To María de la Merced Heredia y Campuzano [BNJM; Augier no. 87]

New York, April 27, 1825

My dearest Mother:

After my last letter I have not had the pleasure of receiving one from you, although to be sure only one war schooner from Havana has arrived, and since it does not run a regular route, it does not carry mail.

In my last letter I told you about my determination to leave in May for Mexico, but now who knows what I will do, since the month of April ends the day after tomorrow, and I still do not have my diploma, nor the letter of credit that Ignacio has offered me. If I cannot embark during the month of May, perhaps I will travel by land to New Orleans with Silvestre and Pancho, and from there, with Pancho, make the short voyage to Alvarado, Tampico or Veracruz. But continue to write me in New York until further notice, and if you want to send the money, even if the money order is made out to me, address the envelope to my friend Don Tomás Gener, who, should I not be here, will cash and deposit it. If they charge you a high fee, then don't send it, since bank shares are very expensive here as well (they charge fees of 18 to 20 percent), and so a good deal of the money would be lost. The dangers on the island of Cuba, although real, are still not imminent.

I had written you a long letter to send with Ignacio Zequeira, but despite my best efforts I could not find him, and so I was left not only with my letter, but also with the one you sent me for him.

On this occasion I am sending a letter from Santiago for Aunt Francisca. I am not enclosing it in another envelope, so as not to increase its cost needlessly. It would not add to its safety in any way, since both are going in the mail.

News from Madrid through March 13 has appeared in the papers here, and they say that the King has signed a decree of amnesty which was to be made public on the 19th, the anniversary of his ascent to the throne.[224] They assure that the king will absolve all those who have been convicted for political reasons since March 1, 1825. Time will tell.

My best regards to my aunts and cousins, especially to Magdalena, my affectionate remembrances to Franco, Osés, Doña Pepa Gómez and Antonino, a thousand embraces for my sisters and do not forget nor fail to write to your most loving

José M^a

P.S. My health is getting visibly better with the spring. May God increase it and give me life so that I may see you again and embrace you.

Tell Aunt Francisca that so as to avoid confusion with the letters after I leave, I have written to Santiago instructing how to address them. He wrote me on March 22, and he and all the family are fine.

My dearest Ignacia: I am very sorry not to have seen Ignacio Zequeira, since I was planning to send with him a little book for you along the lines of the *Telémaco*. Oh well, another time. It is a shame that one cannot do what one wants, since if it were not thus, instead of the book, I would have flown to embrace you.

If I cannot leave in May as I fear may occur, I will have printed some of my poems in a little volume, and you will have a very pretty copy of them.

I was thinking of having a portrait done of me, since I have changed so much since I began to have a beard. But I have been in such bad shape, and so terribly thin up until now, that I have not wanted to make you sad with a faithful copy of my "sorrowful countenance."

Now that, thank God, I have begun to feel like myself again, I will carry through with the plan, and will send the portrait via Matanzas with Luis Ramírez.[225]

Good-bye: write to me whenever you can. I will not give you any advice, since it would be pointless, although you have at your side, thanks to the goodness of God, such a virtuous mother. Never doubt that your happiness is the most fervent wish of your loving brother

José Mª

To María de la Merced Heredia y Campuzano [Augier no. 88]

May 4, 1825

My dearest Mother:

Since I was not able to find Ignacio Zequeira, this letter remained behind with me, as well as the one that Aunt Belén sent me for him, which I am returning. My friend Pancho Ruiz, who is a splendid fellow and who I wish were not leaving, will deliver it to you.[226]

I had the pleasure of receiving, in the *Broway*, my diploma and several letters from you. Your acquiescence to my wishes and your expressions of tenderness have caused me to shed more tears than all my past misfortunes. I foresee that we will be reunited in this world, and without that I would not have endeavored to preserve my life [torn] to seek my fortune in Mexico. My hopes are well founded, and if things do not change in Cuba, I hope that within two or three years I will be able to call you to my side, and we may enjoy a peace never disturbed by tyrants.

Rocafuerte is now serving the Mexican government as ambassador in London, and he has written me recently. You know how partial he always has been to me. He has sent me letters of recommendation, among them one for President Victoria, written with all the ardor of his friendship, nor does he limit himself to empty words, since he also has sent an order for a merchant here to give me $300 for my voyage, even though I never told him that I needed money. I do not plan to accept it, as long as Ignacio continues to help me out as he has done till now. In this way I can preserve the independence that is natural to my character, and not be obligated by favors in any future dealings.

    Ignacio has now sent me the money order so that I can continue to collect my monthly stipend, and the merchant has offered me another for Alvarado or Mexico City.

(continuation)New York, May 5, 1825

On another topic: in my last letter you will have seen that I was thinking of leaving immediately. But after receiving my diploma it has occurred to me that it would be a kind of ingratitude on my part not to give such a good mother a pleasure that is not incompatible with my plans and needs. Instead of going to Alvarado from here, I will wait until the end of June or the first days of July. So, as soon as you receive this letter, get the money order and send it to me in the first ship leaving for New York, or any of these ports: Baltimore, Philadelphia, Boston, Providence (in Rhode Island) or New London, since I will receive it from any of these in three days. Address it like this:

> J. M. Heredia, Esq.
> Absent, to be delivered to Thomas Gener, Esq.
> Care of Messrs. Goodhue & Co.
> New York

    Later, in the first ship coming directly here, you can send me the duplicate, addressed the same way, so that if for some unusual delay they do not find me here, Gener by my order will open the letters and collect the money, and he will put it in the bank. This precaution is only for more safety, since as I say I will wait here until the first days of July. Then I will travel by land (that is, inland along rivers) to New Orleans, along with Pancho García, and from there we will embark for Alvarado or Veracruz. If you cast your eyes upon the sea, you will see that the voyage will be reduced by two-thirds, and the risk of passing near Havana and Matanzas will be avoided. We will leave in October and we will be in Jalapa in the month of November. From there we will arrange our future actions. It will give me great pleasure to travel with Pancho García, such a worthy person in every sense, and bound to me by our previous friendship and our common misfortune.

I repeat that you should not delay a moment in taking care of the money order, or should you choose not to send it, write and tell me so immediately. It is true that the cost of bank shares has risen to 20%, and they will only yield 4%; but one must remember as well that they will be worth the same when the day comes to sell them, which one can do at any time, with the slight loss of a ¼ per cent. Anyway, simply by depositing it, the money will be safe, and if it doesn't gain, nor will it lose. I will act according to the circumstances.

With regard to the *Historia de Venezuela*, I have told you that the situation has changed from six months ago. The struggle for independence has concluded, and what before only seemed like an interminable war of devastation, has become a revolution that is transforming the face of the world. England, Holland, Sweden and the United States now have inscribed in their catalog of nations what five years ago was but a mob of rebels. Bolívar, who in Father's eyes could only seem like an obstinate agitator, is today the tutelary deity of America. Peru, Santa Fe, Quito and Venezuela, one-eighth of the entire world, owe their existence to him, happily acknowledge the ascendancy of his genius, and honor him as an entity somewhere between human and divine. His name is uttered with respect in all of Europe, and is the most beautiful name that the history of this century has presented. All the illustrious names of legislators and warriors, except for that of George Washington, are overshadowed by his soaring greatness. Unfortunately, Father had the misfortune of seeing only the dark and bloody part of the picture, and death snatched him away before the veil that covered the splendor of Bolívar's glory could be removed, as it has been.

The struggle for independence, although concluded, does not yet belong to the annals of history. Now that its fruits have begun to be gathered, its tragedies should not be renewed, but rather buried and forgotten. Why stir up old rancors and divisions by reopening the wounds of the revolution, when nothing can return its victims to life?

I am not afraid of persecution, because the peoples of America are not tyrannical. I never will sacrifice my sentiments for material gain, and in any case it is unlikely that the latter would result from the publication of that work. What is likely is that it would be received badly by both sides, since it does not favor the passions of either.

They will not hold me responsible for my father's opinions, but neither will they think well of me for having published them needlessly. Thus will be closed to me the vast panorama of hope that now opens before me, and, banned by Spaniards and thought ill of by those of the Americas, what will be left for me on this earth?

I hope you will recognize the rightness of these reflections, which you can pass on to Señor Franco, and that you will forgive me for not satisfying your wish in this matter. I would have gone ahead with the publication if I had returned to Havana, since I am not afraid of the hatred of my enemies, but rather of the scorn of those whom I hold in high regard. But I would be very happy to have the copy, since you would keep the original, although if I had known that my sentence would be what it is, I would not have asked you to have the copy made.

I am sending notes for Father Márquez and José Miguel.

Accompanying this letter is one from Santiago, the same one that I had intended to send via the *Cadmus*,[227] and which later I thought better to send with Pancho Ruiz.

My health has improved as better weather has approached. Once past the first shock of distress, I am almost grateful for my sentence, which in a sense has liberated me. Is there any horror comparable to that of going to bed not knowing if dawn will find one in a jail cell? It is true that I am separated from my family, but does that man who, without being tried nor heard, can be sent to perish two thousand leagues from his home as has happened to us, truly have a family? You and my sisters, defended by your very weakness, can live in Havana, but its air would be noxious for me.

So then, my beloved and excellent Mother, be happy with an occurrence that at the cost of some tears has spared you a fountainhead of agony. Right now I have only to fear the troubles common to all men, those illnesses and afflictions to which our mortal nature subjects us. But I am free of the fury and the vengeance of tyrants, which are more terrible and ominous than all the scourges of nature, and I am hopeful that quite soon we will be reunited and live freely and in peace, until our Creator calls us to His side.

My most affectionate regards to all my relatives, especially to Aunt Francisca, Magdalena and Abus, Franco and family, Osés and his father. A thousand embraces for my dear sisters, for Ignacia to whom I would write separately if I had time. Pray to God that the desires of your most loving son may come true.

José M^a

So as not to make this letter more bulky, I have decided to burn the letter from Aunt Belén, which cannot be of any use now since her son is on his way back. There is no point in risking any complications. He is on his way.

To María de la Merced Heredia y Campuzano [BNJM; Augier no. 89]

New York, May 8, 1825

My dearest Mother:

Although I have written you at length in a letter sent with my friend Don Francisco Ruiz, who left for Havana via Matanzas three days ago, since I do not want to miss the opportunity to write you, I am sending you these few lines, which perhaps will arrive in your hands before the aforementioned letter.

In that letter I wrote you that I have decided not to depart yet, so as to satisfy your desire that I wait and deposit the money in the bank. I reiterate that you should send me the money at once, via any ship leaving for Boston, Philadelphia or Baltimore, if there are none for New York, addressing the envelope like this:

> J. M. Heredia, Esq.
> Absent, to be delivered to Thomas Gener, Esq.
> Care of Messrs. Goodhue & Co.
> New York

I plan to leave for New Orleans at the beginning of July, traveling overland with Pancho and Silvestre, and from there Pancho and I will continue on to Alvarado.

Do not think that for this reason I am hurrying you to send me the money. If they charge you a large commission you will have to decide what to do.

With regard to the *Historia de Venezuela*, I have written you at length about this in the aforementioned letter, and here I only will repeat that in the present circumstances its publication is not a good idea. For the rest, I refer you to the letter arriving with Ruiz.

I am in a quandary regarding the present for Antonino, since I would send him either something of such little value and novelty that it would be ridiculous, or else some scientific instrument whose use he would not understand, and therefore would be useless to him. As for books, here there are only foreign ones. Anyway, I will have to figure a way out of this predicament in which my indecisiveness has left me.

The publication of my poems has begun, and within twenty days I will be able to send Ignacia a lovely copy of them. I have omitted the political ones.

The day before yesterday I received two letters from Pérez, the doctor from Jalapa, who is urging me to go there with the most ardent expressions of friendship, offering me lodging in his house while I work out whatever is best for getting established.

Good-bye. My best regards to Osés, Franco and family, Aunt Francisca (to whom I am sending a letter from Santiago via Ruiz), her children, José Miguel and other deserving relatives, all my love to Ignacia, my "son"[228] and the delinquents. And to you I send all my love,

José Mª

My health, thank God, continues to improve, and visibly so, except that now I am full of gray hair.

To María de la Merced Heredia y Campuzano [Augier no. 93]

New York, June 1, 1825 (?)[229]

My dearest Mother:

I have had the pleasure of receiving your letters of April 13 and 20, although it pains me to hear of the illnesses that our household servants suffer. However, you and the rest of the family are well, which is the most important thing.

I consider myself all recovered. I have regained my appetite, my chest ailments and cough have been gone for some twenty days, and my strength is returning rapidly, just because the warm weather has begun. Thanks to my Creator for preserving my life, and if He does so it is not in vain . . . such is my hope.

I hope to receive at any moment the order of payment and the *Historia de Venezuela*. As I told you in the letter that I sent with Pancho

Ruiz, this is not a good time for it to be published, but since that copy is made, I wish to have it.

Nothing is sure yet regarding my trip, except that I am not going to spend another winter here, even if they should appoint me the Great Panjandrum. The trip to New Orleans never got beyond the planning stage, since with the current drought, river navigation is very difficult. Therefore, I believe I will embark for Alvarado from here on a 50-cannon frigate of the Mexican government, which will be leaving within a month or month and a half.

The publication of my poetry is almost done, and at the first opportunity I will send copies to Havana.

I have not yet been able to forward the latest letters to Santo Domingo. As I have told you before, do not enclose them in letters to me, but send them in their own envelope addressed "to Don J. M. Heredia, to be forwarded to . . ." If you do not, I will run the risk of receiving them in Mexico, and this way I will leave orders for them to be forwarded from here.

Good-bye, my Mother. All my love to my sisters and do not despair of being reunited with your most loving son

José M^a

Regards to all my relatives and friends . . .

To María de la Merced Heredia y Campuzano [BNJM; Augier no. 92]

New York, June 29, 1825

My dearest Mother:

I have not had any letters from you for some days, although I attribute that to the same thing that obliges me at times to miss the opportunity of writing you: the lack of news about the departure of ships.

This letter is going via Matanzas and I am sending with it a little package with three copies of my book of poems, one for Ignacia, another for Osés and another for Franco. Ignacia should not think ill of me for not letting her choose which one, and for putting my preference above hers. If she likes the other color better, she can take one of those the next time I send some. I am going to send a batch to Agustín Hernández, and she can choose one from it. And she should not lend it to anyone, because they will get it dirty, as they did with my manuscript copy. If you should see Agustín, tell him what I am planning to do.

I already have told you that I received the *Historia de Venezuela*. I am going to have it bound and will keep it as a precious thing. But also as I have told you, having it published would be injurious to me in the position I find myself in right now.

Agustín will turn over to you any profits from the sale of my book of poems that I will send him.

I still do not know for sure when I will leave here, but it won't be long now. Any letters for Santo Domingo should be sent individually, addressed like this:

>   To José Ma. Heredia
>   New York; to be forwarded to Santiago Garay
>   in Santo Domingo.

If not, they may get lost. If they arrive thus addressed, I will leave orders for them to be routed. In letters to me, now you have only to put, "to José Ma. Heredia, New York."

Good-bye, my dearest Mother, a thousand embraces for my sisters and regards to all my relatives and friends. Do not forget your most loving son

José M^a

To María de la Merced Heredia y Campuzano [Augier no. 97]

New York, August 4, 1825

My dearest Mother:

For quite a few days I have been deprived of the pleasure of receiving letters from you. Lately I received one to send on to Santiago, but nothing for me. I have letters from Ignacio up to mid-July.

On the next available ship I will send 200 copies of my *Poesías* to Agustín Hernández so that he can sell them and hand over the earnings to you. You must reimburse him any fees, if they demand them in customs.

You will have learned by now that France has recognized the independence of Santo Domingo.[230] I am extremely happy about this, since this step will disabuse the whites of the Spanish part of the island of their unreasonable hopes which could lead them to extermination, and, dissipating the fears of the blacks, will enable them to use honest and gentle means to consolidate the peace and union of the two parts of Haiti.

On to another matter. I still do not know when I will leave, but it will not be long now. I never will be explicit about the date, since that could have bad consequences.[231] You will know about my departure once it has taken place.

I would like to have a letter from you to relieve me of the worry I am feeling regarding my son's illness, which you mentioned in your last letter.[232]

Good-bye, dear Mother. A thousand embraces for my sisters and best regards to Señor Franco and family, Aunt Francisca, Magdalena and Abus, all the Angelinos, Domingo del Monte, and Osés. Do not forget your most loving son

José Mª

To María de la Merced Heredia y Campuzano [BNJM; Augier no. 98]

New York, August 10, 1825

Dearest Mother:

I have not had the satisfaction of receiving any letters from you for some days, which has me somewhat worried. I hope nonetheless that all is well at home.

On this occasion I am sending Agustín Hernández a little crate with forty-three copies of my *Poesías*. I am not sending any more, since I don't want there to be any problems upon entry. If there are none, I will send another, larger shipment. I have told him to give you two copies, one for Domingo del Monte and the other so that Ignacia does not get the first one dirty by loaning it to others—the very pretty one I sent her with Mora via Matanzas. I am also telling Agustín that you will pay the cost of any duties, which should be about three *onzas*.

These poems have been very well received here, and the newspapers have praised them extravagantly.[233]

I am very desirous of receiving news from home, and how the person is who has been ill.

I do not yet know the exact date of my trip, but it will not be long now; I wish I were already far from here; but unavoidable circumstances have detained me—among other things, the wait for the money and the *Historia de Caracas*. I have had the latter bound, and have added an introduction that rectifies the intentions expressed in the work, and which under the present circumstances would seem inappropriate.

I had my portrait done and it turned out to be a ridiculous figure that everyone said did not resemble me at all. The painter found someone to buy it, and so now I am a parlor adornment. I don't know if I will manage to have a good one done before I leave.

Good-bye, my most loved and excellent Mother. A thousand embraces for my sisters, and regards to all my relatives and friends. Do not forget your most loving son

José M^a

To María de la Merced Heredia y Campuzano [Augier no. 99]

Aboard the schooner *Chasseur*,[234] at sail off Sandy Hook,
August 22, 1825

My dearest Mother:
After having been detained for more than seven days in New York Bay because of bad weather, today we have finally put to sea.

I have not wanted to miss the opportunity of the pilot going ashore to let you know that I continue in perfect health, thanks to cognac.

The day that I planned to leave I wrote you at greater length, to let you know that I am leaving $500 in New York, deposited in the United States bank. I am repeating it here just in case that letter has gone astray as is not impossible.

I will not fail to write you upon my arrival. Write to me in New York, addressing the letters to Don José Alfonso García—that is, Pepé—whom I have charged with forwarding them.

Those going to Santiago can be sent the same way, but not enclosed in the letters to me, since they are liable to end up in Mexico. I will add the last one I received, in Staten Island, along with yours of July 30, which gave me the pleasure of seeing that you are happy.

Good-bye, my much-loved Mother. Remembrances to all my relatives and friends, especially to Franco and Osés, and a thousand embraces for my dear sisters. Do not fail to love and bless your most loving son

José Mª

My Ignacia: I am exceedingly sorry not to have been able to send you the portrait. I had one done that I didn't want to take because it was not of any use and it was impossible for me to have another made. I will send you one done in wax from Mexico.

I sent you a copy of my *Poesías* with Manuel Mora who went via Matanzas, and later in the *Cadway* which left seven days ago now, I sent Agustín Hernández a crate of the *Poesías*, and I am telling him to give Mamá two or three.

Good-bye. Do not be surprised by the poor handwriting, since the schooner is rocking a great deal. Write me, and do not forget the most tender affection that your brother feels for you.

José Mª

To María de la Merced Heredia y Campuzano [Augier no. 100]

Alvarado, September 16, 1825

My dearest Mother:

Yesterday I arrived in this port, and I am in good health, thank God, despite the rigors of the voyage, which were considerable. Tomorrow I continue on to Veracruz, and from there inland.

This town is misery incarnate, and I am writing these few lines at the home of Estremera.

From Veracruz to Jalapa, I will write you at greater leisure. A thousand embraces for my sisters, and do not forget your most loving son

                                                      José M^a

Do not worry, I am well, very well indeed, and I have been very well received here.

Selected Verse, 1823–1825

A Emilia

Desde el suelo fatal de su destierro
tu triste amigo, Emilia deliciosa,
te dirige su voz; su voz que un día
en los campos de Cuba florecientes
virtud, amor y plácida esperanza
cantó felice, de tu bello labio
mereciendo sonrisa aprobadora
que satisfizo su ambición. Ahora
sólo gemir podrá la triste ausencia
de todo lo que amó, y enfurecido
tronar contra los viles y tiranos
que ajan de nuestra patria desolada
el seno virginal. Su torvo ceño
mostróme el despotismo vengativo
y en torno de mi frente, acumulada
rugió la tempestad. Bajo tu techo
la venganza burlé de los tiranos.
Entonces tu amistad celeste, pura,
mitigaba el horror a las insomnias
de tu amigo proscripto y sus dolores.
Me era dulce admirar tus formas bellas
y atender a tu acento regalado,
cual lo es al miserable encarcelado
el aspecto del cielo y las estrellas.
Horas indefinibles, inmortales,
de angustia tuya y de peligro mío,
¡cómo volaron! —Extranjera nave
arrebatóme por el mar sañudo,
cuyas oscuras turbulentas olas
me apartan ya de playas españolas.

Heme libre por fin; heme distante
de tiranos y siervos. Mas, Emilia,
¡qué mudanza cruël . . . ! Enfurecido
brama el viento invernal: sobre sus alas
vuela y devora el suelo desecado

To Emilia

From his banishment on foreign soil
Your sorrowful friend, o Emilia divine,
His voice directs to you, which erewhile,
In Cuba's flowering fields,
Songs of virtue, love and placid hope
Once intoned, and genial smiles of praise
From you, grateful, earned,
Which his ambition satisfied. Now
His voice can but lament
The absence cruel of all that he did love,
And fulminate against the tyrants vile
Who the virginal breast
Ravage of our devastated isle.
Around my weary brow
The tempest was unleashed, and tyranny
Showed to me its visage stark and cruel.
Beneath your roof a refuge did I find
From despotism's wrath,
And there your friendship, celestial and pure,
Soothed the horrid nights
Your hunted friend did sleeplessly endure.
Your graceful form was sweet unto my eyes
As to my ears your voice,
Even as a glimpse of starry skies
Cheers the prisoner in his lightless cell.
How the vague, immortal hours passed
Of gravest danger mine, and anguish yours,
Until a ship at last
Fetched me off across the wild waves,
And safe delivered me from Spanish shores.

Now I am free. Now from tyrants and slaves
I am removed. But Emilia mine,
What a cruel exchange!
The wintry gale rages. Upon its wings
The biting ice devours the withered earth.

el hielo punzador. Espesa niebla
vela el brillo del sol, y cierra el cielo,
que en dudoso horizonte se confunde
con el oscuro mar. Desnudos gimen
por doquiera los árboles la saña
del viento azotador. Ningún ser vivo
se ve en los campos. Soledad inmensa
reina y desolación, y el mundo yerto
sufre de invierno cruel la tiranía.

¿Y es ésta la mansión que trocar debo
por los campos de luz, el cielo puro,
la verdura inmortal y eternas flores
y las brisas balsámicas del clima
en que el primero sol brilló a mis ojos
entre dulzura y paz . . . ? —Estremecido
me detengo, y agólpanse a mis ojos
lágrimas de furor . . . ¿Qué importa? Emilia,
mi cuerpo sufre, pero mi alma fiera
con noble orgullo y menosprecio aplaude
su libertad. Mis ojos doloridos
no verán ya mecerse de la palma
la copa gallardísima, dorada
por los rayos del sol en occidente;
ni a la sombra de plátano sonante
el ardor burlaré de mediodía,
inundando mi faz en la frescura
que espira el blando céfiro. Mi oído,
en lugar de tu acento regalado,
o del eco apacible y cariñoso
de mi madre, mi hermana y mis amigas,
tan sólo escucha de extranjero idioma
los bárbaros sonidos; pero al menos
no lo fatiga del tirano infame
el clamor insolente, ni el gemido
del esclavo infeliz, ni del azote
el crujir execrable, que emponzoñan
la atmósfera de Cuba. ¡Patria mía,

The fog obstructs the sun and blurs the line
On the far horizon
Where the darkened sea adjoins the sky.
Before the whipping wind,
Everywhere the naked trees do cry.
Not a living soul
Upon the frozen farmlands do I see.
In lonely barrenness the wasted world
Of winter cruel bears the tyranny.

  Is this the new abode which I must trade
For the fields of light, the candid skies,
Eternal blooms, the cool and verdant shade,
The soft, balsamic breezes of the clime
Where first I saw the blessed light of day
In the sweetness of a happy home?
I tremble it to think, and in my eyes
Angry tears appear.
But does it matter? No, Emilia mine.
My body suffers, but my untamed soul,
With scorn for suffering and noble pride,
Applauds its liberty.
My grieving eyes are not for now to see
The noble crown of the swaying palm,
Gilded by the sun's declining rays.
Nor can I escape the midday sun
In the shadow of the plantain tree,
And feel the cooling zephyr gently graze
And caress my face.
My ears your gentle voice are not to hear,
Nor the echo sweet
Of my mother, sisters, and my friends.
And harshly fall upon my waiting ear
The barbarous sounds of a foreign tongue.
At least the clamor of the despot foul
The air no longer rends,
Nor the whimpering of the wretched slave
And the cracking of the brutal whip
That poisons Cuba's air.

idolatrada patria! tu hermosura
goce el mortal en cuyas torpes venas
gire con lentitud la yerta sangre,
sin alterarse al grito lastimoso
de la opresión. En medio de tus campos
de luz vestidos y genial belleza,
sentí mi pecho férvido agitado
por el dolor, como el Oceano[1] brama
cuando le azota el Norte. Por las noches,
cuando la luz de la callada luna
y del limón el delicioso aroma,
llevado en alas de la tibia brisa
a voluptuosa calma convidaban,
mil pensamientos de furor y saña
entre mi pecho hirviendo, me nublaban
el congojado espíritu, y el sueño
en mi abrasada frente no tendía,
sus alas vaporosas. De mi patria
bajo el hermoso desnublado cielo,
no pude resolverme a ser esclavo,
ni consentir que todo en la natura
fuese noble y feliz, menos el hombre.
Miraba ansioso al cielo y a los campos
que en derredor callados se tendían,
y en mi lánguida frente se veían
la palidez mortal y la esperanza.

   Al brillar mi razón, su amor primero
fue la sublime dignidad del hombre,
y al murmurar de *Patria* el dulce nombre,
me llenaba de horror el extranjero.
¡Pluguiese al Cielo, desdichada Cuba,
que tu suelo tan sólo produjese
hierro y soldados! ¡La codicia ibera
no tentáramos, no! Patria adorada,
de tus bosques el aura embalsamada
es al valor, a la virtud funesta.
¿Cómo viendo tu sol radioso, inmenso,

O island fair! My beloved isle!
May you be enjoyed by the man
In whose veins but torpid blood does flow
And to oppression's cry is insensate.
Amidst your glorious fields bathed in light,
Pain my fervid breast did agitate,
Like the sea when angry north winds blow.
In the calm of night,
When the glimmer of the silent moon
And the beguiling fragrance of the lime,
Carried on the breeze's temperate wings,
Invited in the soul a sultry rest,
Yet indignation did my spirit assail
And ire filled my breast.
And of sleep the gauzy, vaporous veil
Did not upon me fall.
Beneath the fair, unclouded Cuban sky
As a slave I could not bear to live,
Nor my consent to give
That all in Nature blessed and noble were
Excepting man. Anxiously I gazed
Upon the sky and fields
That before my eyes in silence spread.
And on my languid brow there could be seen
The gleam of hope and pallid mark of dread.

   Since reason in me dawned, my first desire
The dignity of man has ever been.
The name of any land except my own
In me did only bitter dread inspire.
Unhappy Cuba! If Heaven would ordain
That naught but soldiers brave and sharpened steel
Should from your soil spring!
Then Cuba would not tempt the greed of Spain.
The perfumed air of my beloved isle
To virtue and to valor is adverse.
Why does not your radiant sun inflame

no se inflama en los pechos de tus hijos
generoso valor contra los viles
que te oprimen audaces y devoran?

    ¡Emilia! ¡dulce Emilia! La esperanza
de inocencia, de paz y de ventura
acabó para mí. ¿Qué gozo resta
al que desde la nave fugitiva
en el triste horizonte de la tarde
hundirse vio los montes de su patria,
por la postrera vez? —A la mañana
alzóse el sol, y me mostró desiertos
el firmamento y mar . . . ¡Oh! ¡cuán odiosa
me pareció la mísera existencia!
Bramaba en torno la tormenta fiera,
y yo sentado en la agitada popa
del náufrago bajel, triste y sombrío,
los torvos ojos en el mar fijando,
meditaba de Cuba en el destino
y en sus tiranos viles, y gemía,
y de rubor y cólera temblaba,
mientras el viento en derredor rugía,
y mis sueltos cabellos agitaba.

    ¡Ah! también otros mártires . . . ¡Emilia!
doquier me sigue en ademán severo
del noble Hernández la querida imagen.
¡Eterna paz a tu injuriada sombra,
mi amigo malogrado! Largo tiempo
el gran flujo y reflujo de los años
por Cuba pasará, sin que produzca
otra alma cual la tuya, noble y fiera.
¡Víctima de cobardes y tiranos,
descansa en paz! Si nuestra patria ciega,
su largo sueño sacudiendo, llega
a despertar a libertad y gloria,
honrará, como debe, tu memoria.

The hearts of my fellow countrymen
To take a stand against the tyrants vile
Who my homeland recklessly defile?

   Sweet Emilia! My hopes of innocence,
Of blessed peace and of fortune fair,
Are for me no more. What joy is there
For him who from the swiftly fleeing barque
Saw the mountains of his cherished isle
Sink below the far horizon's line
In the gathering dark?
In the light of dawn, the sky and sea
Endless deserts seemed.
How hateful then my life appeared to me!
When in the howling gale
Upon the reeling deck I did remain
Of the struggling ship,
And fixed my baleful eye upon the sea,
I thought upon my homeland's destiny,
And of its vile tyrants, and I groaned.
In ire and in shame I trembled, too.
While the wind around me raged and moaned
And my loosened locks wildly blew.

   Ah Emilia, martyrs more there are!
The visage of Hernández[2] follows me
With countenance severe that e'er I loved.
May peace upon your slandered shade descend,
Dear, departed friend.
Many a long year shall come and go
Before we are to see
Another soul like yours, as wild and free.
Of cowards and of despots you were prey.
In peace may you rest.
And if our blinded homeland should one day
To glory wake, and to liberty,
Honor it will give your memory.

¡Presto será que refulgente aurora
de libertad sobre su puro cielo
mire Cuba lucir! Tu amigo, Emilia,
de hierro fiero y de venganza armado
a verte volverá, y en voz sublime
entonará de triunfo el himno bello.
Mas si en las lides enemiga fuerza
me postra ensangrentado, por lo menos
no obtendrá mi cadáver tierra extraña,
y regado en mi féretro glorioso
por el llanto de vírgenes y fuertes
me adormiré. La universal ternura
excitaré dichoso, y enlazada
mi lira de dolores con mi espada,
coronarán mi noble sepultura.

Soon a brilliant dawn of liberty
Shall break against a cloudless Cuban sky.
And then, Emilia, I
With angry steel and vengeance armed shall be.
To you I shall return. In voice sublime,
A splendid hymn of triumph I shall sing.
And if the saber of the enemy
Should cut me down, at least
On foreign shores my body will not lie.
When maidens and the strong above me weep,
Their tears will reach me in my glorious grave,
And happy I will sleep.
The tenderness of all I will inspire,
And for my noble tomb a crown shall be
My sword of vengeance and my plaintive lyre.

Placeres de la melancolía[3]

I

    No es dado al hombre de su débil frente
las penas alejar y los dolores,
ni por campos de mirtos y de flores
dirigir el torrente de la vida.
De las pasiones el aliento ardiente
le enajena tal vez, y breves horas
en ilusiones férvidas perdido
osa creerse feliz. ¿Quién no ha sufrido
la fiebre del amor, ni qué alma helada
no probó la dulzura emponzoñada
que en el beso fatal vierte Cupido?
Yo adoré la beldad: cual sol de vida
lució a mis ojos, y bebí encendido
el cáliz del amor hasta las heces.
Mi alma fogosa, turbulenta y fiera,
en todos sus placeres y deseos
al extremo voló; tibias pasiones
nunca en ella cupieron . . . Mas ¡ay! pronto
siguió a los goces y delirio mío
la saciedad, el tedio devorante,
como sigue de otoño al sol brillante
el del invierno pálido y sombrío.
    Tal es la suerte del mortal cuitado:
agitarse y sufrir, después que siente
el vigor de su pecho quebrantado
por su excesivo ardor, que al fin agota
del sentimiento la preciosa fuente.
¿Qué hará el triste? Las flores de la vida
al soplo abrasador de las pasiones
marchitas sentirá. Doquier que mire
será el mundo a sus ojos un desierto,
y el misterioso abismo de la tumba
será de su esperanza único puerto.
Así el piloto en tempestosa noche

The Pleasures of Melancholy

I

   The lot of man is not to cast away
Distress and sorrow from his feeble brow,
Nor guide the torrent of his life through fields
In myrtles decked, and flowers.
From time to time the ardent breath of passion
Deranges him, and fleeting are the hours
When lost in fervid fancies he may think
His happiness complete. Who has not
Endured the fever of love? And what soul
Could coldly scorn to taste the poison sweet
That Cupid pours upon each fatal kiss?
I beauty loved. And to my eyes it seemed
The very sun of life. Inflamed, I drank
Love's cup unto the dregs.
My fiery soul, turbulent and wild,
In all its ardent pleasures and desires
Temperance did not know, and passions mild
Could never in my soul command a place . . .
But oh! How soon did surfeit then conspire
With tedium my passions to consume;
Just as the fiery glow of autumn's sun
Must be replaced by winter's pallid gloom.
   Such it ever is for troubled man:
To worry and to suffer when he feels
His heart that once was stout
Broken by the excess of his ardor,
And parched the precious font of sentiment.
What then will he do? The flowers of life
Withered and consumed by passion's flame
He'll find. Where'er he looks,
A desert to his eyes the world will seem.
The only haven for the battered barque
Of his hope, a lightless tomb will be.
Thus a sailor in the stormy dark

sólo distingue entre su denso velo
el mar furioso y el turbado cielo.
   Entonces tú, gentil Melancolía,
serás bálsamo dulce que suavice
su árido corazón y le consuele,
más que el plácido llanto de la noche
a la agostada flor. Yo tus placeres
voy a cantar, y tu favor imploro.
Ven: tonos blandos a mi voz inspira;
enciéndala tu aliento, y de mi lira
templa con languidez las cuerdas de oro.
   ¿Quién en adversa o próspera fortuna,
no se abandona al vago pensamiento
cuando suspira de la tierra el viento,
y de Cuba en el mar duerme la luna?
¿Quién no ha sentido entonces dilatarse
su corazón, y con placer llevarse
a mil cavilaciones deliciosas
de ventura y amor? ¡Con qué deleite
en los campos bañados por la luna
siguen nuestras miradas pensativas
la sombra de las nubes fugitivas
en océano de luz puro y sereno!
¿Qué encanto hay en la calma de la noche,
del hondo mar en la distante furia,
y halaga el corazón? Melancolía,
tu respiras allí: tu faz amable,
velada entre vapores transparentes,
sonríe con ternura al que en tu seno
busca la paz, y al que de penas lleno
se acoge a ti, con mano compasiva
del rostro enjugas el sudor y llanto.
Mas la disipación furiosa en tanto,
en sus bailes y juegos y festines
hace beber de tedio triste copa
a los que por su halago seducidos
buscan entre sus pérfidas caricias
gozo y felicidad. Mustios, rendidos,
maldecirán al sol, y a su sueño ansioso

Can only through its shifting veils espy
The agitated sea and churning sky.
   Then you, kind Melancholy,
A balsam are to soothe
His arid heart, and consolation bring—
More indeed than placid dew of night
Revives the withered flower. Come to me:
Your pleasures I will sing.
With dulcet tones may you my voice inspire;
Breathe in me your warmth. And of my lyre,
Tune with languor soft each golden string.
   What man in circumstance adverse or fair
Will not drift off in misty reverie,
When softly sighing winds caress the earth,
And Cuba's moon reposes on the sea?
What man has not then felt his swelling heart
Allow a thousand thoughts of luck and love
To carry him away?
With what delight our pensive glances stray,
Following, across the moonlit fields,
The shadows cast by swiftly flying clouds,
Chasing through a sea of tranquil light!
In the calm of night,
How the distant fury of the sea
Enchants and lulls the heart! Melancholy,
You there abide. Your endearing face,
Veiled in vaporous transparency,
Tender smiles at him who on your breast
Solace seeks; with compassionate hand
You dry the sweat and tears
Of the afflicted one who turns to you.
But all the while, dissipation's fury,
In banquets, dances, games,
Does but dispense the cup of ennui
To those who by its empty charm ensnared
Within its false caress
Joy and pleasure seek. Wearily,
They curse the sun, and on a bed recline
Of restless sleep. With worried conscience they

la frente atormentada reclinando,
la suerte trocarán del bello día.
¡Ansia falaz, funesta, cómo impía
me desecaste el corazón! ¡Oh tiempo
de ceguedad y de furor ...! Insano,
de tormento sin fin buscaba dicha,
paz en eterna turbación ... —Empero
a mis ojos el sol brilla más puro
desde que ya, más cuerdo, no alimento
de mi sangre el ardor calenturiento,
soñando gozos y placer futuro.
De la grata ilusión perdí el encanto,
pero hallé de la paz el bien seguro.

II

    Dulce es la soledad, en que su trono
asienta la feliz Melancolía.
Desde la infancia venturosa mía
era mi amor. Aislado, pensativo,
gustábame vagar en la ribera
del ancho mar. Si los airados vientos
su seno hinchaban en tormenta fiera,
mil pensamientos vagos, tumultuosos
me agitaban también, pero tenía
deleite inexplicable, indefinido
aquella confusión. Cuando la calma
reinaba en torno, y el espejo inmenso
del sol en occidente reflejaba
la noble imagen en columna de oro,
yo en éxtasis feliz la contemplaba,
y eran mis escondidos pensamientos
dulces, como el silencio de los campos
de la luna en la luz. Y los pedantes
azotes de la infancia,[4] que querían
subyugar mi razón a sus delirios,
fieros amenazándome decían:
Este niño holgazán y vagabundo
siempre necio ha de ser. Y yo temblaba,

Elect the barren dark o'er noble day.
Fatal, false desire! How my heart
You wasted, ruthlessly! Oh days consumed
In blindness and in frenzy! Still I sought
Delight in endless torment,
In ceaseless desire, peace.
But now the sun shines brighter to my eyes;
No longer do I spur in feverish fury
The raging ardor of my reckless blood
With empty dreams of bliss.
I lost the shimmering vision, its allure,
But now in peace I've found a blessing sure.

II

   Sweet is solitude, where Melancholy
Contented has her throne.
And in my happy childhood, she was
My love. Musing, dreamy and alone,
Along the ocean's shore
I loved to roam. And if the angry winds
In raging storm should swell the ocean's breast,
A thousand tangled thoughts would stir my mind;
And yet, a strange delight
In that untamed confusion did I find.
And when a noble calm
Held gentle sway upon the glassy sea—
A mirror for the sun
Declining west atop a shaft of gold—
Enthralled I would behold
Its slow descent. And my thoughts were mild,
Like the silence of the moonlit fields.
And when, a wayward child,
I underwent the edifying lash
That sought to bend my dreams to reason's rule,
With admonitions cruel
They said of me, "this lazy, aimless boy
Shall ever foolish be."
I hated, yet I did not curse the blows,

mas no los maldecía,
sino de ellos huía,
y en mi apacible soledad lloraba.

III

¡Oh! ¡si Dios de mis males apiadado,
las alas de un espíritu me diera!
¡Cuál por los campos del espacio huyera
de este mundo tan bello y desdichado!
¡Oh! ¡si en él a lo menos me ofreciera
una mujer sensible, que pudiera
fijar mi corazón con sentimientos
menos vivos tal vez, menos violentos
que los que enciende Amor, pero más dulces
y duraderos! En su ingenua frente
el candor y la paz me sonreirían:
de este exceso de vida que me agobia
me aliviara su amor. Su voz piadosa,
de aqueste pecho en la profunda herida
bálsamo de consuelo derramara,
y su trémulo acento disipara
las tinieblas de mi alma entristecida.
    Encarnación de mi ideal esposa,
¡cómo te adoraré . . . ! No por más tiempo
me hagas ansiarte y suspirar en vano;
mira que vuela mi verdor lozano.
¡Ay! ¡ven, y escucha mi rogar piadosa . . . !

IV

¿Quién placer melancólico no goza,
al ver al tiempo con alada planta
los días, los años y los siglos graves
precipitar en el abismo oscuro
de lo que fue? Las épocas brillantes
recorro de la historia . . . ¡Qué furores!
¡Cuadro fatal de crímenes y errores!
Doquier en sangre tíñense las manos;

But from them trembling fled.
In soothing solitude my tears I shed.

III

   Oh! If only God, in His benevolence,
A spirit's wings would give me!
From this lovely, luckless world, away
Through airy fields I'd flee!
Oh! If He at least would deign to find
A woman's heart to love me tenderly,
And settle this heart of mine
With sentiments less ardent, it may be,
Than those that Love inflames,
But sweeter and more lasting! I would see
Upon her face sincerity and peace;
This oppressive excess of life I feel
Her love would mitigate.
With consolation mild her voice would pour
A balm of comfort on my wounded breast,
And its trembling tone would gently part
The shadows that enshroud my doleful heart.
   Incarnation of my ideal wife,
How I will adore you . . . !
Do not make me wait for you in vain.
Come! My verdant years do swiftly flee;
With compassion kind attend my plea . . . !

IV

   What man does not take melancholy joy
To witness time with its wínged foot
Cast days and years and solemn centuries
Into the dark abyss of yesterday?
When history's brilliant epochs I survey,
What furors do I see!
A spectacle of error and of crime!
The hands of men are stained in others' blood;
Fanatic or deranged,

los hombres fascinados o furiosos
ya son juguetes viles de facciosos,
ya siervos miserables de tiranos.
Pueblos a pueblos el dominio ceden;
y del orbe sangriento, desolado,
desaparecen, como en mar airado
las olas a las olas se suceden.
 De Babilonia, Menfis y Palmira
entre los mudos restos el viajero
se horroriza de ver su estrago fiero,
y con profunda lástima suspira.
¡Campos americanos! en vosotros
lágrimas verterá. ¿Qué pueblo ignora
vuestro nombre y desdicha? Circundado
por tenebrosa nube un hemisferio,
ocultábase al otro; mas osado
forzó Colón el borrascoso imperio
del Oceano feroz. La frágil nave
por los yermos de un mar desconocido
en silencio volaba; la vil chusma
pálida, yerta, con terror profundo,
a la patria querida
tornaba ya la resonante prora,
cuando a sus ojos refulgente aurora
las playas reveló del nuevo mundo.
 ¡Hombres feroces! La severa historia
en páginas sangrientas eterniza
de sus atrocidades la memoria.
Al esfuerzo terrible de su espada
cayó el templo del sol, y el trono altivo
de Acamapich . . . Las infelices sombras
de los reyes aztecas olvidados
a evocar me atreví sobre sus tumbas,
y del polvo a mi voz se levantaron,
y su inmenso dolor me revelaron.
¿Dó fue la raza candorosa y pura
que las Antillas habitó? —La hiere
del vencedor el hierro furibundo,
tiembla, gime, perece,
y como niebla al sol, desaparece.

For agitators some are vile toys,
Some for tyrants wretchedly are slaves.
Realm to realm dominion does concede,
And from this bloody, godforsaken sphere
Perforce will disappear,
As on the ocean, waves to waves succeed.
 The traveler who walks the mute remains
Of Babylonia, Memphis and Palmyra,
The ravages of time with horror sees,
And moved to pity, sighs.
O plains of sorrowful America!
The traveler will shed a bitter tear
Your misfortune to regard. Your name
To every nation is known,
But once you were a shrouded hemisphere,
Until Columbus came
To subdue the empire of the sea.
The fragile ship in lonely silence flew
Across the desolate, uncharted deep.
With terror pale, the crew
Toward their beloved homeland turned their prow;
And in the light of dawn, with sails unfurled,
To their astonished eyes
Appeared the shoreline of another world.
 Oh ferocious men! History
Chronicles in pages soaked with blood
The memory of their atrocities.
The temple of the sun, the haughty throne
Of Acamapich, fell before their sword . . .
Upon their tombs I once dared to invoke
The dim and doleful shades
Of long-ago forgotten Aztec kings.[5]
Summoned from the dust,
Of their boundless pain they spoke to me.
And the fair Antilles:
Where is their candid race of yesteryear?
They fall before the victors' ruthless steel.
They tremble, whimper, die;
Like mist before the sun they disappear.

Sediento de saber, infatigable,
del Tíber, del Jordán y del Eurotas
las aguas beberé, y en sus orillas
asentado en escombros solitarios
de quebrantadas míseras naciones,
me daré a meditar: altas lecciones,
altos ejemplos sacará mi mente
de su desolación: ¡cuánto es sublime
la voz de los sepulcros y ruinas!
Allí tu inspiración pura y solemne,
¡oh Musa del saber! mi voz anime.
Y tú también, genial Melancolía,
me seguirás doquiera suspirando,
o en mi lecho tu frente reclinando,
harás a mi descanso compañía.

V

¡Cuánto es plácida y tierna la memoria
de los que amamos, cuando ya la muerte
a nuestro amor los arrancó! La tumba
encierra las inmóviles cenizas;
los ligeros espíritus pasean
en el aire sereno de la noche
en torno de los que aman, y responden
a sus dulces recuerdos y suspiros
en misteriosa comunión. Creedme;
no lo dudéis: por esto son tan dulces
las solitarias lágrimas vertidas
en la tumba del padre, del esposo
o del amante, y el herido pecho
ama su llanto y su dolor piadoso.
    ¿Oh tú, que para mí fuiste en la tierra
de Dios augusta imagen! ¡Cuántas horas
desde el momento que cerró tu vida
por mí pasaron, llenas de amargura
y de intenso dolor! Sombra querida
del mejor de los padres, en el cielo
recibe de mi pecho lastimado

In thirst for wisdom, tireless, I will go
The ancient waters to drink
Of the Tiber, Jordan and Eurotas.
Along their banks, among forlorn remains
Of nations that are broken, come to naught,
I'll lose myself in thought.
And noble lessons will my mind derive
From their desolation. How sublime
Is the voice that speaks from ruins and tombs!
O wisdom's muse! Animate my voice
With inspiration absolute and grave.
And Melancholy, you will walk with me,
Sighing at my side, companion kind,
Or in my rest keep me company,
Next to me upon my bed reclined.

V

How peaceful is the tender memory
Of those we loved, when from our loving arms
Bitter death has taken them away!
Quiet rest their ashes in the tomb.
But in the tranquil air at end of day,
The airy spirits come to hover 'round
Those whom they love; and to their memories
And tender sighs they give a hushed reply
In mystical accord.
Believe me. Do not doubt it. That is why
The tears we shed upon a father's grave,
Or that of husband or beloved, are sweet.
And that is why beyond all disbelief,
The wounded heart can learn to love its grief.

O you, who were for me upon this earth
The august image of God!
How many bitter hours have I known
And how I've mourned, since He called you home!
O spirit most beloved
Of the best of fathers, in Paradise
Receive the gratitude eternally

la eterna gratitud. Mi dócil mente
con atención profunda recogía
de tu boca elocuente en las palabras
el saber, la verdad: aun de tu frente
en la serena majestad leía
altas lecciones de virtud. Tus pasos,
tus miradas, tu voz, tus pensamientos
eran paz y virtud. ¡Con qué dulzura
de mi pecho impaciente reprimías
el ardimiento, la fiereza . . . ! El cielo
contra el ciego furor de los malvados
sirviéndote de asilo, me dejara
entre borrascas mil . . . ¡Ay! a lo menos
iré a morir en tu sepulcro, y junto
a tu polvo sagrado
reclinaré mi polvo atormentado,
que al eco de tres sílabas funestas
aun allí temblará. Mas tu memoria
será, mientras respire, mi consuelo,
y grato y dulce el solitario llanto
que la consagre, más que gozo alguno
del miserable suelo.
¡No me abandones, Padre, desde el cielo!

VI

  ¡Patria . . . ! ¡Nombre cual triste delicioso
al peregrino mísero, que vaga
lejos del suelo que nacer le viera!
¡Ay! ¿Nunca de sus árboles la sombra
refrescará su dolorida frente?
¿Cuándo en la noche el músico ruido
de las palmas y plátanos sonantes
vendrá feliz a regalar mi oído?
¡Cuántas dulzuras ¡ay! se desconocen
hasta perderse! No: nunca los campos
de Cuba parecieron a mis ojos
de más beldad y gentileza ornados,
que hoy a mi congojada fantasía.

Of a grieving son. My docile mind
All your thoughtful words did ever heed,
And many lessons wise
Upon your very brow oft did I read,
Whose tranquil majesty
Lofty truths and peaceful virtue spoke.
And virtuous were your thoughts, your voice, your glance.
How sweetly you would scold me
And check the fierce impatience in my breast!
Now that Heaven where at last you rest
From the violence of blind and wicked men
Has left me to endure a thousand storms,
Won't it let me then
Die upon your grave? There I'll join
Your sacred dust with mine;
And mine will tremble there to recall
Three syllables that direly echo still.⁶
But now, while yet I breathe, your memory
I consecrate with solitary tears;
And these are sweet and gratifying, more
Than any joy on earth.
In this vale of sorrows I must be.
From heaven, Father, do not abandon me!

VI

 Homeland! Such a sad and lovely word
For the wretched wanderer who strays
Far from his native ground!
When will its deep and verdant island shade
Refresh his troubled brow?
When evening falls, when will the tuneful sound
Of its rustling palms and plantain trees
Fall gently on my ear?
How many pleasures dear
We thoughtlessly enjoy, unaware,
Until they're lost! Never did the fields
Of Cuba to my heedless eyes appear
As gracious and as fair

¡Recuerdo triste de maldad y llanto!
Cuando esperaba paz el alma mía,
redobló la Fortuna sus rigores,
y de persecución y de furores
pasó tronando el borrascoso día.
Desde entonces mis ojos anhelantes
miran a Cuba, y a su nombre solo
de lágrimas se arrasan. Por la noche
entre el bronco rugir del viento airado
suena el himno infeliz del desterrado.
O si el Oceano inmóvil se adormece
de junio y julio en las ardientes calmas,
ansioso busco en la distante brisa
la voz de sus arroyos y sus palmas.
   ¡Oh! no me condenéis a que aquí gima,
como en huerta de escarchas abrasada
se marchita entre vidrios encerrada
la planta estéril de distinto clima.
Mi entusiasmo feliz yace apagado:
en mis manos ¡oh lira! te rompiste.
¿Cuando sopla del Norte el viento triste,
puede algún corazón no estar helado?
¿Dó están las brisas de la fresca noche,
de la mágica luna inspiradora
el tibio resplandor, y del naranjo
y del mango suavísimo el aroma?
¿Dónde las nubecillas, que flotando
en el azul sereno de la esfera,
islas de paz y gloria semejaban?
Tiende la noche aquí su oscuro velo;
el mundo se adormece inmóvil, mudo,
y el aire punza, y bajo el filo agudo
del hielo afinador centella el cielo.
Brillante está a los ojos, pero frío,
frío como la muerte. Yo lo admiro,
mas no lo puedo amar, porque me mata,
y por el sol del trópico suspiro.

As today to my anguished fancy.
How sad and bitter is it to recall
The turn that Fortune took,
Unleashing storms of fury from the skies,
When my soul expected blessings all.
And since then, my longing, anxious eyes
To Cuba look, and at its very name,
Brim with sudden tears.
In the angry howling of the wind
Sounds the wretched, wandering exile's hymn.
Or if the drowsy sea immobile lies
In the summer calms,
In the distant breeze I seek to hear
The murmur of its rivers and its palms.

   Oh leave me not here to cry alone
Like a sterile plant from other climes,
Withered, in glass encased,
In a garden that frost has laid to waste.
My happy inspiration lies consumed;
Your strings, o Lyre, were broken in my hands.
When the north wind blows,
Will any heart before its blast not freeze?
Where is the temperate night with its breeze?
And the moon that inspiration lends
As it softly glows?
And the scent of mango and orange trees?
Where are the little clouds that gently float
In the placid azure of the sky,
Like islands of glory and peace?
Here the night extends its darkling veil.
The world in silence sleeps, all movements cease.
The air stabs. The stars glitter and spark
Beneath the icy edge of the sharpening knife.
It is brilliant to the eyes, but cold.
Its beauty I remark,
But love it I cannot; it takes my life,
And I long for the tropical sun.

Vuela, viento del Norte, y a los campos
de mi patria querida
lleva mi llanto, y a mi madre tierna,
murmura mi dolor . . .

VII

A ti me acojo, fiel Melancolía.
Alivia mi penar; a ti consagro
el resto de mi vida miserable.
Siempre eres bella, interesante, amable,
ya nos renueves los pasados días,
ya tristemente plácida sonrías
en la pálida frente de una hermosa,
cuando la enfermedad feroz anuble
su edad primaveral. Benigna diosa,
tu bálsamo de paz y de consuelo
vierte a mi alma abatida,
hasta que vaya a descansar al cielo
de este delirio que se llama vida.

To the temperate fields
Of my beloved isle, o North Wind, fly!
And to my mother, whisper of my pain.
Tell her how I cry . . .

VII

   To you I turn, faithful Melancholy:
Ease my pain. I dedicate to you
The rest of my wretched days.
You are ever lovely, charming, kind.
Whether bygone times you bring to mind,
Or with sadness smile
Upon the pallid brow of a maiden fair
Struck in her prime with cruel infirmity.
O goddess benevolent,
Pour upon my tired, despondent soul
Your balm of consolation and of peace
Until from this dream that some call life,
In heaven's endless rest I find release.

Atenas y Palmira

    Al contemplar las áticas llanuras
en la serena cumbre del Himeto,
espectáculo espléndido se goza.
Vense grupos de palmas, que otro tiempo
oyeron de Platón la voz divina,
y entre masas brillantes de verdura
alza el olivo su apacible frente.
Cubre la viña el ondulante suelo
de esmeraldas y púrpura, y los valles
en diluvio de luz el sol inunda.
Entre tantas bellezas majestosa
con marmóreo esplendor domina Atenas.
En sus dóricos templos y columnas
juega la luz rosada,
y con mágica tinta
el contorno fugaz colora y pinta.

    ¡Cuadro admirable y delicioso! Empero
goza placer más puro y más sublime
el solitario y pensador viajero
que a la luz del crepúsculo sombrío,
entre un oceano de caliente arena,
contempla el esqueleto de Palmira,
de alto silencio y soledad cercado.
¡Desolación inmensa! El obelisco,
cual roble anciano, se levanta al cielo
con triste majestad, y el cardo infausto,
brotando en grietas del marmóreo techo,
al viento sirio silba. En los salones
do la elegancia y el poder moraron,
hoy la culebra solitaria gira.
En el suelo de templos quebrantados
crecen los pinos, y en las anchas calles,
que antes hirvieron en rumor y vida,
se mira ondear la hierba silenciosa.
Doquier yacen columnas derribadas
unas sobre otras, y en la gran llanura

Athens and Palmyra

   How splendid is the view the traveler sees,
When pausing on serene Hymettus hill
He contemplates the plains of Attica.
Palm trees cluster which in former times
The voice divine of Plato did attend.
The olive tree its peaceful brow does raise
Amid the verdant groves.
The rolling fields are overspread with vines
Bejeweled with amethyst and emerald; vales
Are flooded with the sun's engulfing light.
Above such loveliness,
Towers Athens in marble majesty.
A ruddy light now falls
Upon its Doric columns, temples high,
And with beguiling hue
Does color and diffuse their fading lines.

   A noble and enchanting sight! And yet,
A pleasure more complete and more sublime
Awaits the lonely, pensive wayfarer
Who in the somber light of evenfall,
Amid a burning sea of shifting sand,
Palmyra's skeleton does behold,
In silence draped and deepest solitude.
A desolation vast! The obelisk,
Like an ancient oak skyward soars
In mournful majesty; the brambles wild,
Springing from the cracks of marble roofs,
Whistle in the wind. In ruined halls
Where elegance and power once did dwell,
Now coils the lonely snake.
And in the floors of temples, wrecked and rent,
Pine trees grow. In streets
That teemed in other days with sound and life,
The silent grasses bend before the wind.
Columns lie, fallen here and there,
One upon the other; in the plain.

incontables parecen los despojos
de la grandeza y del poder pasado.
Arcos, palacios, templos y obeliscos
forman un laberinto pavoroso
en que inmóvil se asienta
el silencioso genio de las ruinas,
y altas verdades, máximas divinas
de su frente el dolor al sabio cuenta.

Countless seem the spoils
Of grandeur and of power, ages gone.
Obelisks and arches, mansions, temples,
A frightful labyrinth form.
Unmoving, in that place,
The silent Spirit of the ruins dwells,
Who lofty truths and formulas divine,
With anguished brow, speaks unto the wise.

A Washington

Primero en paz y en guerra,
primero en el afecto de tu patria,
y en la veneración del universo,
viva imagen de Dios sobre la tierra,
libertador, legislador y justo,
Washington inmortal, oye benigno
el débil canto, de tu gloria indigno,
con que voy a ensalzar tu nombre augusto.

¿Te pintaré indignado
a la voz de la patria dolorida
volar al arduo campo de la gloria,
y como Jove en el Olimpo armado
a la suerte mandar y a la victoria?
Magnánimo apareces;
ríndese Boston, y respira libre.
Vanamente el tirano
cuarenta mil esclavos lanza fiero
para extirpar el nombre americano.
Tú, sin baldón, al número cediste,
y acallando el espíritu guerrero,
a tu gloria la patria preferiste.
Así del pueblo eterno los caudillos
al vencedor Aníbal contemplaron
con inmutable frente,
y la invasión rugiente
a la Púnica playa rechazaron.

Mas luego, en noche de feliz memoria,
del Delaware el vacilante hielo
ofreció a tu valor y patrio celo
el camino del triunfo y de la gloria.
La soberbia británica humillada
es por último en York, y su caudillo
rinde a tus pies la poderosa espada.
El universo atónito saluda
a la triunfante América, y te adora,

To Washington

   First in peace and war,
And in your countrymen's hearts,
And in the veneration of the world;
Replica of God upon the earth,
Liberator, legislator, just:
O Washington immortal, deign to hear
This song of praise, unworthy of your fame,
With which I would extol your august name.

   Shall I dare to paint your righteous wrath,
As in answer to your nation's plea,
To the field of glory, swift you fly,
And like Olympian Jove for battle armed,
Victory and fate itself command?
Magnanimous you let the enemy flee.
The British quit the field, Boston is free.
But now the tyrant's rage in vain does cast
Forty thousand slaves across the sea
The very name "America" to erase
From the earth. Before a force so vast,
Honorably you yield, place nation first,
And your warrior's fame and glory last.
Just as the consuls of eternal Rome,
With visage undismayed,
Hannibal the Conqueror did regard,
And chose the call of battle to ignore,
Disdaining to invade the Punic shore.[7]

   But later, on that night enshrined in time,
Your valor and your patriotic zeal
Find upon the fragile, fractured ice
Of the Delaware victory's path.
Then at last, humbled British pride
Capitulates on Yorktown's bloodied fields,
And at your feet, his sword the vanquished yields.
The universe hastens to proclaim
America triumphant, and you adores,

mientras que la metrópoli sañuda
tu gloria bella y su baldón devora.
Mas cuando por la paz inútil viste
de Libertad la espada en tu alta mano,
el poder soberano
como insufrible carga depusiste.

   Alzado a la primer magistratura,
de tu patria la suerte coronaste,
y en cimientos eternos afirmaste
la paz, la libertad sublime y pura.
De años y gloria y de virtud cargado,
con mano vencedora
regir te vieron el humilde arado.
Con Sócrates divino te asentaste
de la Fama en el templo,
y a la virtud, con inmortal ejemplo,
la fe del universo conservaste.

   Cuando en noble retiro,
de oro y de crimen y ambición ajeno,
tu espléndida carrera coronabas,
en este bello asilo respirabas
pobre, modesto y entre libres libre.
¡Oh Potomac! del orgulloso Tíber
no envidies, no, la delincuente gloria,
que no recuerda un héroe como el tuyo
del orbe todo la sangrienta historia.

   Por la Francia feroz amenazada
vuelve la patria del peligro al día,
y en unánime voto al héroe fía
de Libertad y América la espada.
Los rayos de la gloria
vuelven a ornar su venerable frente . . .
Mas ¡ay! desapareció, volando al cielo,
como de nubes en brillante velo
hunde el sol su cabeza en occidente.

While Mother England must endure its shame,
Raging at the mention of your name.
And when, with peace, the sword of liberty
Rests idle in your hand,
You hasten sovereign power to abjure
As a weight too heavy to endure.

   Then called to highest office,
The fortune of your nation to complete,
You set it on foundation firm and fast:
An edifice of peace and liberty.
With years and glory, and with virtue weighed,
And with the hand that once a sword did wield,
The humble plow you guide
In furrows straight. With Socrates divine
In Fame's temple sure your place you claim,
And with your virtue ever as example,
The faith of all creation you maintain.

   When released at last from cares of office,
Your splendid race now run,
In this tranquil refuge you retire,
Far from the bane of lucre and ambition,
Modest, humble, free among the free.
Do not envy, o noblest Potomac,
The dissolute glory of the Tiber.
For hero such as he who walked your shore
This bloodstained world has never seen before.

   Now the nation once again in peril,
Threatened by a sanguinary France,
With one accord, entrusts to its old hero
The righteous sword of American liberty.
Once again, rays of shining glory
Adorn your venerable brow . . .[8]
Alas! Too fleeting is their noble glow,
A fading nimbus in the darkening west,
As Heaven calls you to your final rest.

¡Oh Washington! Protegen tu sepulcro
las copas de los árboles ancianos
que plantaron tus manos,
y lo cubre la bóveda celeste.
Aun el aire que en torno se respira,
el que tú respirabas,
paz y santa virtud al pecho inspira.

En la tumba modesta,
que guarda tus cenizas por tesoro,
ni luce el mármol, ni centella el oro,
ni entallado laurel, ni palmas veo.
¿Para qué, si es un mundo
a tu gloria inmortal digno trofeo?
Con estupor profundo
por tu genio creador lo miro alzado
hasta la cumbre de moral grandeza.
Potente y con virtud; libre y tranquilo;
esclavo de las leyes;
del universo asilo;
asombro de naciones y de reyes.

O Washington! The crowns of stately trees
Planted by your hands,
Stand silent vigil by your hallowed grave,
And the vault of heaven stretches o'er.
The very airs that once you did respire
And waft around me now,
In my breast tranquility inspire.

Upon the modest tomb[9]
Whose treasure is your glorious remains,
Nor gold nor gleaming marble do I see,
Nor laurel carved, nor palm of victory.
What would they serve, when the only trophy
Worthy of your greatness is a nation?
In astonishment I see it rise,
Virtuous and powerful and free,
To heights of just and moral majesty.
From your inventive genius, bold it springs,
Only bound by laws,
A refuge to the world,
The wonderment of nations and of kings.

Niágara

    Templad mi lira, dádmela,[10] que siento
en mi alma estremecida y agitada
arder la inspiración. ¡Oh! ¡cuánto tiempo
en tinieblas pasó, sin que mi frente
brillase con su luz . . . ! Niágara undoso,
tu sublime terror sólo podría
tornarme el don divino, que ensañada
me robó del dolor la mano impía.

    Torrente prodigioso, calma, calla
tu trueno aterrador: disipa un tanto
las tinieblas que en torno te circundan,
déjame contemplar tu faz serena,
y de entusiasmo ardiente mi alma llena.
Yo digno soy de contemplarte: siempre
lo común y mezquino desdeñando,
ansié por lo terrífico y sublime.
Al despeñarse el huracán furioso,
al retumbar sobre mi frente el rayo,
palpitando gocé: vi al Océano,
azotado por austro proceloso,
combatir mi bajel, y ante mis plantas
vórtice hirviente abrir, y amé el peligro.
Mas del mar la fiereza
en mi alma no produjo
la profunda impresión que tu grandeza.

    Sereno corres, majestoso; y luego
en ásperos peñascos quebrantando,
te abalanzas violento, arrebatado,
como el destino irresistible y ciego.
¿Qué voz humana describir podría
de la sirte rugiente
la aterradora faz? El alma mía
en vago pensamiento se confunde
al mirar esa férvida corriente,
que en vano quiere la turbada vista

Niagara

My lyre! Give me my lyre!
For in my kindled soul I feel
Inspiration's flame.
How long in gloom it did abide,
And I without its light . . . !
Niagara, your terror sublime alone
Could give me back the gift divine
That sorrow had me denied.

Prodigious torrent: temper
Your terrible thunder. Dispel
The darkness that surrounds you;
Let me behold your face serene,
And with ardor fill my soul.
Worthy to behold you,
The mean and common I have ever spurned,
And craved the fearsome and sublime.
At the blast of the furious hurricane,
As lightning flashed above,
I reveled, trembling. The Ocean churned,
And whipped by winds, assailed my ship,
Opening chasms at my feet,
And I its peril loved.
Yet even tempests of the sea,
Made less impression on my soul,
Than you, in your majesty.

Serenely do you flow, until
On crags rudely dashed,
Madly you hurtle, fall away,
Like destiny, compelling, blind.
What human voice would dare portray
The terrifying face
Of that roaring cliff? My mind,
Disconcertedly,
Contemplates the current swift,
Which in vain my sight would chase

en su vuelo seguir al borde oscuro
del precipicio altísimo: mil ondas,
cual pensamiento rápidas pasando,
chocan, y se enfurecen,
y otras mil y otras mil ya las alcanzan,
y entre espuma y fragor desaparecen.

¡Ved! ¡llegan, saltan! El abismo horrendo
devora los torrentes despeñados:
crúzanse en él mil iris, y asordados
vuelven los bosques el fragor tremendo.
En las rígidas peñas
rómpese el agua: vaporosa nube
con elástica fuerza
llena el abismo en torbellino, sube,
gira en torno, y al éter
luminosa pirámide levanta,
y por sobre los montes que le cercan
al solitario cazador espanta.

Mas ¿qué en ti busca mi anhelante vista
con inútil afán? ¿Por qué no miro
alrededor de tu caverna inmensa
las palmas ¡ay! las palmas deliciosas,
que en las llanuras de mi ardiente patria
nacen del sol a la sonrisa, y crecen,
y al soplo de las brisas del Oceano,
bajo un cielo purísimo se mecen?

Este recuerdo a mi pesar me viene . . .
Nada ¡oh Niágara! falta a tu destino,
ni otra corona que el agreste pino
a tu terrible majestad conviene.
La palma, y mirto, y delicada rosa,
muelle placer inspiren y ocio blando
en frívolo jardín: a ti la suerte
guardó más digno objeto, más sublime.
El alma libre, generosa, fuerte,
viene, te ve, se asombra,

To the very precipice.
A thousand passing waves,
Quick as thought itself,
Clash and career.
A thousand more displace them, then
In foam and thunder disappear.

See how they bound! The dire abyss
Devours the plunging flood
Amidst iridescent bows,
While the forest returns the deafening roar.
On boulders in the yawning depths,
The torrents crash; vaporous clouds
In tensile filaments spin and soar
And to the ether rise
In luminous pyramids.
The hunter, in the circling hills,
Beholds them in surprise.

But what does my anxious eye
In you so vainly seek? Why
Around your cave immense
Do I not see the graceful palms
That on my island's ardent plain
Are born beneath a smiling sun,
'Neath azure skies untroubled grow,
And sway as ocean breezes blow?

Unbidden is this memory . . .
Oh, Niagara! You lack for naught.
No crown besides the rugged pine
Befits your fearsome majesty.
Let the palm and myrtle and rose
Enchantments inspire, and leisure sweet,
In beguiling gardens. Your destiny
Loftier purposes contains.
The free and generous soul
Comes here, sees you, is amazed,

el mezquino deleite menosprecia,
y aun se siente elevar cuando te nombra.

　¡Omnipotente Dios! En otros climas[11]
vi monstruos execrables
blasfemando tu nombre sacrosanto,
sembrar error y fanatismo impío,
los campos inundar en sangre y llanto,
de hermanos atizar la infanda guerra,
y desolar frenéticos la tierra.
Vilos, y el pecho se inflamó a su vista
en grave indignación. Por otra parte
vi mentidos filósofos, que osaban
escrutar tus misterios, ultrajarte,
y de impiedad al lamentable abismo
a los míseros hombres arrastraban.
Por eso te buscó mi débil mente
en la sublime soledad: ahora
entera se abre a ti; tu mano siente
en esta inmensidad que me circunda,
y tu profunda voz hiere mi seno
de este raudal en el eterno trueno.

　¡Asombroso torrente!
¡Cómo tu vista el ánimo enajena,
y de terror y admiración me llena!
¿Do tu origen está? ¿Quién fertiliza
por tantos siglos tu inexhausta fuente?
¿Qué poderosa mano
hace que al recibirte
no rebose en la tierra el Océano?[12]

　Abrió el Señor su mano omnipotente;
cubrió tu faz de nubes agitadas,
dio su voz a tus aguas despeñadas,
y ornó con su arco tu terrible frente.
¡Ciego, profundo, infatigable corres,
como el torrente oscuro de los siglos
en insondable eternidad . . . ! ¡Al hombre

Is exalted at your name,
And idle pleasures disdains.

 Almighty God! In other climes
I have seen execrable men
Your holy name blaspheme,
Impious fanaticism sow,
Fields engulf in blood and tears,
Lay waste in war the very earth,
And turn brother into foe.
I saw these, and my heart would swell
In righteous wrath. I saw as well
Presumed philosophers
Dare to probe your mysteries,
Insult you, and to the yawning hell
Of impiety drag their fellow men.
That is why my mind sought you
In solitude sublime;
It opens now to you, and knows
Your hand in this immensity
That surrounds me. Your voice profound
Reverberates in my breast,
In the torrent's thundering sound.

 Astounding cataract!
How the sight of you enthralls,
And dread and awe inspires.
Where is your source? From what spring
Do you flow unceasingly?
What compelling hand
Ensures that by your swelling flood
The sea does not deluge the land?

 God his mighty hand unclenched,
In shifting clouds obscured your face,
Gave your waters his thundering voice
And crowned you with his radiant bow.
Headlong, blind, you ever race
Like the onrush of the centuries,
Boundless, timeless . . . ! And so a man sees

huyen así las ilusiones gratas,
los florecientes días,
y despierta al dolor . . . ! ¡Ay! Agostada
yace mi juventud, mi faz marchita,
y la profunda pena que me agita
ruga mi frente de dolor nublada.

   Nunca tanto sentí como este día
mi soledad y mísero abandono
y lamentable desamor . . . ¿Podría
en edad borrascosa
sin amor ser feliz . . . ? ¡Oh! ¡si una hermosa
mi cariño fijase,
y de este abismo al borde turbulento
mi vago pensamiento
y ardiente admiración acompañase!
¡Cómo gozara, viéndola cubrirse
de leve palidez, y ser más bella
en su dulce terror, y sonreírse
al sostenerla mis amantes brazos . . . !
¡Delirios de virtud . . . ! ¡Ay! ¡Desterrado,
sin patria, sin amores,
sólo miro ante mí llanto y dolores!

   ¡Niágara poderoso!
¡Adiós! ¡Adiós! Dentro de pocos años
ya devorado habrá la tumba fría
a tu débil cantor. ¡Duren mis versos
cual tu gloria inmortal! ¡Pueda piadoso
viéndote algún viajero,
dar un suspiro a la memoria mía!
Y al abismarse Febo en occidente,
feliz yo vuele do el Señor me llama,
y al escuchar los ecos de mi fama,
alce en las nubes la radiosa frente.

His fond illusions swept away—
His strong and vital years—
And wakes to naught but woe!
Alas! My youth is gone,
And clouded by my sorrow,
My brow is lined, my face is wan.

   Never before today
Have I such abandonment known,
And lack of love . . . At an age
Of youthful ardor, can a man
Find happiness alone?
Oh! If only a lovely one
Would capture my affection
And follow me in my wandering thoughts
And fervent admiration
To the edge of this abyss!
How I would thrill to see her pale,
In her terror sweet,
And then see her smile, absolved of fears
In my loving arms' embrace . . .
Ah, virtuous dreams! An exile
I am, loveless, alone,
Before me, only pain and tears.

   Mighty Niagara! Goodbye! Goodbye!
In too few years, the icy tomb
Will your frail bard devour.
But may my verses yet endure
Like your eternal glory.
May some traveler, stopping near,
In memory of me a sigh allow,
And in heaven to where I am called,
At the final sunset hour
I will hear the echoes of my fame,
And raise in the clouds my shining brow.

Proyecto

    De un mundo débil, corrompido y vano
menosprecié la calma fastidiosa,
y amé desde mi infancia tormentosa
las mujeres, la guerra, el Oceáno.

    ¡El Océano . . . ! ¿Quién que haya sentido
su pulso fuertemente conmovido
al danzar en las ondas agitadas,
olvidarlo podrá? Si el despotismo
al orbe abruma con su férreo cetro,
será mi asilo el mar. Sobre su abismo
de noble orgullo y de venganza lleno,
mis velas desplegando al aire vano,
daré un corsario más al Oceáno,
un peregrino más a su hondo seno.

    Y ¿por qué no? Cuando la esclava tierra
marchita y devorada
por el aliento impuro de la guerra,
doblando al yugo la cerviz domada,
niegue al valor asilo,
yo en los campos del piélago profundo
haré la guerra al despotismo fiero,
libre y altivo en el sumiso mundo.
De la opresión sangrienta y coronada
ni temo el odio, ni al favor impetro.
Mi rojo pabellón será mi cetro,
y mi dominio mi cubierta armada.

    Cuando los aristócratas odiosos,
vampiros de mi patria despiadados,
quieran templar sus nervios relajados
por goces crapulosos,

Project

    The calm of a weak, corrupted world
Ever was irksome to me.
From boyhood on I've only loved
Women, war and the sea.

    The sea! What man who has ever felt
Of its surge the heave and fall
When dancing in its roiled waves,
Would fail to heed its call?

    If tyranny with its iron fist
Should ever oppress the world,
Refuge I'll find in the ocean's void,
To the winds my sails unfurled.

    A corsair brave I'll learn to be,
With vengeance filled and pride,
And when the earth by the scourge of war
Is consumed and sorely tried,

    Bends its neck to oppression's yoke,
And refuge to valor denies,
I'll find my freedom on the open sea,
As my ship its billows plies.

    War I'll declare on tyranny,
Free in a world of the meek.
The hatred of despots I'll never fear,
And never their favor seek.

    My domain will be my armored ship,
My scepter, a flag of red.
And when the odious aristocrats
Who my country have savagely bled,

    Seek to brace their tired nerves
By dissolute pleasures unmanned,

en el aire genial del Oceáno,
sobre ellos tenderé mi airada mano,
como águila feroz sobre la presa.
Sufrirán servidumbre sin combate,
y opulento rescate
partirán mis valientes compañeros.

   Bajo del yugo bárbaro que imponen
a la igualdad invocarán: vestidos
con el tosco buriel de marineros,
me servirán cobardes y abatidos.
Pondré a mis plantas su soberbia fiera,
temblarán mis enojos,
y ni a fijar se atreverán los ojos
sobre mi frente pálida y severa.

In the healthful airs of the ocean wide,
Upon them I'll lay my hand.

   With cool resolve I'll swiftly fall
Like an eagle upon its prey,
And my comrades and I will soon enjoy
The ransom they shall pay.

   Humbly they'll serve in sailors' wool,
Equality they'll invoke.
But they'll suffer now what they once imposed:
Of tyranny the yoke.

   At my feet they'll yield their haughty pride,
Before my ire they'll bow,
And never dare to raise their eyes
To my pale and pitiless brow.

Himno del desterrado

    Reina el sol, y las olas serenas
corta en torno la prora triunfante,
y hondo rastro de espuma brillante
va dejando la nave en el mar.
    ¡*Tierra*! claman; ansiosos miramos
al confín del sereno horizonte,
y a lo lejos descúbrese un monte . . .
Le conozco . . . ¡Ojos tristes, llorad!

    Es el *Pan* . . . En su falda respiran
el amigo más fino y constante,
mis amigas preciosas, mi amante . . .
¡Qué tesoros de amor tengo allí!
    Y más lejos, mis dulces hermanas,
y mi madre, mi madre adorada,
de silencio y dolores cercada
se consume gimiendo por mí.

    Cuba, Cuba, que vida me diste,
dulce tierra de luz y hermosura,
¡cuánto sueño de gloria y ventura
tengo unido a tu suelo feliz!
    ¡Y te vuelvo a mirar . . . ! Cuán severo
hoy me oprime el rigor de mi suerte!
La opresión me amenaza con muerte
en los campos do al mundo nací.

    Mas, ¿qué importa que truene el tirano?
Pobre, sí, pero libre me encuentro;
sola el alma del alma es el centro;
¿qué es el oro sin gloria ni paz?

The Exile's Hymn

    Beneath a fiery sun the conquering prow
Sharply cleaves the peaceful, flowing waves,
And in its wake, across the ocean deep
The ship a trail of shining lather paves.

    Land! they cry, and anxiously we look
To the distant boundary of the skies.
A mountain on the blue horizon shows . . .
I know it well . . . Oh weep, my grieving eyes!

    It is *El Pan* . . . and there upon its slope
Lives a friend unwavering and true,
Maidens dear to me, my beloved . . .
There abide the treasures that I knew!

    And farther still, all my sisters dear,
And my mother, precious to my heart.
In silent grief she slowly pines away,
Weeping for me since we've been apart.

    Cuba, in whose bosom I was born,
Cuba, land of loveliness and light:
What dreams of happy fortune and of glory
Me with your beloved shores unite!

    From afar I see you once again!
But grim oppression threatens me with death.
A destiny most cruel would sure await me,
In that land where first I drew a breath.

    But let the tyrant thunder in his rage.
Poor I am, but honorable and free.
The soul is but the center of the soul.
What is gold without tranquility?

Aunque errante y proscripto me miro,
y me oprime el destino severo,
por el cetro del déspota ibero
no quisiera mi suerte trocar.

Pues perdí la ilusión de la dicha,
dame ¡oh gloria! tu aliento divino.
¿Osaré maldecir mi destino,
cuando puedo vencer o morir?
Aun habrá corazones en Cuba
que me envidien de mártir la suerte,
y prefieran espléndida muerte
a su amargo azaroso vivir.

De un tumulto de males cercado
el patriota inmutable y seguro,
o medita en el tiempo futuro,
o contempla en el tiempo que fue.
Cual los Andes en luz inundados
a las nubes superan serenos,
escuchando a los rayos y truenos
retumbar hondamente a su pie.

¡Dulce Cuba! en tu seno se miran
en su grado más alto y profundo,
la belleza del físico mundo,
los horrores del mundo moral.
Te hizo el cielo la flor de la tierra;
mas tu fuerza y destinos ignoras,
y de España en el déspota adoras
al demonio sangriento del mal.

¿Ya qué importa que al cielo te tiendas
de verdura perenne vestida,
y la frente de palmas ceñida
a los besos ofrezcas del mar,

A life of wandering exile I must lead.
Of cruelest fate I feel the piercing sting.
And yet I would not change my destiny
For the scepter of the Spanish king.

And since my dream of happiness is lost,
O glory, let me feel your breath divine!
Dare I reprehend my luckless fate
When to triumph or to die, alone is mine?

Still in Cuba there are surely hearts
Who envy me my martyr's destiny,
And might prefer to die a splendid death
And not to live in fear and bitterly.

Surrounded by a host of tangled ills,
The patriot, immutable and fast,
Thinks upon the times that are to come
Or contemplates the times that now are past.

Just as the Andes, piercing through the clouds,
Bathed in purest light, serenely glow,
And see the lightning flash, hear the thunder
Rumble deeply in the vales below.

Cuba fair! Within your breast one finds
In the most profound and high degree,
Of the natural world, loveliness,
Of the moral world, depravity.

Heaven made of you an earthly flower,
Yet you your strength and destiny ignore,
And in the Spanish despot who commands you,
An evil, bloody demon you adore.

What does it matter if beneath the heavens
You lie bedecked in constant greenery,
And, your brow enwreathed in swaying palms,
You offer kisses to the shining sea.

si el clamor del tirano insolente,
del esclavo el gemir lastimoso,
y el crujir del azote horroroso
se oye sólo en tus campos sonar?

   Bajo el peso del vicio insolente
la virtud desfallece oprimida,
y a los crímenes y oro vendida
de las leyes la fuerza se ve.
   Y mil necios, que grandes se juzgan
con honores al peso comprados,
al tirano idolatran, postrados
de su trono sacrílego al pie.

   Al poder el aliento se oponga,
y a la muerte contraste la muerte;
la constancia encadena la suerte;
siempre vence quien sabe morir.
   Enlacemos un nombre glorioso
de los siglos al rápido vuelo;
elevemos los ojos al cielo,
y a los años que están por venir.

   Vale más a la espada enemiga
presentar el impávido pecho,
que yacer de dolor en un lecho,
y mil muertes muriendo sufrir.
   Que la gloria en las lides anima
el ardor del patriota constante,
y circunda con halo brillante
de su muerte el momento feliz.

   ¿A la sangre teméis . . . ? En las lides
vale más derramarla a raudales,
que arrastrarla en sus torpes canales
entre vicios, angustias y horror.

If the tyrant's raging fulminations
And of the wretched slave the piteous moan,
And the cracking of the dreaded whip
In your fields reverberate alone?

Virtue lies oppressed and defeated
Beneath the weight of insolence and vice
And the force of law is e'er corrupted,
For gold exchanged at the highest price.

A thousand utter fools, self-satisfied,
Before the despot lie abject and prone;
With honors purchased by the highest bidder,
They worship at his sacrilegious throne.

Let bravery oppose itself to power,
For constancy the hand of fate enchains,
Let death with death contend in open battle,
Who fears not death then victory attains.

Let us join a name of lasting glory
To the centuries that swiftly fly,
Let us set our eyes upon the future
And elevate our vision to the sky.

To bare a fearless breast before the sword
Of the enemy is worth much more
Than to die upon an old man's bed,
And lingering, a thousand deaths endure.

For glory in the raging of the battle
The ardor of the patriot does incite,
And surrounds him with a brilliant halo
When he at last must perish in the fight.

Is it blood you fear? How much better
In copious amounts it is to shed
Than to feel it slacken in your veins
In vice consumed, in loathing and in dread.

¿Qué tenéis? Ni aun sepulcro seguro
en el suelo infelice cubano.
¿Nuestra sangre no sirve al tirano
para abono del suelo español?

   Si es verdad que los pueblos no pueden
existir sino en dura cadena,
y que el cielo feroz los condena
a ignominia y eterna opresión;
   de verdad tan funesta mi pecho
el horror melancólico abjura,
por seguir la sublime locura
de Washington y Bruto y Catón.

   ¡Cuba! al fin te verás libre y pura
como el aire de luz que respiras,
cual las ondas hirvientes que miras
de tus playas la arena besar.
   Aunque viles traidores le sirvan,
del tirano es inútil la saña,
que no en vano entre Cuba y España
tiende inmenso sus olas el mar.

What have you then? Within poor Cuba's soil
Not e'en a sheltered grave will you attain.
Does not our blood but serve the tyrant vile
To fertilize the soil of distant Spain?

If it is true that free from chains and shackles
The peoples of the world can never be,
And that a fearsome Heaven e'er condemns them
To oppression and indignity,

The melancholy of that dreadful truth
My stubborn heart cannot but disavow.
Of Washington, of Brutus and of Cato
The noble madness only I'll allow.

Cuba! Pure and free you'll someday live,
As pure and free as your radiant air,
And as the churning waves that embrace you
And rush ashore to kiss your beaches fair.

Although vile traitors bow before him,
The fury of the tyrant is in vain.
For vast extend the waves of the ocean
Between Cuba and the wrath of Spain.

Vuelta al Sur

    Vuela el buque: las playas oscuras
a la vista se pierden ya lejos,
cual de Febo a los vivos reflejos
se disipa confuso vapor.
    Y la vista sin límites corre
por el mar a mis ojos abierto,
y en el cielo profundo, desierto,
reina puro el espléndido sol.

    Del aliento genial de la brisa
nuestras velas nevadas llenamos,
y entre luz y delicia volamos
a los climas serenos del Sur.
    A tus hielos adiós, Norte triste;
de tu invierno finaron las penas,
y ya siento que hierven mis venas,
prometiéndome fuerza y salud.

    ¡Salve, cielo del Sur delicioso!
Este sol prodigóme la vida,
y sus rayos en mi alma encendida
concentraron hoguera fatal.
    De mi edad las amables primicias
a tus hijas rendí por despojos,
y la llama que aun arde en mis ojos
bien demuestra cual supe yo amar.

    ¡Oh recuerdos de paz y ventura!
¡Cómo el sol en tu bello occidente
inundaba en su luz dulcemente
de mi amada la cándida faz!
    ¡Cómo yo del naranjo a la sombra
en su seno mi frente posaba,
y en sus labios de rosa libaba
del deleite la copa falaz!

Return to the South

    The ship speeds on; the distant shores
Vanish to my sight,
Just as gauzy threads of mist
Dissolve in Phoebus's light.

    My unencumbered eye surveys
The ocean's boundless sweep;
The splendid sun holds fiery court
In the sky's fathomless deep.

    Before the brisk, genial breeze
Our vessel swiftly flies;
In radiance and bliss we race
To tranquil southern skies.

    Farewell to your rigors, icy North;
Farewell to winter's pains.
Foretelling days of strength and health,
Warmth courses through my veins.

    Hail, delightful southern sky!
Yours was the sun whose rays
First stirred the ardors of my soul
And kindled a fatal blaze.

    The spoils of my tender youth
Your maidens took as prize,
And how I loved, how much and well,
Still flames there, in my eyes.

    Oh memories of peace, of bliss!
Your sun, declining west,
Bathed my beloved in its light,
And soft her face caressed.

    How I, in the shade of the orange trees,
On her breast would my brow repose,
And drink the cup of false delight,
As I sipped from her lips of rose!

*Mas vinieron después negros días
de opresión, de discordias y saña,
y los hijos odiosos de España
de mi patria me osaron lanzar.
    Para excluirme por siempre de Cuba,
mi cadalso en los campos levantan,
y su triunfo los pérfidos cantan
al mirarme sin patria ni hogar.*

    ¡Dulce Cuba! en tus aras sagradas
la ventura inmolé de mi vida,
y mirando tu causa perdida,
mis amores y amigos dejé.
    Mas tal vez no está lejos el día
(¡cuál me anima tan bella esperanza!)
en que armado con hierro y venganza
a tus viles tirano veré.

    ¡Cielo hermoso del Sur! Compasivo
tú me tornas la fuerza y aliento,
y mitigas el duro tormento
con que rasga mi seno el dolor.
    Al sentir tu benéfico influjo,
no al destino mi labio maldice,
ni me juzgo del todo infelice
mientras pueda lucirme tu sol.

    ¡Adiós, hielos! —¡Oh lira de Cuba!
cobra ya tu feliz armonía,
y del Sur en las alas envía
himno fiel de esperanza y amor.
    Por la saña del Norte inclemente
destrozadas tus cuerdas se miran;
mas las brisas, que tibias suspiran,
te restauran a vida y vigor.

But then came days, foreboding, dark,
When wrath and oppression would reign,
And banished I was from the land of my birth
By the odious sons of Spain.

To keep me e'er from my native land
They prepare a waiting cell,
And sing perfidious songs of glee,
While I must homeless dwell.

Sweet Cuba! On your sacred pyre
My life was a holocaust.
I left behind my loves, my friends,
Your cause forever lost.

And yet perchance the day draws near
(How hope fills me with zeal!)
When your tyrants I'll confront
With vengeance armed, and steel.

Fair southern skies, compassionate,
My ardor you restore,
And for my breast, so torn with grief
By torment's blade, are the cure.

With your beneficent influence,
I'll not my fate malign,
Nor think myself unfortunate
Whene'er your sun may shine.

Farewell to ice! O Cuba's lyre!
Glad harmonies now employ,
And wafting forth on southern wings,
Send hymns of hope and joy.

Your strings, o Lyre, were broken, rent
By the North Wind's knife;
But warm winds, sighing soft,
Restore your strength and life.

Yo te pulso, y tus ecos despiertan
en mis ojos marchitos el llanto . . .
¡Cuál me alivias! Tu plácido encanto
la existencia me fuerza a sentir.
   ¡Lira fiel, compañera querida
en sublime delicia y dolores!
de ciprés y de lánguidas flores
ya te debes por siempre ceñir.

   ¡Siempre . . . ! No, que en la lid generosa
tronarás con acento sublime,
cuando Cuba sus hijos reanime,
y su estrella miremos brillar.
   ¡Yo con ellos! Si el hierro enemigo
en la férvida lid me derrumba,
y a otros mundos conduce mi tumba,
mundos son de justicia y paz.

   Y las musas y Cuba doliente
cubrirán de laureles mi pira,
do enlazadas mi fúnebre lira
y mi espada veránse brillar.
   "¡Libertad," clamarán, "en su pecho
inflamó de su aliento la llama!"
Y si caigo, mi espléndida fama
a los siglos futuros irá.

I touch you now, and sudden tears
My weary eyes revive;
And under your enchanting spell
I once more feel alive.

In sorrows and delights sublime,
Lyre you are kind!
May cypress leaves and languid blooms
Forever 'round you wind.

Forever . . . ! No, for yet in strife
You'll thunder with voice divine,
When Cuba spurs her sons to fight
And her star in the heavens will shine.

With them I'll go! And if in the fight,
Cut down by steel I should be,
Justice I'll find in the world to come,
And sweet tranquility.

Then Cuba and the muses nine
Will drape with laurels my pyre,
Where e'er will clasp in close embrace,
My sword and my mournful lyre.

"Freedom," they'll cry, "within his breast
Kindled a lasting flame."
And if I fall, for eternity
Shall live my splendid fame.

Inmortalidad

    Cuando en el éter fúlgido y sereno
arden los astros por la noche umbría,
el pecho de feliz melancolía
y confuso pavor siéntese lleno.

    ¡Ay! ¡así girarán cuando en el seno
duerma yo inmóvil de la tumba fría . . . !
Entre el orgullo y la flaqueza mía
con ansia inútil suspirando peno.

    Pero, ¿qué digo? —Irrevocable suerte
también los astros a morir destina,
y verán por la edad su luz nublada.

    Mas superior al tiempo y a la muerte
mi alma, verá del mundo la ruina,
a la futura eternidad ligada.

Immortality

When stars illuminate the shadowy night
And in their ethereal realm serenely glow,
The soul a melancholy joy can know,
And fills with doubt and disconcerted fright.

Alas! When I in frigid tomb shall lie,
They yet upon eternal wheels shall ride;
And caught between my weakness and my pride,
In sore anxiety I vainly sigh.

But no! The same unyielding fate applies
To the stars themselves, whose destiny
Is to fade and vanish from the skies.

While transcending death my soul shall see
How in time the world in ruin lies,
My soul to live for all eternity.

Notes

Notes to Introduction

1. The years around the centennial of Heredia's death saw the publication of some of the most complete biographies of him, including González del Valle's chronology (1938) and study of Heredia's time in Cuba (1939), and Mejía Ricart's life and works study (1941). The editions of Heredia's work by Lacoste de Arufe (1939) and Valdés y de la Torre (1939) offer comprehensive biographies. García Garófalo's excellent biography (1945) goes far beyond the focus on Heredia's time in Mexico suggested in its title. See also the biography by Díaz (1973). José María Heredia is not to be confused with his relative, the Cuban-born French poet José-María de Heredia (1842–1905).

2. Heredia's sisters were Ignacia (b. 1808), Rafaela (b. 1815), María Concepción (b. ?), and María Dolores (b. 1820). See Cipriano de Utrera 140.

3. Heredia frequently alludes in his letters to the manuscript of his father's memoir and history of the independence struggles in Venezuela. He asks his mother to have a copy made and sent to him in New York, with the thought of editing and publishing it there. But in a letter to his mother of May 5, 1825 (see herein), he indicates a change of heart, seeing the anti-Bolivarian stance of his father as out of date and possibly dangerous to his own prospects in the wake of the triumph of the Spanish American revolutions. Heredia senior's memoirs were eventually published in Paris in 1895 with a biography of its author by Enrique Piñeyro. See bibliography.

4. Heredia published a shorter version of this poem in his New York *Poesías* (1825) with the title "Fragmentos descriptivos de un poema mexicano." He published a definitive, extended version in the 1832 Toluca edition of his poetry, with the title "En el teocalli de Cholula." Given that he developed the poem over the years, it is misleading to date it to 1820, as anthologies often do.

5. Del Monte's promotion of Heredia's work began as early as that eventful year of 1823. On March 31, Del Monte placed an announcement in Havana's

Revisor político y literario of a planned edition of Heredia's work, soliciting subscriptions for its publication. In it he hails Heredia as "perhaps the first who, devoting himself from an early age to the study of the classics, has made the Cuban lyre reverberate with delicate and noble sounds." Del Monte sees Heredia as being in the vanguard of a new generation of Cuban poets who, following models of good taste from the Spanish peninsula, will "take advantage of the enviable qualities that adorn the inhabitants of a sweet and temperate zone, and who will worthily employ the advantageous disposition with which nature has blessed the happy sons of the most beautiful of the Antilles" (Del Monte 10, 12).

6. On the *Soles y Rayos* conspiracy and the involvement of its principal figures, see Morales y Morales, chapter 3. Garrigó is another fundamental source on the conspiracy.

7. See Moore for a recreation of Heredia's life in New York City. Upon his untimely death in 1949 at age forty, Moore left behind extensive notes and other materials that constitute a significant contribution to Heredia studies. The Ernest R. Moore papers are held in the Syracuse University archives.

8. An important example is the anonymous novel *Jicoténcal*, published in Philadelphia in 1826. The novel is a historical romance set in Mexico at the time of the Conquest, and is notable for its anti-colonial ideas. It is widely assumed that its author was a member or members of the expatriate Spanish or Spanish American community in the United States. Garland helpfully reviews the scholarship on the topic, and defends the proposition that Félix Varela was the author. The novel is sometimes attributed to Heredia, and even has been republished with him indicated as the author, but the attribution is highly speculative. Varela's incendiary periodical *El Habanero* (1824–1826) was published first in Philadelphia by Stavely and then in New York by Behr and Kahl, the same press that published Heredia's *Poesías*. See Rojas for the topic of Philadelphia as the center for pro-independence and pro-republican publications by Varela, Vicente Rocafuerte, Manuel Lorenzo de Vidaurre, and other Spanish American émigrés in Philadelphia in the 1820s. See Kanellos and Martell on the topic of early Spanish-language periodicals in the United States.

9. According to Cipriano de Utrera (141–42), the couple's surviving children were José de Jesús (1836–1923), María Merced (1833–?), and Loreto Jacoba (1839–1910).

10. "¿Quién cantará tus brisas y tus palmas, / tu sol de fuego, tu brillante cielo? / [. . .] por ti clamaba en el destierro impío, / y hoy condena la pérfida fortuna / a suelo extraño su cadáver frío . . ." (*Poesías selectas* 202).

11. Villaverde 90. The definitive, extended version of Villaverde's novel was published in New York in 1882.

12. According to Augier, the letter was published in *El indicador constitucional*, a Havana newspaper (Heredia, *Obra poética* 21).

13. Torres-Cuevas and Soucy both explore the overlap between masonic networks and rites and the *Soles y Rayos* and *Gran Legión* groups.

14. The letter is dated April 1, 1836. It is cited by Lacoste de Arufe in Heredia, *Poesías, discursos y cartas*, vol. 1, pp. CXLV–CXLVI.

15. Cited by Lacoste de Arufe in Heredia, *Poesías, discursos y cartas*, vol. 1, p. CLII.

16. Cited in Heredia, *Poesías, discursos y cartas*, vol. 2, pp. 29–30.

17. At least one of Del Monte's edits suggests a desire to elude censorship. In his letter describing Philadelphia, Heredia refers to the "fierce and generous *republicans*" among whom the aristocrat Joseph Bonaparte resides in Bordentown, New Jersey. Under Del Monte's hand, the phrase becomes "fierce and generous *people*." Méndez (51–52) suggests that journals like *La moda o recreo semanal del bello sexo*, which were intended for a female readership and dealt mostly with artistic and literary matters, gave editors and contributing writers cover to express potentially controversial aesthetic and social ideas. The edit by Del Monte, however, suggests that such journals were not beyond the scrutiny of government censors. Heredia himself had briefly edited a journal for women in Havana in 1821: the *Biblioteca de damas*.

18. See McKinsey, Gassen, and Mulvey for the meaning of Niagara for nineteenth-century travelers, the development of a tourist infrastructure in New York State, and the Catskill and Niagara regions as destinations for artists and writers.

19. The topic is treated in Howe, chapter 6.

20. Early on, the Erie Canal inspired a corpus of poetry, travelogues, letters, and sketches, within which Heredia's letters deserve to take their place. See Hecht.

21. In several letters, Heredia discusses the injustice done to Clinton when he was removed from the Erie Canal Commission. Clinton was a key figure in American freemasonry, having served as Grand Master of both the Grand Lodge of New York and the Grand Encampment of Knights Templar, which he also helped to found. Perhaps Heredia's sympathies for him derived in part from a masonic connection.

22. There is little or no sustained denunciation of slavery in Heredia's work. His mother owned domestic slaves, his Uncle Ignacio's coffee plantation was worked by slaves, and his family in general was connected among the Matanzas landowning class whose wealth depended upon slave labor. An expression of aversion to the suffering of slaves surfaces occasionally in Heredia's verse, as in "A Emilia," herein. In a letter to his mother of September 2, 1824, Heredia advises his mother against buying slaves with some money that she has come into, mentioning "pangs of conscience," although ultimately emphasizing that they are "a bad investment."

23. *New York American*, August 6, 1825. Moore (288–91) reproduces the complete review and the editor's preface, and suggests that the review's author was Félix Varela.

24. Cited in Moore 285. Moore proposes that the author of this review was William Cullen Bryant. Moore reproduces the cover page of Heredia's translation as printed in 1825 and offers important commentary on it (283–87).

25. In 1828, Bryant published an adaptation of an early poem by Heredia, "En una tempestad" ["The Hurricane"]. On Bryant's "Hispanophilia," see Peterson.

26. Orjuela resolved the question of who was responsible for the translation of Heredia's poem. José De Onís ("The Alleged Acquaintance . . .") settled the matter of whether or not Bryant and Heredia knew each other personally by bringing to light a letter from 1849 in which Bryant stated: "I came to New York in 1825 soon after the publication of Heredia's volume, but I never had any personal acquaintance with him and regret that I can give you no more information concerning his sojourn in this country" (219).

27. Among the important mid-twentieth-century studies that documented this phenomenon are Helman (1946), Onís (1952), Stimson (1954), Williams (1955), and González (1962). In more recent years, the topic has received a new impulse in the context of transnational and transatlantic studies. See, for example, Gruesz (2002), Brickhouse (2004), Lazo (2005), and Jaksic (2007). In the pages of these studies can be found important discussions of Heredia.

28. el ósculo santo / de amistad fraternal.

29. On the topic of the possible annexation of Cuba by the United States, see Pérez.

30. Also worthy of note is a review of Heredia's works contained in a larger, anonymous review of "The Poetry of Spanish America" in the *North American Review*, vol. 68, no. 142, 1849, pp. 129–60; it includes a translation of a fragment of Heredia's "Himno del desterrado" and most of "La estación de los nortes."

31. Ellis translates Heredia's letter from Niagara along with his poem of that name. Aparicio Laurencio (Heredia, *Selected Poems*) gathers the following: James Kennedy's translations of "A mi esposa," "A mi caballo," and "Poesía"; versions of "La estación de los nortes" by James Kennedy and W. H. Hurlbut; a prose version of "Al sol" by Alice Stone Blackwell; the well-known version of "Niagara" in which Bryant collaborated, and Bryant's translation of "En una tempestad"; one stanza of "En el aniversario del 4 de julio de 1776" translated by Minna Carolina Smith; "A la estrella de Venus" and "Oda a la noche" published by Gertrudis Vingut; a short fragment of "A Emilia" by Clarence Hills; a fragment of "El himno del desterrado" attributed to W. H. Hurlbut; and the sonnet "Inmortalidad" published by Vingut.

32. "To whom shall I dedicate these poems if not to the best of friends, to him who loves me more than a brother, to you, my Ignacio? When, defying the waves of the ocean that separate us, they arrive in your hands, read them in the tranquil shade where many of them were written, where I thought I would end my days, peacefully, at your side. But an unforeseen hurricane ruined all my innocent hopes . . ."

33. Heredia announces Alfonso's arrival in New York in a letter to his Uncle Ignacio of June 2, 1824, included herein.

34. González del Valle published Heredia's surviving letters to Alfonso in 1937. In that edition he also reproduced Heredia's dedication to Alfonso of his translation of Chénier's 1792 tragedy *Caius Gracchus* in which Heredia eulogizes his recently deceased friend, recalling when Alfonso "voluntarily crossed the sea, and poured the balm of consolation upon the breast of [his] banished friend." He also says: "When I was about to expire in your arms along the frozen shores of the Hudson, I survived thanks to the hope that your strength of character and your patriotism inspired in me . . ." (*Del epistolario*, 24). According to González del Valle (19), Alfonso died of the same consumptive illness that would take Heredia's life. Alfonso had returned from New York to Cuba in late 1825, apparently via a route that included Niagara, the Ohio and Mississippi Rivers, and New Orleans. He wrote Heredia from New Orleans on December 10 of that year, as Heredia acknowledged in his letter addressed to Silvestre in Havana in March 1826 (*Del epistolario* 18). Domingo del Monte published some of Alfonso's notes from his North America travels in *La moda o recreo semanal del bello sexo* in June 1830.

35. Cristóbal Madan y Madan, born in Havana in 1806, was a few years younger than Heredia. He was from a prominent Cuban landowning and commercial family of Irish origin. See Santa Cruz y Mallén, vol. 5, p. 166.

36. García Marruz sorts out the conflicts in the friendship between Heredia and Del Monte and their ongoing collaboration, including Del Monte's important work as defender, promoter, and corrector of Heredia's poetry.

37. These letters are cited by Augier in Heredia, *Obra poética* 540–41.

38. In the journal *Miscelánea: Periódico Crítico y Literario* (2ª época), which he edited and published in Toluca, Mexico, in 1831, Heredia reproduced an 1804 essay by Manuel José Quintana, "Sobre la rima y el verso suelto." The essay defends blank verse against its detractors.

39. Augier reveals that "among the papers of doctor Vidal Morales, preserved in the Biblioteca Nacional José Martí . . . in Havana, there appears a photograph of the first page of what seems to be the original or draft of this poem, beneath the title 'Verses written after seeing the panoramas of Athens and Palmyra'" (Heredia, *Obra poética* 561).

40. Copies of the guide to the display survive, with the various elements of the painting numbered and labeled (*Exhibition at the Rotunda*).

41. Mejía Ricart (p. 123, n. 387) quotes the letter in which Gener describes Heredia's poem as he read it in the guest book. Gener indicated that the poem had eleven *estrofas* (stanzas), which corresponds to the number of sections in which the poem is divided in both the 1825 and 1832 editions. Neither the version of the poem enclosed in the letter to Ignacio nor that inscribed in the guestbook at Niagara is extant.

42. Méndez (166) and González (*Heredia, primogénito* 113–16) posit the influence of Byron and note that Heredia's poem precedes by some years the "Canción del pirata" (1835), a Romantic classic by the Spanish poet José de Espronceda.

43. See herein Heredia's letter to his mother of January 28, 1825.

44. Augier (*Obra poética* 542) indicates that the poem was published in *El Águila Mexicana* on October 20, 1825.

45. *North American Review*, vol. 68, no. 142, Jan. 1849, pp. 139–40. Augier (*Obra poética* 543) affirms that review and translation were by W. H. Hurlbut. The translation also appears in Heredia, *Selected Poems* 41–42.

46. Augier (*Obra poética* 542) includes the four stanzas in his notes to the poem, which he indicates first appeared in *El Amigo del Pueblo* (México) 1, 3 (August 15, 1827).

47. The essay, "Fama póstuma," appeared in *Miscelánea: Periódico Crítico y Literario*, tomo 1, Sept. 1829. "Inmortalidad" appeared in the journal *Minerva* (no. 2, 1834, pp. 115–18), which Heredia edited in Mexico and to which he was the primary contributor.

48. The Spanish version of the poems is taken from Heredia's 1832 Toluca edition of his *Poesías*, with some modernizations of spelling and punctuation.

Notes to Selected Letters

1. In her biography (Heredia, *Poesías, discursos y cartas*, vol. 1, pp. LIII–LIV) Lacoste de Arufe cites documents that reveal that Heredia's son José de Jesús Heredia destroyed the original copy of this letter because of its controversial nature.

2. On Betancourt, see introduction. According to Garrigó (248), Guillermo Aranguren died during the criminal proceedings against the *Caballeros Racionales*.

3. The original reads: "aquellos dos testigos la ameritaban demasiado." Another possible translation could be "those two witnesses gave ample evidence that would lead to my imprisonment." Either translation captures the idea that Aranguren and Betancourt incriminated Heredia to save their own skins. Morales y Morales (52) indicates that Betancourt in fact was spared the harsh sentences that were dealt to others involved in the *Caballeros Racionales* conspiracy.

4. Morales y Morales notes that, in an effort to discredit totally the *Soles y Rayos* movement, conservatives in Cuba along with Captain General Francisco Dionisio Vives alleged that the conspirators were planning an uprising of the island's population of color (41). The violence of the slave uprising that accompanied Haiti's revolution a few decades before was never far from the minds of Cuba's white population.

5. The San Juan River is one of three that flow through Matanzas and into its bay. The love interest in Matanzas that Heredia seems to be on the verge

of naming was most likely Dolores Junco, the *Lola* to whom he had devoted a number of poems.

6. Augier (Heredia, *Epistolario* 73) indicates that this letter was first published in the Mexican journal *El Iris*, no. 26, June 1826, pp. 99–102.

7. Tarpaulin Cove is found on Naushon Island, off the southern coast of Massachusetts. Note the error of the letter's date: November has 30 days. In Augier's edition, the year appears as "1826 [1823]." It would seem that the error of the year, at least, was on the part of *El Iris*.

8. The Castillo de San Severino was a colonial-era fortress that protected Matanzas Bay. From the early 1800s on it served as a military prison.

9. Almost two years later, Heredia would be inspired to write his "Himno del desterrado" (see herein) upon catching a glimpse of the Pan de Matanzas peak during his voyage from New York to Alvarado, Mexico.

10. Earlier that year, Heredia had journeyed to the city of Puerto Príncipe (today Camagüey) to be formally admitted to the bar. Lacoste de Arufe (Heredia, *Poesías, discursos y cartas*, vol. 1, pp. XLIII–XLIV) reproduces the June 9, 1823, document that recognized Heredia's completion of his legal studies in Havana's Universidad de San Gerónimo and licensed him to practice law.

11. A reference to Milton's *Paradise Lost* (1667). A translation into Spanish of Milton's epic by Benito Ramón de Hermida was published in Madrid in 1814.

12. Regrettably, the diary to which Heredia alludes is not known to posterity.

13. Probably the Boston shipping merchant Daniel C. Bacon.

14. During his brief time in Boston, Heredia also acquired a copy of the tragedy *Saul* by Vittorio Alfieri (1749–1803) and undertook its translation into Spanish from the Italian. See herein the note to his letter to his mother of December 11, 1824.

15. In Spanish: "*. . . bien que a pesar de todo eso no te parece saco de paja el famoso buque.*" Heredia apparently is using a code name for some stately lady of Matanzas who had caught Ignacio's attention.

16. *Pájaro bobo* in Spanish.

17. Goodhue & Co., founded by Jonathan Goodhue in 1809, was a premier merchant house in New York City through much of the nineteenth century, with far-flung shipping and import/export interests. See Barrett 23–25. It is not clear who Bodan was.

18. The Arango family, who gave Heredia refuge on the family plantation before his flight to the United States.

19. Heredia sends frequent greetings to Chea, who seems to be the same Doña María la Goicochea who is a family friend or a companion to his Uncle Ignacio.

20. Perhaps the father of one of Heredia's early love interests, Isabel Rueda y Ponce de León ("Belisa" or "Lesbia" in Heredia's poetry). The Ruedas were

neighbors of the Heredias in Matanzas. See González del Valle, *Heredia en la Habana* 23, 39. Several *Soles y Rayos* conspirators also were named Rueda (Morales y Morales 46, 52).

21. The original reads: "... *si ha pasado a conocimiento al Juez de letras quiénes son capitulares este año?*" Given that Heredia has just mentioned the legal proceedings against the *Soles y Rayos* conspirators, it would seem that here he is referring to their continued roundup and interrogations. But the language is ambiguous.

22. This *adulador* is another example of the many acquaintances that Heredia shared with his uncle, and to whom he refers cryptically in his letters.

23. John Latting was an American merchant established in Matanzas.

24. In the Augier edition there appears only an ellipsis at this point in the letter, but in the original in the BNJM, along with the ellipsis there also appears indistinctly what may be the capital letter "A." Assuming that is indeed what Heredia intended, the reference is certainly to José Arango, to whom Heredia alludes with similar circumspection in other letters. In addition, in the original letter the name of the captain is carefully scratched out, but Harding is certainly whom Heredia is referencing. It is interesting to note the degree to which Captain Harding served as intermediary between Heredia (and perhaps others among the conspirators) and his/their friends and relations in Cuba, and Heredia's care not to implicate the good captain.

25. Luciano Ramos was another of the *Caballeros Racionales* who fled to the United States. Like Heredia, he eventually was to receive the maximum penalty imposed upon the conspirators of exile to Spain. See Morales y Morales 52 and Garrigó 249. It would seem that within just four months Ramos was back in Cuba, since in a letter to his mother dated April 23, 1824 (see herein), Heredia notes: "I believe that Luciano will give you a lengthy account of me; let me know if he is already in Matanzas." There are no subsequent mentions of Ramos in Heredia's letters from the United States.

26. Caraballo, apparently a fellow Cuban exile, and with whom Heredia would share lodgings in New York, is not listed by Morales y Morales nor by Garrigó among the *Soles y Rayos* conspirators.

27. In this letter, and in many subsequent ones, Heredia includes a postscript for his eldest and favorite sister, Ignacia.

28. In the original, "*a la persona.*" It is not clear what Heredia's motives were for not wanting to name this person.

29. Heredia's aunt Francisca (1780–1849) was his mother's sister; among her children was a daughter, Magdalena. See Cipriano de Utrera 133.

30. *Pache* in Augier. *Pachis* is closer to what appears in the original letter in the BNJM, although it is difficult to read.

31. The fellow expatriate Juan de Acosta, whom Heredia references a number of times in his letters, was part of Heredia's circle in New York and accompanied him to Niagara Falls. Garrigó (249) lists a Juan Miguel de Acosta among the Matanzas conspirators.

32. The Marchioness in question was perhaps the Marquesa de Prado Ameno (María de la Concepción Aparicio del Manzano y Justiz), owner of the *Los Molinos* plantation where the Arango family resided and where Heredia found refuge before his flight to the United States. The Marquesa del Prado Ameno is the same known to posterity as the owner and tormentor of Juan Francisco Manzano, whose *Autobiography of a Slave* is a classic of Cuban literature. Manzano (1797–1854) obtained his freedom from slavery; a poet and playwright, he was a protégé of Domingo del Monte.

33. Tomás Gener (1787–1835), born in Spain but a resident of Matanzas, Cuba, after 1808, was one of the three Cuban delegates to the Spanish *Cortes*, along with Leonardo Santos Suárez and Félix Varela; the three men had just arrived in the United States after the dissolution of that body by Ferdinand VII and being charged with treason. Of the three, Gener was perhaps the one whom Heredia was closest to; he mentions him on a number of occasions in his letters from the United States.

34. While in New York, Heredia served as intermediary for the sending of letters between the Heredia family in Cuba and relatives in Santo Domingo. Heredia's wording here (*"a ver si se puede sacar algún partido de lo que allí tenemos"*) suggests that the Cuban Heredias still had property in Santo Domingo.

35. Heredia refers here to his mother's cousin Belén Caro Campuzano Polanco. Belén married Manuel de Zequeira y Arango (1764–1846), an important Cuban poet in his own right. Ignacio and Joaquín were sons of the couple, and would have been around Heredia's age.

36. In the original Spanish, *gentuza*. María de la Merced and her daughters had household slaves in their home in Matanzas.

37. In the original, "*el oprobio de la naturaleza.*" It is not clear to whom Heredia is referring, although upon leaving Cuba for the United States, it seems that Heredia thought that his friend Domingo del Monte had betrayed him. See introduction and the letter to Del Monte, herein.

38. *Betancourt:* Antonio Betancourt, the fellow member of the *Caballeros Racionales* who had implicated Heredia in the conspiracy. See introduction.

39. It seems likely that Heredia is referring to some volume of the work of Jean-François Ducis (1733–1816), who adapted in French, among others, the Shakespearean tragedies that Heredia mentions. In the inventory of his library that Heredia made in Toluca in 1832 (held in the Biblioteca Nacional José Martí), Heredia lists, in the section on French theater, a volume of "Ducis, teatro y poesías."

40. María de la Merced's older sister María de los Ángeles (1777–1830), married to Antonio José Angulo. See Cipriano de Utrera 132–33.

41. Heredia's Aunt Francisca married Simón Garay (1771–1815) who returned to Santo Domingo from Cuba in 1809 (see Augier's introduction to Heredia's *Epistolario*, 20). Heredia frequently mentions forwarding letters between his aunt and her son Santiago Garay (1803–1877) in Santo Domingo, and he maintained his own correspondence with his Dominican cousin, born the same year as he. For the names and dates of Francisca and her children, see Cipriano de Utrera 133.

42. Perhaps this anonymous friend was Luciano Ramos, who returned to Cuba sometime in the late winter or early spring of 1824. Whomever it is that Heredia refers to here, his cohabitation with him predates his time in the United States. At the time of writing this letter, Heredia had been in the United States only for about two months.

43. At some point in the preceding weeks, Heredia had moved from 44 Broadway to 88 Maiden Lane, so it is unclear to which family he is referring.

44. Micaela was Heredia's cousin, daughter of his paternal aunt María de los Dolores (1774–1802), second wife of José Tiburcio Sterling del Monte.

45. In the original: "*la presentación de Perucho, y prisión de Herrera y Arango. (. . .) ¿Se ha querido suponer que tenían algo con los Soles?*" Perucho is, apparently, another *Soles y Rayos* conspirator whose willingness to give testimony about the plot has left Heredia indignant. Herrera may have been Francisco de Herrera, who, according to Morales y Morales (51), was a ringleader in Matanzas of a group of *gente de color* who claimed membership in the *Caballeros Racionales*. If this is the Herrera in question, Heredia's indignation would square with his overall denial that the *Caballeros* sought to foment an uprising of slaves and other people of color. Garrigó (248) lists a José Arango Lache among the imprisoned Matanzas conspirators.

46. This is the first statement on Heredia's part in his extant correspondence that his letters were at best liable to fall into the wrong hands and at worst be intercepted and examined by the authorities in Cuba.

47. *Conventículo matemático*: Perhaps an allusion to meetings of freemasons. See introduction.

48. Garrigó (249) lists a Bernardo Navarro among the Matanzas conspirators who fled prosecution.

49. The monetary term used by Heredia here is *reales*, which was 1/8 of a Spanish dollar (in Spanish, a *peso* or *real de a ocho*). The Spanish dollar was still in use in the United States in the early nineteenth century. The present volume uses the word *dollar* when Heredia uses *peso*, and a dollar sign when Heredia uses that.

50. Probably Gardiner Greene Howland (1787–1851) of the New York mercantile house G.G. and S. Howland, founded in 1816, and which began with "a schooner in the Matanzas trade" (Ingham 628).

51. In a letter to his mother of May 15, 1824, Heredia would complain of the fees that he was charged to receive a pair of cashmere shorts that she or Uncle Ignacio apparently had sent to him, doubtlessly with the cold New York winters in mind.

52. In the original, humorously: "*. . . y solté el money.*"

53. On Antonio Betancourt, see introduction.

54. A seeming non sequitur. Because Heredia underlines *en Boston,* the phrase must have a special meaning understood by Ignacio. Given that in the next paragraph Heredia alludes to Betancourt's drinking, perhaps *en Boston* means something like *in his cups.*

55. A reference to the tsunami that devastated the Peruvian port city of Callao, following the great earthquake of 1746.

56. Perhaps Luciano Ramos, who around this time returned to Cuba. Because Ramos was a major figure in the *Caballeros Racionales*, his return to Cuba was sensitive, and this would explain Heredia's reluctance to name him here.

57. Jesús María was Ignacio's coffee plantation near Matanzas.

58. Perhaps Fénelon's highly influential *Les aventures de Télémaque*, first published in 1699 and with many subsequent translations and editions. In the inventory of his library that he made in Toluca in 1832, Heredia lists a two-volume *Telémaco* classified among French authors and works.

59. See Heredia's letter to Ignacio of June 2, 1824, in which he unleashes his contempt for Sotico, who apparently worked in Ignacio's law office in Matanzas.

60. In the original, *resguardos*. Apparently some sort of business form that Ignacio had requested of Heredia.

61. It is not clear why Heredia is reluctant to give the full name of the New York merchant via whom Ignacio is to correspond with his nephew.

62. Because *Tió* is a Catalonian name, and Heredia has mentioned several times that friend Jaime Tió is soon to leave for Matanzas, the reference here must be to him.

63. The name in the original letter in the BNJN is difficult to read, but seems to be *Western*, although Augier reads *Wertern*. Heredia mentions a Captain Western in another letter to Ignacio of October 8, 1824 (herein).

64. Heredia appears to follow the line of thinking that saw Ossian's work as authentic, ancient Gaelic epic poetry, and not a forgery, which was the early and continued accusation made against Ossian's "translator," the Scottish poet James MacPherson (1736–1796). Some of Heredia's Ossian translations appeared in the 1832 Toluca edition of his poetry. Chapman categorizes and dates Heredia's various Ossian translations and demonstrates the influence in them of the translations of Ossian into Italian by Melchiore Cesarotti (1730–1808).

65. The sentence in the original is obscure: "*¿Sabes que me provoca a risa cuando me figuro cuál andaría por los conventículos, y qué estrañote pasearía en Broadway?*" The translation offered here is speculative. The Señor de la Riva alluded to by Heredia was probably Juan Rivas Vértiz, a prominent politician in the pro-Independence movement in his native Yucatán. Rivas Vértiz was a freemason (thus the second reference in Heredia's letters to Ignacio of New York *conventículos*; see the letter to Ignacio of February 21, 1824, herein). For a more complete account of Rivas Vértiz, see the footnote to Heredia's letter to Ignacio of October 8, 1824, herein.

66. Augier no. 36. On Silvestre Alfonso, see introduction. See also González del Valle, *Del epistolario*.

67. Dolores Junco and Isabel Rueda y Ponce de León.

68. González del Valle (*Del epistolario* 11) identifies Tato as Anastasio Carrillo y Arango. Morales y Morales (52) lists an Antonio de Céspedes among

the Matanzas *Caballeros Racionales*, and notes that Céspedes died before the final sentence of the *Soles y Rayos* conspirators was handed down.

69. In his letter to Ignacio of February 28, Heredia announced his intention to send some books to Pepilla Arango via Jaime Tió. Thus, the family referenced here is undoubtedly the Arangos, and because in the original the masculine *amigo* is used, the "friend" alluded to (as always, cautiously) by Heredia is Pepilla's father, José Arango.

70. Garrigó (217–31) includes the "Parecer fiscal en la causa seguida por conspiración de los 'Soles de Bolívar,'" which may be the document that Heredia refers to here. He is not named in it, although the document offers a thorough accounting of the Matanzas conspirators, including the names of those who had fled imprisonment. José Franco, a friend of the Heredia family, was *oidor*, or judge, in the *Real Audiencia de Puerto Príncipe*, which had jurisdiction over the island of Cuba and beyond. Heredia may have lodged with the Franco family in 1823 when he went to Puerto Príncipe to secure his legal diploma. Franco also paid Heredia for the review of some overdue legal cases. See González del Valle, *Heredia en la Habana* 38–39. The judge's ongoing concern for Heredia during his exile is evident from the latter's letters. It would seem that because Heredia was not named in the document in question, Franco had reason to believe that his return to the island was feasible.

71. The monthly $50 stipend from Ignacio that kept Heredia afloat financially.

72. Heredia is referring to some kind of written commentary penned by José Arango regarding Heredia's controversial letter to Francisco Hernández Morejón, whom, here and elsewhere, he flippantly calls "Pancho." In his letter to Ignacio of April 23, 1824 (herein), he once again asks Ignacio to procure him a copy.

73. Heredia frequently sends regards to Antonio Angulo in his letters, and references him as a member of the law profession able to give accurate news about the conspiracy hearings underway in Cuba. Heredia's Aunt María de los Ángeles was married to Antonio José Angulo, and they had a son Antonio María Ramón, a few years older than Heredia and perhaps a lawyer like his cousin. Another son, José Miguel, married Heredia's sister Ignacia in 1835. See Cipriano de Utrera 132, 140.

74. In the original *pobre hermano!* Heredia sometimes refers to his uncle in those brotherly terms, which we have modified to avoid confusion.

75. Heredia's letter to Hernández Morejón upon escaping from Cuba. María de la Merced clearly worried that the letter had compromised rather than exculpated her son.

76. The rest of this short paragraph is damaged and illegible in the original in the BNJM.

77. Others are mentioned in this closing, but the fragments that remain of this paragraph in the damaged original in the BNJM do not allow for an accurate rendering.

78. Heredia met the Spaniard Blas Osés during his first stay in Mexico, between 1819 and 1821. Like Heredia, Osés was in the law profession, and was a man of letters who encouraged and advised Heredia in his poetic pursuits. Beginning in 1821 the two men collaborated in the publication in Havana of the short-lived journal the *Biblioteca de damas*. See González del Valle, *Heredia en la Habana* 35–36.

79. This son of Don Agustín Hernández must be the same Agustín Hernández whom Heredia references in other letters as a roommate during his first months in New York. Sources do not list Hernández as one of the *Soles y Rayos* conspirators, and the reasons for his stay in the United States and his return to Cuba are not clear.

80. In a letter to his mother of January 2, 1837, Heredia would reference an "extremely tiresome" (*fastidiosísimo*) Father Márquez who came to visit him in Havana during his short stay in Cuba.

81. Morales y Morales (52) lists Francisco García Medina among the principal Matanzas conspirators, and notes that, like Heredia, he eventually was sentenced to banishment from Cuba. Garrigó (249) indicates that García Medina held the degree of *licenciado*—a lawyer, like Heredia—and counts him among the conspirators who fled Cuba. García was in New York by July of 1824, and Heredia begins to reference him in his letters as one of his group of exiled friends. As late as June 2 (see Heredia's letter to Ignacio of that date herein), Heredia apparently thought that García was still in Cuba.

82. Cipriano de Utrera lists no uncle of that name on either side of Heredia's family.

83. Perhaps Dolores Junco, Heredia's recent love interest.

84. The Second Bank of the United States was designed by William Strickland (1788–1854); construction lasted from 1818 to 1824.

85. The bones of this mastodon had been discovered on the farm of John Masten, near Newburgh, New York. Thanks to the efforts of Charles Wilson Peale, the skeleton was excavated and reconstructed, was the centerpiece for a natural history museum created by Peale in Philadelphia, and became a national sensation. See Sellers.

86. Heredia almost certainly took this legend from handbills that Peale printed to advertise the mastodon bones that were his museum's primary attraction. The handbills (see reproduction in Sellers 146) quoted part of the text of an article that appeared in *The American Museum or Universal Magazine* (vol. 8, 1790, pp. 284–85) on the mastodon bones. The article cites the Shawnee legend, which Heredia synthesizes point for point.

87. In his "En el teocalli de Cholula" and in other poems, Heredia expresses similar sentiments regarding the historical cycle of cataclysmic destruction and the fall of civilizations, destined to be forgotten by succeeding ones.

88. The Fairmount Water Works in the form that Heredia saw them were constructed between 1819 and 1822.

89. The Chestnut Street Theater, designed by architect William Strickland, was constructed between 1822 and 1824 and destroyed by fire in 1856.

90. In several letters to Ignacio, Heredia alludes to someone named Jaureguiberry, who seems to have been an inside joke between Heredia and his uncle. This gentleman apparently was a mildly annoying or intrusive presence in the spot in Ignacio's coffee grove where nephew and uncle had spent many happy hours in conversation.

91. Among the attractions of the Philadelphia Museum was the "physiognotrace," a device for tracing the outline of a patron's head and transferring its shape to a piece of paper. The center of the paper was cut out, and the outline was placed against a black background to create a silhouette. The device could produce multiple copies. See illustration in Sellers 192.

92. Osés and Hazard must have come through with Heredia's request. The 1832 Toluca inventory of Heredia's library lists a four-volume edition of Meléndez Valdés's verse, most likely his *Poesías* published in Madrid by the Imprenta Real in 1820.

93. Juan de Acosta: see the footnote to Heredia's letter to his mother of December 19, 1823. At the time of Heredia's visit to Philadelphia, Father Félix Varela resided there and was embarking upon the publication of his journal *El Habanero*. In the 1820s, Philadelphia was a hotbed of political activism and pro-republican publication among Spanish American émigrés like Varela and Heredia's personal friend, the Ecuadorian Vicente Rocafuerte (see Rojas), but in his letters about his Philadelphia trip Heredia remains mum about his lodgings and his personal contacts in the city.

94. Joseph Bonaparte (1768–1844) was the eldest brother of the emperor Napoleon, by whom he was placed upon the thrones of Naples and Sicily (1806–1808) and Spain (1808–1813). Upon his brother's abdication, and with the Bonaparte clan in disgrace, Joseph escaped to the United States, establishing himself in Philadelphia with the self-designated title Count of Survilliers. He purchased a large property at Point Breeze near Bordentown, New Jersey, where he built a grand estate. While Joseph was visiting New York in January 1820, his Point Breeze mansion burned to the ground, despite the efforts of his Bordentown neighbors to save it. However, they were able to rescue most of the extremely valuable contents of the house. Joseph built a new house at Point Breeze and resided there until his definite relocation to Europe in 1841.

95. Perhaps the unchaperoned woman with whom Heredia happened to coincide on the steamboat was Annette Savage (1800–1865), Joseph's American mistress.

96. Heredia does not entirely capture the tone and spirit of Joseph's letter. Joseph was most impressed that his Bordentown neighbors were not only courageous in their attempts to extinguish the blaze, but also delivered to him *de la manière la plus scrupuleuse* all the valuable items that they rescued from the

burning house. A bit less arrogantly than Heredia alleges, Joseph writes: "Ceci m'a prouvé à quel point les habitants de Bordentown apprécient l'intérêt qu'ils m'ont toujours inspiré" [This has proven to me the degree to which the inhabitants of Bordentown appreciate the concern they have always inspired in me] (quoted in Bertin 79). He goes on in the letter to praise the innate goodness of men and the happy state of the American people. The temporary bad feelings that the letter caused may have had more to do with Joseph's neighbors resenting that their honesty could even be doubted (Ross 255).

97. In the edited version of this letter for *La Moda o Recreo Semanal del Bello Sexo*, Del Monte replaced the politically charged word *republicanos* with the neutral word *gente*, no doubt because of sensitivity on the part of the Spanish authorities regarding republican sentiments in Cuba. The present translation is based on the original, full text of the letter, held in the Escoto collection at Harvard's Houghton Library.

98. Like others of his generation, Heredia seems to have admired Napoleon Bonaparte's genius and deplored his despotic tendencies. See his sonnet "Napoleón" (1823) and his letter to Ignacio of June 2, 1824, in which he contrasts Napoleon with Washington. While no great fan of the Bonaparte brothers, in the present letter Heredia goes relatively easy on Joseph. As Rojas notes (222), the elder Bonaparte brother was well received in the United States and was friendly with figures whom Heredia admired and who, like Heredia, had masonic connections.

99. The identity of this Lucas is unclear. Perhaps it was Lucas Alamán, the prominent Mexican conservative and monarchist who may have met the Bonaparte brothers in Europe.

100. Another example of Heredia's caution with regard to José Arango, the friend and benefactor who provided Heredia refuge when the order was given for his arrest.

101. On Betancourt, see the introduction and previous references to him in Heredia's letter to Francisco Hernández Morejón of November 6, 1823, his letter to his mother of January 24, 1824, and his letter to Ignacio of February 21, 1824. Heredia had good reason to consider himself well rid of his former fellow conspirator.

102. Or perhaps *Borthimbort*. The instances of the appearance of this name in Heredia's letters are difficult to read in the originals in the Escoto collection and the BNJM. The name seems similar to *Borthiry* and other such Basque names.

103. The phrase *por parte de las autoridades* is not present in Augier's edition, which is based on the version of Heredia's letter published in Havana in *La Moda o Recreo Semanal del Bello Sexo*. Once again, it would seem that Del Monte edited out wording that might give offense to government authorities in Cuba.

104. I owe the rendering "one may kill a man with his fists" to Onís (*The United States as Seen* 85). But the original reads *a puñaladas*, which according to DRAE is clearly "with a *puñal*," that is, a dagger. *Puñetazo* would make more sense.

105. Juan José Hernández y Cano. On the death in captivity of this conspirator, see the introduction and the poem "To Emilia," herein.

106. Francisco Hernández Morejón, the primary judge in the legal proceedings.

107. Most likely Heredia's uncle, José Tiburcio Sterling del Monte, who married first one and then another of Heredia's aunts on his father's side. In a letter to his mother of July 4, 1823, from Puerto Príncipe, Heredia describes Sterling's poor health, because of which, since his arrival from Puerto Rico, Sterling had not been able to attend the Audiencia to which he had been appointed as *oidor*.

108. Probably his younger sisters, *las fascinerosas [facinerosas]*.

109. Apparently Pía and Felipa Fernández, family friends who complained when Heredia did not send them his regards in his letters. See Heredia's letter to his mother of April 23, 1824.

110. The route that Heredia describes corresponds closely to the so-called "Fashionable Tour," which took travelers up the Hudson to Albany and the springs at Saratoga, west by stage and canal to Niagara, northeast through Canada to Montreal and Quebec, then south through Vermont and New York State back to Albany, east to Boston, and back to New York via Rhode Island and Connecticut. Davison's guide to the Fashionable Tour (see bibliography herein) was published in 1825, a year after Heredia's trip, but by 1824 the route was already becoming established, facilitated by the near completion of the Erie Canal. Heredia's extant letters do not describe his return trip. He may have simply retraced his route from Niagara to New York City via the Canal and the Hudson.

111. On the importance of Chateaubriand for Heredia, see introduction.

112. Morales y Morales (52) indicates that Juan Francisco Ruiz was among the Matanzas conspirators who ultimately were dealt a lesser sentence of a fine of 1,000 pesos. On Silvestre Alfonso, see introduction and Heredia's letter to him of February 28, 1824, herein. In his letter to Ignacio of June 2, 1824, Heredia indicates that both men had recently arrived in New York on the *Robert Fulton* as part of a larger group of Cuban exiles. The exile of Ruiz would be short; in his letter to his mother of May 4, 1825, Heredia speaks of Ruiz's imminent return to Cuba.

113. Heredia's fellow Matanzas conspirators who turned testimony against him. Information in Morales y Morales (52) and Garrigó (247–49) suggests that Betancourt, Andux, Portillo, and Mihoura all ultimately received minor sentences for their participation in the conspiracy. As noted earlier, Garrigó lists a D. Guillermo Aranguren as among the Matanzas conspirators who died in prison before being sentenced.

114. Heredia's letters make clear that family friend and *oidor* José Franco made repeated efforts to clear Heredia's name so that he might return to Cuba, offers that Heredia refused because of his unwillingness to accept anything resembling a pardon; Heredia considered himself innocent of any wrongdoing.

115. On this work by José Francisco Heredia, eventually published as the *Memorias sobre las revoluciones de Venezuela*, see the note to the introduction herein.

116. Heredia expresses this thought with a saying for which there is no good English equivalent: *"No está para tafetanes la Magdalena, ni yo para amoríos."*

117. Nena is probably a nickname for Magdalena, his Aunt Francisca's daughter to whom Heredia almost always sends greetings along with her mother.

118. Heredia is referring to José Teurbe Tolón, one of the principal Matanzas conspirators. See Morales y Morales 37, 52 and Garrigó 248.

119. Tarrero and Madruga were *Soles y Rayos* conspirators in Matanzas. Garrigó (204–7) includes the court record of Madruga's testimony in prison on October 10, 1823, in which he vehemently denied any involvement with the conspiracy. See also Morales y Morales 37, 51, 52. According to Trelles y Govín (11), José Teurbe Tolón escaped from prison in Havana with Tarrero and Madruga on May 24, 1824. If Trelles y Govin has that date right, it is remarkable that Heredia could be writing about Teurbe Tolón's presence in New York as early as June 2. In March 1825, Teurbe Tolón relocated to Mexico (Trelles y Govín 11), from which in late 1826 or early 1827 he departed for Philadelphia to serve as Mexican vice-consul, as indicated in a letter from Heredia to Silvestre Alfonso of December 22, 1826.

120. With regard to "La batalla de Lora," Chapman (231–32) explains that "it would seem likely that Ignacio was the one who mislaid it. After more than fifty years it came to light in Matanzas, in the possession of Heredia's daughter Loreto; she delivered it to Vidal Morales y Morales, who then prepared it for publication in the *Revista de Cuba* in 1879 (IV, 201–212)."

121. Mejía Ricart (316, n. 768) cites a series of articles by José Güell y Renté in the Madrid periodical *La América*, in which the latter cites Manuel José Quintana as saying "Heredia is a great poet. Heredia will not die and does honor to America."

122. Heredia's "A la noche" was published in the 1825 New York edition of his *Poesías*. With regard to "Imistona," Chapman (232) notes that "whether Ignacio complied [with Heredia's request to pass on the poem to Pepilla Arango] or not is an open question, but in any event 'Inistona' dropped from sight for over 115 years. At length Francisco González del Valle came upon a copy of it while going through the papers of the Matanzas scholar José Augusto Escoto, and it was made a part of the *Poesías completas* in 1941." Chapman (232, n. 3) proposes that Heredia's title is properly spelled "Inistona" and not "Imistona."

123. *Jaulas* in the original. According to Haddad, the Vauxhall Garden "was surrounded by a high board fence, with entrances on Broadway and Bowery Road. Alcoves for seating were discreetly arranged along the inner perimeter of the garden fence; they provided areas of elegant seclusion, and afforded many a young gentleman the privacy required for courtship." Haddad explains that the garden was established ca. 1803 by a Frenchman named Delacroix. It survived until 1859.

124. On the Ecuadorian Vicente Rocafuerte, see the note to Heredia's letter to Ignacio of April 23, 1824.

125. Rocafuerte translated Adams's "An Address Delivered at the Request of the Committee of Arrangements for Celebrating the Anniversary of Independence, at the City of Washington on the Fourth of July 1821 upon the Occasion of Reading the Declaration of Independence" and included it in his *Ideas necesarias a todo pueblo americano independiente, que quiera ser libre* (Philadelphia: D. Huntington, 1821).

126. Garrigó (250) lists a José Govín among the Matanzas *Soles y Rayos* conspirators who were not charged. He was doubtlessly the *licenciado* José Govín y Aday (?–1851), who was prominent in Matanzas politics. See Santa Cruz y Mallén, vol. 2, p. 19.

127. *Fue* and *Diatifas*: these names are correctly transcribed from the original letter in the BNJM, but it is unclear to whom Heredia is referring.

128. Sotico and Corneta would seem to be employees in Ignacio's law office, in which Heredia had worked for a while, probably as a law student.

129. José Antonio Saco (1797–1879) was to be one of the most prominent men of letters in nineteenth-century Cuba. During his stay in in the United States (1824–1832), he co-directed with Félix Varela the weekly journal *Mensajero Semanal*, which published and helped to promote Heredia's poetry. Saco was a prominent defender of Heredia in the 1828–1829 polemic stirred by Ramón María de la Sagra's negative published critiques of Heredia's poetry. See González del Valle, *Heredia en la Habana* 44–50.

130. The paddle-wheeler *Robert Fulton* was a pioneering steam-powered vessel built for service between New York and New Orleans, with stops in Havana and Charleston. It began operation in 1820, and was converted to sail in 1825. The Cuban gentlemen who made this trip in 1824 were enjoying the most advanced naval technology of the moment. The Havana to Charleston run took about four days, and the Charleston to New York leg another four. See Morrison 436–37, and Frajola and Baird.

131. Perhaps Domingo del Monte or Dolores Junco.

132. Until the summer that Heredia made his Hudson River trip, the monopoly on steamboat travel between New York City and Albany was held by Robert R. Livingston Jr.'s North River Steam Navigation Company, which ran the ships that Heredia mentions. That company had debuted with the maiden voyage of the "Clermont" (as it is remembered, although it was not called that at the time) in 1807. According to Gassan (91), the fare before the breakup of Livingston's monopoly by the Supreme Court in March 1824 was $7 each way. Gassan notes that post-monopoly competition began a precipitous reduction in prices; in June of 1824, the North River Company dropped its weekday fare to $5, and all fares were reduced to $2 in July. It would seem that if Heredia's trip had occurred a few weeks later, he would have saved $4 each way.

133. An error on Heredia's part. West Point is on the west bank of the Hudson.

134. Sugarloaf Mountain (elevation 900 feet) is in the town of Fishkill, New York.

135. The highest peak in the Catskills is Slide Mountain at 4,180 feet. The highest peaks in New York are in the Adirondacks, which Heredia did not see on his way to Niagara.

136. Heredia's description of the Catskills here may owe something to Washington Irving's in the opening paragraphs of "Rip Van Winkle" (1819). The editor thanks an anonymous reader of the manuscript of the present volume for this observation.

137. In his letters describing his trip to Niagara along the Erie Canal, Heredia cites from an article in the *North American Review* (vol. 14, no. 34, Jan. 1822). The estimate of two thousand sloops plying the Hudson probably comes from this article (237).

138. The Albany Academy, founded in 1813.

139. Later in in the nineteenth century, Gibbonsville was incorporated into West Troy, which later in turn was incorporated into the present town of Watervliet, New York.

140. Cable ferries.

141. Heredia must have cited from another reference that he had taken with him on his trip, for this bit of text is not in the *North American Review* article in question.

142. *North American Review*, vol. 14, no. 34, Jan. 1822, p. 241. Heredia translates this and subsequent citations into Spanish.

143. Tonawanda Creek

144. Letter to Ignacio of April 24, 1824, herein.

145. Heredia uses the Spanish term *fanega*, the old Spanish bushel. It is unclear if he has just translated "bushel" to "fanega" from his source or has made the conversion.

146. The Maumee and the Great Miami Rivers, respectively.

147. Heredia translates from the *North American Review*, vol. 14, no. 34, Jan. 1822, p. 246. This passage from "A shortcut . . ." to ". . . the river Mississippi" is actually an embedded quote from *Public Documents Relating to the New York Canals, Which Are to Connect the Western and Northern Lakes with the Atlantic Ocean; With an Introduction* (New York, 1821), p. ix.

148. *North American Review*, vol. 14, no. 34, Jan. 1822, p. 247.

149. *North American Review*, vol. 14, no. 34, Jan. 1822, p. 241.

150. Heredia began his canal journey in Schenectady, rather than in Albany, because there were twenty-seven locks between those two cities, which were only about twenty miles apart. "A trip on the canal between these two points took at least 24 hours and lasted even longer when too many boats were in use. Because

of the amount of time required to traverse this section of the canal, nearly all of the boats carried heavy cargoes and few passengers. After all, passengers could reach Schenectady from Albany in three hours by stagecoach for less than $1 a ticket" (McNeese 97).

151. On Jaureguiberry, see the note to Heredia's letter to Ignacio of April 15, 1824.

152. A concerted effort to produce maple sugar in large quantities to supply markets on the Eastern seaboard had taken place from 1789–1795. Led by William Cooper, this effort sought to replace the refined white sugar imported from the West Indies with this New York-produced maple sugar, not only as a profitable commercial venture but also with the added humanitarian benefit of replacing a form of production that depended on massive use of slave labor with local production by small farmers. See Taylor 119–34.

153. "Cuando en Oriente / reina glorioso el sol, y las espigas / se mueven ondeando al blando soplo / del aura matinal, el valle todo / un piélago dorado representa." Eugenio de Tapia Garcia (Spain, 1776–1860), "Epístola a un amigo."

154. Heredia does not indicate the source of this quote; perhaps it came from some sort of promotional literature or guidebook relating to the canal.

155. At the time of Heredia's trip, canal boats crossed the Seneca River by being lowered to river level by locks. When the canal was enlarged in the mid-nineteenth century, an aqueduct of stone arches was built to carry the canal over the river.

156. For much of the nineteenth century, the salt springs near Onondaga Lake and present-day Syracuse produced the greater part of the salt consumed in the United States.

157. Heredia was not alone in finding amusement in the grandiose classical and historical names of these newly founded towns in the New York State interior. In *Travels in North America* (1828), the Englishman Basil Hall would write: "It has been the fashion of travelers in America, I am told . . . to ridicule the practice of giving to unknown and inconsiderable villages, the names of places long hallowed by classical recollections. I was disposed, however, at one time to think, that there was nothing absurd in the matter. I did not deny that, on first looking at the map, and more particularly on hearing stage-drivers and stage passengers, talking of Troy, Ithaca, and Rome, and still more when I heard them speaking of the towns of Cicero, Homer, or Manlius, an involuntary smile found its way to the lips, followed often by a good hearty laugh." Text in Hecht 42.

158. This is a speculative translation of the word that Heredia uses: *tumbas*. The context suggests that Heredia refers to the piles of wood resulting from the clearing of land. The verb *tumbar* can mean to fell trees. The noun *tumbas* does not appear in dictionaries of *cubanismos* or other regional dictionaries consulted, but in the *Diccionario de la Real Academia Española*, *tumbar* appears as an equivalent of *desmontar* (to clear land) in Cuba and Venezuela.

159. The final stretch of the canal to Buffalo was completed in November 1825. It included the flight of five locks at Lockport that mounted the formidable Niagara escarpment. In the summer of 1824, the last leg of the trip to Niagara still was by stagecoach.

160. The Spanish *vara* was roughly the equivalent of a modern yard.

161. The Eagle Hotel in Manchester (which later became the Village of Niagara Falls, later incorporated into the city of Niagara Falls) was run by General Parkhurst Whitney. When taken over by Whitney in 1819, it was a one-room log tavern; Whitney enlarged it, and it became the first important hotel on the United States side of the falls.

162. Here and in the next paragraph in Augier, *Kingston*, an error.

163. Perhaps Navy Island.

164. Augier follows the manuscript copy in the BNJM in indicating *200 feet*, but this is an error. The ridge of the Horseshoe Falls on the Canadian side is roughly 2,200 feet wide.

165. Heredia may have carried with him John Morison Duncan's *Travels Through Parts of the United States and Canada in 1818 and 1819*, published in British and American editions in 1823. In a number of particulars, Heredia's letter coincides with Duncan's description of his visits to Niagara Falls. For example, Duncan reads as follows: "Various opinions prevail as to the most favourable situation for viewing the falls. (. . .) From the Table Rock the spectator has a more complete view of the Great Fall. (. . .) At the bottom of the precipice you more adequately appreciate the vastness of the foaming cataracts, their tremendous sound, the terror of the impending precipice, and the boiling of the mighty flood, but to these characteristics your view is confined" (48–49).

166. In Augier as in the manuscript copy in the BNJM, *Goat Island*, an error. Augustus Porter (1769–1849) and his brother Peter Buell Porter (1773–1844) purchased Goat Island in 1816, and were active in developing the Niagara Falls area for industry and tourism. They built the bridge to Goat Island, and the tourist establishments described by Heredia on Bath Island in the middle of the Niagara River between Goat Island and the shoreline. Bath Island is today known as Green Island.

167. As earlier noted, Ignacio's coffee plantation near Matanzas.

168. Heredia cites from *Atala*. The French reads: "c'est moins un fleuve qu'une mer, dont les torrents se pressent à la bouche béante d'un gouffre" (Chateaubriand 77).

169. The Pavilion Hotel, the best hotel at Niagara at the time, was built in 1822 by Canadian ex-frontier smuggler and entrepreneur William Forsyth.

170. Heredia may have borrowed this anecdote in part from John Howison, *Sketches of Upper Canada* (Edinburgh, 1821), which he goes on to cite at length in this same letter. Howison reads: "Many years ago, an Indian, while attempting to cross the river above the Falls, in a canoe, had his paddle struck from his

hands by the rapidity of the current. He was immediately hurried toward the cataract, and, seeing that death was inevitable, he covered his head with his cloak, and resigned himself to destruction. However, when he approached the edge of the cataract, shuddering nature revolted so strongly, that he was seen to start up and stretch out his arms; but the canoe upset, and he was instantly ingulfed [sic] amidst the fury of the boiling surge" (101).

171. Accurately following Howison, who calls this part of the St. Lawrence River "the Lake of the Thousand Islands," Heredia uses the term "*el lago de las mil islas.*"

172. Howison 98–99. With only minor errors, Heredia translates Howison word for word in his letter. Interestingly, he omits with ellipses the clause "as if the windows of heaven were opened to pour another deluge upon the earth." In the paragraph that follows this one, Heredia suggests as an original idea that of the waters of Niagara as a second Biblical flood, but it seems likely that he has borrowed the idea from Howison.

173. Heredia's anecdote resembles Duncan's recollection of a spot where an embankment near Table Rock had collapsed: "From within a few feet of where I stood, the bank which had formerly run forward nearly in a straight line towards the Table Rock, now presented a great concavity. The foot path along which I had formerly walked, and the bushes behind which I had stood, had all disappeared—the rock upon whose deceitful support they rested, had suddenly given way, from top to bottom, and a mass . . . about 160 feet in length, and from 30 to 40 in breadth, upon which I had formerly imagined myself in security, now lay shattered into ten thousand fragments at the bottom of the precipice. I cannot describe my emotions in contemplating the scene before me. I had trod where the foot of man will never tread again . . ." (41–42).

174. More evidence that Cuban authorities were opening Heredia's correspondence sent through the regular mails.

175. Apparently, José Francisco Heredia's younger brother Domingo, progenitor of the French wing of the Heredia family that would include the Cuban-French poet José-María de Heredia (1842–1905). It would seem from context that María de la Merced's brother-in-law had given her a sum of two thousand pesos or dollars (see Heredia's letter to his mother of September 18, 1824), and she was looking for advice as to how to invest it.

176. On Madan, see introduction.

177. Moore, p. 257: "From the Battery it was only a short walk up Broadway to the boarding house of Cristóbal Madan, at number 61. Madan, a Cuban employed by Goodhue & Company, exporters, was an unofficial welcomer of many Cuban exiles, who called him 'the Consul of Cuba.'" Lisandro Pérez (64–66, 70–72, 75–77, 155–58) traces Madan's subsequent story, including his involvement with groups favoring the U.S. annexation of Cuba.

178. "Who kisses your hand." The passage in italics was written by Heredia in English. Heredia is translating, perhaps playfully in keeping with the overall tone of the letter, the formal Spanish closing Q.B.S.M. (*que besa su mano*).

179. Captain General of Cuba Francisco Dionisio Vives.

180. Heredia often sends greetings to Abus in the closing of his letters, but the identity of Dirichity is unclear.

181. Heredia's younger sisters Rafaela (1815–?) and María Dolores (1820–1840).

182. Heredia's father José Francisco held a post in Pensacola in Spanish Florida from 1806 until 1810. His sister Ignacia was born there. See Lacoste de Arufe, xvii.

183. Heredia missed by a few weeks the arrival in New York of the Marquis de Lafayette as he began his celebrated tour of the United States.

184. In 1810, José Francisco Heredia, in his role as *oidor* of the Audiencia de Caracas, was commissioned by the Captain General of Cuba, the Marqués de Someruelos, to mediate in the rebellion that was brewing in various cities in Venezuela following the 1808 abdication of Ferdinand VII. The Marqués del Toro (Francisco José Rodríguez del Toro e Ibarra) figured prominently as military leader in the various phases of the revolutionary movement in Venezuela. See Vázquez Cienfuegos.

185. In the original, ". . . *y me dé ocasión de servirle.*"

186. In 1815, when *oidor* in the Audiencia de Caracas, Heredia's father José Francisco requested permission from the Spanish secretary of state to publish an *Idea del gobierno eclesiástico y civil de la España ultramarina o Indias occidentales*, a readable compendium of the so-called *Laws of the Indies*, issued over time by the Spanish crown for the governance of the Spanish colonies. In that request, José Francisco indicated that the first volume of this projected two-volume work was complete. See Chacón y Calvo 66–72 for the text of that request.

187. In letters written to his mother a few weeks later (November 6 and November 17, 1824), Heredia would allude to a work on the "legislation of the Indies" by or in the hands of someone named Cristo, in which María de la Merced had a financial interest. It seems probable that the work in question is the aforementioned one by José Francisco Heredia on the Laws of the Indies, which Heredia has already indicated is in the hands of Ignacio Heredia. Heredia is so cryptic in these references that it is difficult to sort out what the matter was about. Since the work was apparently in manuscript form, in separate notebooks, perhaps some were in Ignacio's possession, and others in Cristo's.

188. It would seem that María de las Mercedes had revealed in her letter to Heredia that some family acquaintance was avoiding her, probably because of the shadow cast over the family by Heredia's implication in the conspiracy and status as political fugitive.

189. Perhaps Heredia was anticipating that his old friend, the Spaniard Blas Osés, could be persuaded to visit him in the United States. The reference to Blas in this same paragraph helps to reinforce this possibility.

190. The United States and Guatemala had established formal diplomatic relations the previous month, on August 4, 1824. Guatemala was at that time a member of the Federal Republic of Central America. Perhaps Heredia had received an offer to work in the employ of that body.

191. Another reference to the "Fernández girls," who apparently hoped that Heredia could cash a money order from Galicia in New York.

192. *Telémaco*: see the note to Heredia's letter to Ignacio of February 21, 1824.

193. Garrigó (248) lists José Manuel Ponce among the Matanzas conspirators, and the Cirilo who was Heredia's friend in New York may have been his brother: Francisco José Cirilo Ponce de León y Espinosa (1797–1840).

194. The Guaire River flows through Caracas, Venezuela. Venezuela at the time was part of the nation that existed from 1819 to 1831 officially named the *República de Colombia*, often referred to today as *Gran Colombia*.

195. Both men were among the Matanzas conspirators. See Morales y Morales 37, 52 and Garrigó 248. Melitón Lamar (b. 1798) was of the same Lamar family in Matanzas to whom Heredia sends frequent greetings in his letters. After his exile in New York, he went on to Colombia, where he pursued a naval career, losing an arm in battle while serving aboard the corvette *Bolívar* (Santa Cruz y Mallén, vol. 2, p. 244).

196. Certain details in this paragraph, and in another reference to "Señor de la Riva" in Heredia's letter to Ignacio of February 24, 1824, suggest that the gentleman in question was Colonel Juan Rivas Vértiz. Rivas Vértiz, a fellow freemason, was prominent in politics in his native Yucatán, where he was elected provincial *jefe político* in July 1820 (Sotelo Regil 215–16). The *San Roberto* alluded to here by Heredia is surely the coffee plantation of that name near Matanzas, which Rivas Vértiz sold in 1821 (Barcia 84). Heredia references some sort of legal trouble that Rivas Vértiz faced, the nature of which is unclear; however, it is worthy of note that Rivas Vértiz was tried and jailed by a political rival in Yucatán during the brief reign of Iturbide (Sotelo Regil 300)—that is, sometime between May 1822 and March 1823.

197. José Teurbe Tolón. See the note to Heredia's letter to Ignacio of June 2, 1824.

198. That is, *I.H.*, Ignacio's initials.

199. Speculative translation of *"sabiendo ya con la que pierde."*

200. José Luis Alfonso y García de Medina (1810–1881). When Heredia wrote this letter, Alfonso y García was just fourteen years old. In 1824 he went from his native Havana to New York, where he studied for several years under the tutelage of Father Félix Varela. He would go on to a distinguished career

as an author in diverse subjects. See "Alfonso y García de Medina, José Luis," *Diccionario de la literatura cubana.*

201. Garrigó (217–31) includes the *Parecer fiscal en la causa seguida por conspiración de los "Soles de Bolívar,"* emitted by the *licenciado* Juan Francisco Cascales in Havana, January 14, 1824. At the end of this document, Cascales makes an emphatic plea for relative leniency regarding the *Soles y Rayos* conspirators. Assuming that this is the document in question, it appears that Heredia found a jarring discrepancy between that plea and the ongoing government persecution of said conspirators.

202. In the original Spanish in Heredia's letter: "... es la desgracia / menos cruel soportada que tenida." Heredia cites from his translation of *Saul* by Vittorio Alfieri (1749–1803); in Heredia's definitive translation, the lines read: "La derrota / es mejor soportada que temida" (Act II, Scene II). Heredia busied himself with this translation during his first days of exile in the United States, as revealed in the following note to the play when he retouched it and published it thirteen years later: "In December of 1823, I found myself in Boston, in a very painful situation. Snatched suddenly by the whirlwind of revolution from Cuba's flowered shores to the terrible winter of New England, relegated to absolute isolation by my ignorance of English, ill, without books, tormented by painful memories and gloomy expectations, I was devoured by the most profound melancholy. By luck I happened upon the tragedies of Alfieri; using hand gestures I was able to buy them, and reading them helped to soothe my soul in its misfortune. I began then the translation of *Saul*, with no other aim than to distract myself during my hours of sadness and tedium. A few days later I ran across two friends and fellow expatriates. The three of us recovered the use of the spoken word, and gave ourselves over to effusions of pain and affection. We shared in all things from that moment on, and we took continuous pleasure in recalling the past and planning the future. If *señores* Ramos and Caraballo should happen upon these lines, I think they will not deny themselves a sigh upon recalling the tender intimacy and boundless trust that presided over our relationship in those days, which I remember with the warmest feelings." Cited and translated from the edition of Heredia's *Saúl* in the *Revista de Cuba*, vol. 7, 1880, pp. 58–59.

203. Biographers affirm that the school in question was Victor Bancel's French school. Bancel was a French-speaking refugee from Santo Domingo. He took over this fashionable New York school, which had been founded as *L'École Économique* by General Victor Moreau and the Baron Jean Guillaume Hyde de Neuville. It was located on Anthony Street, today Worth Street. See Meehan 403. Deák elaborates on the role of the Baron and Baroness Hyde de Neuville in the establishment of this school "for the large New York population of impoverished French émigrés who had fled the troubled islands of Santo Domingo and Cuba" (10). Interestingly, DeWitt Clinton served as president of the school from at least

1814 to 1825 (Fitzpatrick 103–5). This establishes another link between Heredia and the illustrious Clinton for whom he repeatedly expressed admiration, and with whom he may have had masonic ties.

204. In other letters included herein, Heredia refers facetiously to the Anglo-Americans among whom he lived as "Muslims" and "Greeks," usually in the context of his difficulties in mastering English. Given that, it is perhaps safe to say that his use of "Jews" here is not to be taken as an anti-Semitic slight.

205. *Madan's son* would be Cristóbal Madan y Madan.

206. Heredia's friend Blas Osés, whom he references frequently in his letters.

207. From context, it would seem that Heredia here is talking not about the manuscript work by his father to which he refers in his letters as the *Historia de Venezuela,* but to some other work by José Francisco, today unknown.

208. Heredia surely is referring to his uncle Manuel, to whom he also refers disdainfully in the letter of January 20, 1825, which follows. Manuel Cayetano de Carrerá y Colina, married to a younger sister of Heredia's father (see Cipriano de Utrera 126), was born in Coro, Venezuela, of a Spanish father and Venezuelan mother. A royalist officer, he led the resistance in the Castillo San Felipe in the battle for Puerto Cabello; he was wounded on the day of the Castillo's capitulation on November 10, 1823, which brought the War of Independence in Venezuela to a successful end. With other defeated royalists, he removed to Cuba.

209. Heredia may be referring to the Spanish American privateers that attacked Spanish shipping from ports in the United States during the Wars of Independence, thus complicating the United States' posture of neutrality and its relationship with Spain. See Head and Lazo.

210. There is a discrepancy here and in the following letters regarding the date of the letter from his mother of which Heredia acknowledges receipt.

211. Following Mexico's independence from Spain, Agustín de Iturbide reigned briefly (1822–1823) as emperor of Mexico. He was executed on July 19, 1824.

212. *El gordo* in the original. Obviously an affectionate reference to Ignacio.

213. In a letter to his mother from Cuernavaca, Mexico, of March 2, 1828, Heredia would write: "I have received letters from Antonino in which he asks me to send him angels and magi (*reyes magos*). I wish with all my heart to be able to please him and his excellent parents, but how in the world can I send those trifles to him when, given the detours involved, it is lucky to be able to get a letter through?" (*Epistolario,* ed. Augier, 342). Given Heredia's preoccupation, expressed in several letters, with sending Antonio or "Antonino" gifts, perhaps he had a special relationship with him, such as that of godfather to godson.

214. In the *Lives of the Twelve Caesars,* Suetonius praises the emperor Titus for his kindness, generosity, and other virtues.

215. Heredia is referring to the Battle of Ayacucho, December 9, 1824.

216. The letter is also in Figarola 19–21.

217. In September 1823, Del Monte accepted a position as secretary and legal counsel to the mayor of the town of Guane in Pinar del Río province in western Cuba. He remained in that remote outpost for fewer than five months (Martínez Carmenate 110, n. 3). Del Monte was there at the time of the order for Heredia's arrest and flight from Cuba. Apparently Del Monte was ill received in Guane, which, along with other rumors, led Heredia to suspect that his friend was in league with the persecutors of the *Soles y Rayos* conspirators. See Martínez Carmenate 108–9; García Marruz 21–24, 124–25.

218. "I have such a heart in my breast that exults in disasters, a heart that takes pleasure in struggling with fate, and overcoming it." Heredia quotes from the first act of Vincenzo Monti's tragedy *Caio Gracco* (1802). In later years, Heredia would adapt Marie-Joseph Chénier's tragedy *Caius Gracchus*.

219. Lines from Heredia's "A mi caballo" (1821).

220. "But thou suggestest a tremendous doubt / To me, a Roman, Roman as thou art; / But thou dost not offend me: in thy breast / The vile suspicion never had arisen, / No never . . ." (Alfieri 195). Heredia quotes from Act V of Vittorio Alfieri's tragedy *Virginia* (1777–1783). Significantly, Alfieri also was the author of *L'America libera* (1781–1783), a series of odes to the American Revolution.

221. It seems that Heredia is mentioning both Angulo brothers in this paragraph. Perhaps the lawyer Angulo was advising Heredia to petition for a pardon.

222. This is the first reference in Heredia's extant letters to his *Poesías*, published in the summer of 1825 by the New York press of Behr and Kahl. The volume was ready to send by June 29, as Heredia's letter to his mother, herein, indicates.

223. As earlier indicated, Ignacio Zequeira was the son of Heredia's mother's cousin. See the note to Heredia's letter to his mother of January 4, 1824.

224. After the forced abdication of Charles IV, his son Ferdinand VII ascended to the throne of Spain on March 19, 1808.

225. Garrigó (249) lists a Luis Ramírez among the Matanzas conspirators who fled.

226. Ruiz received the light sentence of a fine for his participation in the *Soles y Rayos* conspiracy and apparently was free to return to Cuba after less than a year in exile. See Morales y Morales 52.

227. *Cadmus*: Perhaps the same American merchant ship that had carried the Marquis de Lafayette to the United States the year before to begin his triumphant tour.

228. In subsequent letters written from Mexico, it becomes clear that Heredia affectionately refers to one of his sisters—most likely the youngest—as his "son."

229. In Augier, the letter appears with the date July 1, 1825, but details in the letter indicate that this may be incorrect. We have taken the liberty of speculating that the letter was written on *June* 1, 1825.

230. On April 17, 1825, an agreement was reached by which France would recognize the independence of Haiti (formerly St. Domingue), and Haiti would pay France a sizable indemnity.

231. Perhaps Heredia was worried that he might be apprehended by the Spanish authorities if a ship carrying him to Mexico were compelled to put into a Cuban port.

232. Heredia refers to one of his sisters. See the note to his letter to María de la Merced of May 8, 1825.

233. Probably an allusion to the review of Heredia's *Poesías* that appeared on August 6, 1825, in the *New York American*. See introduction.

234. Perhaps the privateer affectionately known as the "Pride of Baltimore," launched in that city in 1812. The *Chasseur* won a notable victory over HMS *St. Lawrence* on February 26, 1815, off Havana.

Notes to Selected Verse

1. The Toluca edition sometimes marks the word *océano* as *oceano* or *oceáno*, according to the metric or rhyme needs of the line in question. In this case, for example, the *ea* needs to be diphthongized in order for the line not to exceed eleven syllables.

2. Doctor Juan José Hernández y Cano, a prominent member of the *Caballeros Racionales* group who died in Havana, perhaps by poisoning, shortly after his release from prison.

3. As early as the 1825 New York edition, Heredia's poem bore an epigraph from the Spanish poet Manuel José Quintana: "Yo lloraré, pero amaré mi llanto, / y amaré mi dolor" [I will weep, but I will love my weeping / and I will love my pain].

4. Both the 1825 New York and the 1832 Toluca editions place a comma after *pedantes*. Eliminating the comma makes *pedantes* a modifier of *azotes*—arguably a more coherent reading.

5. A reference to Heredia's poem "Las sombras" [The Shades"].

6. Heredia scholars have speculated variously on what the "*tres sílabas funestas*" in the poem might refer to, but the poet's intent remains a mystery.

7. A reader of Plutarch's *Parallel Lives*, Heredia knew that Washington's military tactics vis-à-vis the British were comparable to those of Fabius Maximus, who successfully waged a war of attrition against Hannibal and the Carthaginians.

8. At the outset of the so-called Quasi-War with France in 1798, President John Adams persuaded Washington to re-emerge from retirement and take control of the American armed forces. The Quasi-War led to no land engagements, but Washington did help to reconstitute and organize the United States military during his last months.

9. If he did travel to Mount Vernon, the tomb that Heredia would have seen is the so-called "old tomb," the very simple family vault that still exists on the grounds of the estate. In 1831, the remains of George and Martha Washington, along with those of other family members, were moved to a new brick tomb familiar to visitors to the site today.

10. In the 1825 version, the first line reads "Dadme mi lira, dádmela, que siento . . ."

11. The 1825 version of the poem does not include the next eight lines. They either were composed and added later or deliberately excluded from the 1825 edition. Assuming the latter, this is another example of Heredia suppressing politically charged lines or entire poems from his New York *Poesías*.

12. Here and elsewhere, Heredia marks *océano* as *oceáno* in order to pick up an opportune rhyme, in this case with the word *mano*, two lines before.

Works Cited

Alfieri, Vittorio. *The Tragedies of Vittorio Alfieri, Complete, Including his Posthumous Works, Translated from the Italian*. Edited and translated by Edgar Alfred Bowring, vol. 1, London, 1876.
"Alfonso y García de Medina, José Luis." *Diccionario de literatura cubana*, https://linkgua-digital.com/.
Barcia, Manuel. *The Great African Slave Revolt of 1825: Cuba and the Fight for Freedom in Matanzas*. Louisiana State UP, 2012.
Barnstone, Willis. *The Poetics of Translation: History, Theory, Practice*. Yale UP, 1993.
Barrett, Walter. *The Old Merchants of New York City*. Vol. 1, New York, 1885.
Bertin, Georges. *Joseph Bonaparte en Amérique*. Paris, 1893.
Brickhouse, Anna. *Transamerican Literary Relations and the Nineteenth-Century Public Sphere*. Cambridge UP, 2004.
Chacón y Calvo, José María. *Criticismo y libertad: evocación de José Francisco Heredia, regente de Caracas*. La Habana, Secretaría de Educación, Dirección de Cultura, 1939.
Chapman, Arnold. "Heredia's Ossian Translations." *Hispanic Review*, vol. 23, no. 3, 1955, pp. 231–36.
Chateaubriand, François-René de. *Atala*. Edited by Oscar Kuhns, D.C. Heath & Co., 1905.
Cipriano de Utrera, Fray. *Heredia*. Ciudad Trujillo, Editorial Franciscana, 1939.
Davison, Gideon M. *The Fashionable Tour, in 1825. An Excursion to the Springs, Niagara, Quebec and Boston*. Saratoga Springs, G.M. Davison, 1825.
Deák, Gloria-Gilda. *Passage to America: Celebrated European Visitors in Search of the American Adventure*. I.B. Tauris, 2013.
Del Monte, Domingo. "Primeros versos de Heredia." *Revista de la Biblioteca Nacional José Martí*, no. 4, 1953, pp. 9–12.
Díaz, Lomberto. *Heredia, primer romántico hispanoamericano*. Ediciones Géminis, 1973.
Duncan, John Morison. *Travels through Parts of the United States and Canada in 1818 and 1819*. Vol. 2, Glasgow, 1823.

Ellis, Keith, editor and translator. *First Poet of the Americas: José María Heredia and "Niagara Falls."* Editorial José Martí, 2010.

———, editor and translator. *Torrente Prodigioso: A Cuban Poet at Niagara Falls.* Lugus Libros Latin America, 1998.

Exhibition at the Rotunda, Chamber-Street. Description of the Panorama Picture of Athens, As It Is Now. New York, 1825.

Figarola Caneda, Domingo, editor. *Centón epistolario de Domingo del Monte.* Vol. 1, La Habana, Imprenta "El Siglo Veinte," 1923.

Fitzpatrick, Edward A. *The Educational Views and Influence of DeWitt Clinton.* 1911. Arno Press, 1969.

Frajola, Richard C., and James Baird. "The Pioneer Steamship *Robert Fulton*." *The Chronicle of the U.S. Classic Postal Issues*, vol. 63, no. 2, 2011, pp. 115–19.

García Garófalo y Mesa, Manuel. *Vida de José María Heredia en México, 1825–1839.* Ediciones Botas, 1945.

García Marruz, Fina. *Estudios Delmontinos.* Ediciones Unión, 2008.

Garland, Marissa. "The Authorship of Jicoténcal." *Hispania*, vol. 88, no. 3, 2005, pp. 445–55.

Garrigó, Roque E. *Historia documentada de la conspiración de los Soles y Rayos de Bolívar.* Vol. 2, La Habana, Imprenta "El Siglo XX," 1929.

Gassan, Richard H. *The Birth of American Tourism: New York, the Hudson Valley, and American Culture, 1790–1830.* U of Massachusetts P, 2008.

Gómez de Avellaneda, Gertrudis. *Poesías selectas.* Edited by Benito Varela Jácome, Editorial Bruguera, 1968.

González, Manuel Pedro. "Bryant y Heredia: dos grandes pioneros de las relaciones culturales inter-americanas." *Revista Nacional de Cultura* (Caracas, Venezuela), vol. 25, no. 155, 1962, pp. 43–56.

———. *José María Heredia, primogénito del Romanticismo hispano.* El Colegio de México, 1955.

González del Valle, Francisco. *Cronología herediana (1803–1839).* La Habana, Secretaría de Educación, Dirección de Cultura, 1938.

———. *Del epistolario de Heredia. Cartas a Silvestre Alfonso.* La Habana, Secretaría de Educación, Dirección de Cultura, 1937.

———. *Heredia en la Habana.* Municipio de la Habana, 1939.

Gruesz, Kirsten Silva. *Ambassadors of Culture: The Transamerican Origins of Latino Writing.* Princeton UP, 2002.

Haddad, Ann. "Vauxhall Garden: The Coney Island of Its Day." *Merchant's House Museum*, http://merchantshouse.org/blog/vauxhall-garden/.

Head, David. *Privateers of the Americas: Spanish American Privateering from the United States in the Early Republic.* U of Georgia P, 2015.

Hecht, Roger W. *The Erie Canal Reader, 1790–1950.* Syracuse UP, 2003.

Helman, Edith F. "Early Interest in Spanish in New England (1815–1835)." *Hispania*, vol. 29, no. 3, 1946, pp. 339–51.

Heredia, José Francisco. *Memorias sobre las revoluciones de Venezuela*. Edited by Enrique Piñeyro, París, 1895.
Heredia, José María. *Antología herediana*. Edited by Emilio Valdés y de la Torre, La Habana, Imprenta "El Siglo XX," 1939.
———. *Epistolario de José María Heredia*. Edited by Ángel Augier, Editorial Letras Cubanas, 2005.
———. *Obra poética*. Edited by Ángel Augier, Editorial Letras Cubanas, 1993.
———. *Poesías*. New York, 1825.
———. *Poesías*. 2nd ed., Toluca, 1832. 2 vols.
———. *Poesías, discursos y cartas*. Edited by María Lacoste de Arufe, La Habana, Cultural, S.A., 1939. 2 vols.
———. *Selected Poems in English Translation*. Edited by Ángel Aparicio Laurencio, Ediciones Universal, 1970.
Howe, Daniel Walker. *What Hath God Wrought: The Transformation of America, 1815–1848*. Oxford UP, 2007.
Howison, John. *Sketches of Upper Canada, Domestic, Local, and Characteristic: To Which Are Added Practical Details for the Information of Emigrants of Every Class and Some Recollections of the United States of America*. Edinburgh, London, 1821.
Ingham, John N. *Biographical Dictionary of American Business Leaders*. Vol. 2, Greenwood Press, 1983.
Jaksic, Iván. *The Hispanic World and American Intellectual Life, 1820–1880*. Palgrave Macmillan, 2007.
Kanellos, Nicolás, and Helvetia Martell. *Hispanic Periodicals in the United States, Origins to 1960: A Brief History and Comprehensive Bibliography*. Arte Público Press, 2000.
Lazo, Rodrigo. *Writing to Cuba: Filibustering and Cuban Exiles in the United States*. U of North Carolina P, 2005.
Martínez Carmenate, Urbano. *Domingo del Monte y su tiempo*. Ediciones Unión, 1997.
McKinsey, Elizabeth. *Niagara Falls: Icon of the American Sublime*. Cambridge UP, 1985.
McNeese, Tim. *The Erie Canal: Linking the Great Lakes*. Chelsea House, 2009.
Meehan, Thomas F. "Catholic Literary New York, 1800–1840." *The Catholic Historical Review*, vol. 4, no. 4, 1919, pp. 399–414.
Mejía Ricart, Gustavo Adolfo. *José María Heredia y sus obras*. La Habana, Molina y Cia., 1941.
Méndez, Roberto. *José María Heredia: la utopía restituida*. Editorial Oriente, 2003.
Moore, Ernest R. "José María Heredia in New York, 1824–1825." *Symposium*, vol. 5, 1951, pp. 256–91.
Morales y Morales, Vidal. *Iniciadores y primeros mártires de la revolución cubana*. 1901. Vol. 1, La Habana, Cultural, 1931.
Morrison, John H. *History of American Steam Navigation*. W.F. Sametz & Co., 1903.
Mulvey, Christopher. "New York to Niagara by Way of the Hudson and the Erie." *The Cambridge Companion to American Travel Writing*, edited by Alfred Bendixen and Judith Hamera, Cambridge UP, 2009, pp. 46–61.

Onís, José de. "The Alleged Acquaintance of William Cullen Bryant and José María Heredia." *Hispanic Review*, vol. 25, no. 3, 1957, pp. 217–20.

———. *The United States as Seen by Spanish American Writers*. Hispanic Institute in the United States, 1952.

Orjuela, Héctor H. "Revaloración de una vieja polémica literaria: William Cullen Bryant y la oda 'Niágara' de José María Heredia." *Thesaurus: Boletín del Instituto Caro y Cuervo*, vol. 19, 1964, pp. 248–73.

Percival, James Gates. *The Poetical Works of James Gates Percival with a Biographical Sketch*. Vol. 2, Boston, 1863.

Pérez, Lisandro. *Sugar, Cigars, and Revolution: the Making of Cuban New York*. New York UP, 2018.

Pérez, Louis A., Jr. *Cuba and the United States: Ties of Singular Intimacy*. 3rd ed., U of Georgia P, 2003.

Peterson, Roy M. "Bryant as a Hispanophile." *Hispania*, vol. 16, no. 4, 1933, pp. 401–12.

Rojas, Rafael. "Traductores de la libertad: el americanismo de los primeros republicanos." *Historia de los intelectuales en América Latina*, edited by Jorge Meyers, vol. 1, Katz Editores, 2008, pp. 205–26.

Ross, Michael. *The Reluctant King: Joseph Bonaparte, King of the Two Sicilies and Spain*. Mason/Charter, 1977.

Santa Cruz y Mallén, Francisco Xavier de. *Historia de familias cubanas*. Editorial Hércules, 1940–1952. 9 vols.

Sellers, Charles Coleman. *Mr. Peale's Museum: Charles Wilson Peale and the First Popular Museum of Natural Science and Art*. W.W. Norton & Co., 1980.

Sotelo Regil, Luis F. *Campeche en la historia*. Vol. 1, México, Imprenta "Manuel León Sánchez," 1963.

Soucy, Dominique. *Masonería y nación: redes masónicas y políticas en la construcción identitaria cubana (1811–1902)*. Ediciones Idea, 2006.

Stimson, Frederick S. "The Beginning of American Hispanism, 1770–1830." *Hispania*, vol. 37, no. 4, 1954, pp. 482–89.

Taylor, Alan. *William Cooper's Town: Power and Persuasion on the Frontier of the Early American Republic*. Alfred A. Knopf, 1995.

Torres-Cuevas, Eduardo. *Historia de la masonería cubana: seis ensayos*. Imagen Contemporánea, 2004.

Trelles y Govín, Carlos M. *Matanzas en la independencia de Cuba*. La Habana, Imprenta "Avisador Comercial," 1928.

Vázquez Cienfuegos, Sigfrido. "La comisión de Heredia de 1810: la preocupación cubana ante el inicio del proceso independentista venezolano." *Las independencias hispanoamericanas: un debate para siempre*, edited by Rogelio Altez, Bucaramanga, Dirección Cultural de la Universidad Industrial de Santander, 2012, pp. 221–69.

Villaverde, Cirilo. *Cecilia Valdés*. Edited by Sibylle Fischer, translated by Helen Lane, Oxford UP, 2005.

Williams, Stanley T. *The Spanish Background of American Literature*. Yale UP, 1955. 2 vols.

Index

Acosta, Juan de, 14, 45, 53, 73, 84, 103, 118, 130, 242n31
Adams, John Quincy, 86, 252n125
Alamán, Lucas, 75, 249n99
Albany, NY, Heredia on, 91–93
Alfieri, Vittorio, 6, 259n202; *Saul*, 136, 241n14, 259n202; *Virginia*, 148, 261n220
Alfonso y García, José Luis ("Pepé"), 136, 139, 141, 165, 258n200
Alfonso y Soler, Silvestre Luis, 24, 58, 62, 64, 65, 81, 87, 130, 134, 139, 153, 159, 239n34, 250n112
Andux, Manuel, 82, 120, 250n113
Angulo, Antonio José, 243n40, 246n73
Angulo, Antonio María Ramón, 61, 64, 65, 150, 246n73, 261n221
Angulo, José Miguel, 83, 139, 150, 158, 246n73, 261n221
Angulo, María de los Ángeles, 50, 243n40, 246n73
Angulo, Merced, 60
Arango, José, 43, 54, 57, 60, 76, 242n24, 246n69, 246n72, 249n100
Arango, Josefa ("Pepilla"), 4, 41, 51, 54, 57, 85, 128, 246n69; letter to, 35–38; poem addressed to, 24, 25, 169–77
Arango Lache, José, 51, 244n45

Aranguren, Juan Guillermo, 33, 34, 82, 120, 240nn2–3, 250n113
Augier, Ángel, 25
Ayacucho, Battle of, 260n215

Bacon, Daniel C., 39–40, 41–42, 45, 241n13
Bancel, Victor, 259n203
Bello, Andrés, 20
Betancourt, Antonio, 11, 33, 49, 53, 76, 82, 120, 240n3, 243n38, 250n113
Bolívar, Simón, 145, 157
Bonaparte, Joseph, 2, 14, 17, 74–75, 237n17, 248nn94–96, 249n98
Bonaparte, Napoleon, 2, 20, 85, 248n94, 249n98
Borthiribort, Pedro, 76, 87, 249n102
Boston, Heredia on, 39–40
Brutus, Marcus Junius, 224–25
Bryant, William Cullen, 19, 30, 238nn24–26, 238n31
Burr, Aaron, 88
Burton, Robert, 26
Byron, George Gordon, Lord, 28, 240n42

Caballeros Racionales, 4, 9, 11, 25–26, 33–34, 58, 240nn2–3, 244n45, 246n68

Campuzano Polanco, Belén Caro, 47, 155, 159, 243n35
Caraballo, Miguel María, 5, 42, 44, 53, 55, 75, 114, 242n26, 259n202
Carrerá y Colina, Manuel Cayetano de, 113, 138, 139, 260n208
Carrillo y Arango, Anastasio ("Tatao"), 58, 245n68
Cascales, Juan Francisco, 259n201
Cato, Marcus Porcius, 10, 55, 62, 224–25
Cervantes, Miguel de, allusions to *Don Quixote*, 138, 155
Céspedes, Antonio de, 58, 245n68
Chateaubriand, François-René de, 15, 81, 109, 255n168
Clinton, DeWitt, 1, 17, 78, 95, 237n21, 259n203
Cole, Thomas, 15
Coleridge, Samuel T., 31
Columbus, Christopher, 186–87
Cooper, James Fenimore, 28
Crawford, William H., 86

Davison, Gideon M., 250n110
Del Monte, Domingo, 4, 6, 9, 12–13, 31, 62, 64, 65, 86–87, 163–64, 235n5, 239n34, 239n36, 243n37, 261n217; editing by, 237n17, 249n97, 249n103; on Heredia's travel writings, 13–14; letter to, 25, 146–48
Demosthenes, 10, 55, 62
destierro and *desterrado* concept, 5, 8
Ducis, Jean-François, 49, 243n39
Duncan, John Morison, 255n165, 256n173

Erie Canal, 15–16, 17, 93–97, 100, 101–03, 237n20, 253n150, 254n155, 255n159

Espronceda, José de, 240n42

Fénelon, François de, 54, 128, 135, 154, 245n58
Ferdinand VII, 145, 154, 257n184, 261n224
Fernández, Pía and Felipa, 72, 80–81, 250n109, 258n191
Franco, José, 58, 59, 61, 63, 82, 124, 125–27, 140, 142, 144, 146, 158, 161, 246n70, 250n114
freemasonry, 7, 11–12, 237n13, 237n21, 244n47, 245n65, 249n98, 258n196, 260n203
Freneau, Philip, 27

Garay, Santiago, 50, 152, 154, 158, 160, 162, 243n41
García Medina, Francisco ("Pancho"), 64, 65, 72, 87, 118, 125, 150, 156, 247n81
Gener, Tomás, 5, 11, 28, 45–46, 152, 153, 156, 159, 239n41, 243n33
Goffe, William, and Edward Whalley, 116
Goicochea, María la ("Chea"), 41, 52, 76, 118, 123, 131–32, 241n19
Gómez de Avellaneda, Gertrudis, 8
González del Valle, Francisco, 239n34, 251n122
Goodhue, Jonathan, 241n17
Govín y Aday, José, 86, 252n126
Gran Legión del Águila Negra, 7, 11, 237n13

Haiti, 2, 163, 240n4, 262n230
Hall, Basil, 254n157
Hamilton, Alexander, 88
Hannibal, 200–201, 262n7
Harding, Captain, 42–44, 242n24

Heredia, Ignacia (sister), 15, 44, 48, 51, 59, 61, 80, 158, 160, 161, 164, 242n27, 246n73; postscripts to, 126, 127, 128, 135, 151, 154–55, 165

Heredia, José de Jesús (son), 8, 236n9, 240n1

Heredia, José María: birth and family background of, 2; in Cuba, 1–4, 7–9, 12–13; education of, 2–4; influences on, 3, 15; in Mexico, 3, 6–8, 12, 23, 29, 144, 149, 165–66; reputation and legacy of, 8–9, 12–13; translations and adaptations by, 3, 6–7, 18–19, 31, 56–58, 85, 245n64, 251n120, 251n122; travel writings of, 13–18, 66–71, 73–75, 87–112, 115–17

BOOKS:
Jicoténcal (questionably attributed novel), 236n8
Lecciones de Historia Universal, 7
Poesías, 6, 7, 12, 17, 18, 24, 26–29, 58, 151, 154, 160, 161–65, 235n4, 240n48, 245n64, 261n222, 263n11

POEMS:
"A Emilia," 6, 24, 25–26, 30, 168–77, 237n22, 238n31
"A la estrella de Venus," 238n31
"A la noche," 85, 251n122
"A mi caballo," 148, 238n31
"A mi esposa," 238n31
"A Washington," 6, 27, 30, 200–205
"Al sol," 238n31
"Atenas y Palmira," 26–27, 30, 196–99, 239n39
"En el aniversario del 4 de julio de 1776," 238n31
"En el teocalli de Cholula," 3, 6, 235n4, 247n87
"En una tempestad," 238n25, 238n31
"Himno del desterrado," 6, 8, 9, 29, 31, 218–25, 238nn30–31, 240nn44–45, 241n9
"Imistona," 85, 251n122
"Inmortalidad," 30, 31, 232–33, 238n31, 240n47
"La batalla de Lora," 85, 251n120
"La estación de los nortes," 238nn30–31
"Las sombras," 262n5
"Napoleón," 249n98
"Niágara," 6, 14, 15, 16, 19–20, 21, 28, 29, 30, 108, 206–13, 238n26, 238n31, 239n41, 263nn10–11
"Oda a la noche," 85, 238n31, 251n122
"Placeres de la Melancólia," 6, 26, 30, 178–95, 262n3
"Poesía," 238n31
"Proyecto," 28, 30, 214–17
"Vuelta al Sur," 29, 30, 31, 226–31, 240n46

Heredia, María Merced and Loreto Jacoba (daughters), 8, 236n9, 251n120

Heredia, Rafaela and María Dolores (sisters), 121, 235n2, 257n181, 261n228

Heredia y Campuzano, Ignacio (uncle), 3, 5, 10, 11, 61–63, 65, 80–81, 120, 121, 123, 128, 133, 135, 141–43, 150, 153, 155–56, 162, 260n212; letters to, 13–14, 22, 23–24, 27–28, 38–42, 49, 51–57, 59–60, 66–71, 73–79, 84–112, 115–18, 129–32

Heredia y Campuzano, María de la Merced (mother), 2–5, 7, 11, 34,

Heredia y Campuzano, María de la Merced *(continued)* 56–60, 244n51, 257nn187–88; letters to, 15, 18, 22–23, 25, 41, 42–51, 61–65, 71–73, 79–84, 112–13, 119–29, 132–46, 148–66; slaves and, 237n22, 243n36

Heredia y Campuzano, María Francisca (aunt) and Magdalena (cousin), 44, 50, 59, 61, 64, 73, 80, 83, 119, 121, 128, 134–35, 137–38, 142, 143, 149, 152–54, 160, 163, 251n117; biographical details on, 242n29, 243n41

Heredia y Mieses, Domingo (uncle), 113, 119, 128, 134, 256n175

Heredia y Mieses, José Francisco (father), 2–3, 22, 257n182, 257n184, 257nn186–87; *Historia de la América*, 137, 260n207; *Memorias sobre las revoluciones de Venezuela*, 83, 122–25, 149–50, 157–58, 159, 160–62, 164, 235n3

Hernández, Agustín, 63, 64–65, 71, 72, 80, 83, 122, 162–65, 247n79

Hernández, Pedro, 41, 54, 71, 76, 118, 131

Hernández Morejón, Francisco ("Pancho"), 9, 13, 23, 60, 62, 76, 79, 82, 246n72, 246n75, 250n106; letter to, 33–35

Hernández y Cano, Juan José, 26, 79, 174–75, 262n2

Herrera, Francisco de, 51, 244n45

Homer, 56, 85, 86

Howison, John, 15, 111, 255–56nn170–72

Howland, Gardiner Greene, 52, 54, 60, 72, 76, 114, 244n50

Irving, Washington, 20, 253n136

Iturbide, Agustín de, 142, 145, 260n211

Jackson, Andrew, 86

Junco, Dolores ("Lola"), 58, 65, 87, 118, 241n5, 245n67, 247n83, 252n131

Keats, John, 26

La Fontaine, Jean de, 114

Lafayette, Marquis de, 257n183, 261n227

Lamar, Melitón, 130, 258n195

Lanas, Félix, 41, 52, 87

Latting, John, 42, 52, 76, 242n23

Lee, Henry, 27

Leyes de Indias, Las, 123, 134, 257nn186–87

Little Falls, NY, Heredia on, 98

Longfellow, Henry Wadsworth, 19, 31

Madan y Madan, Cristóbal, 5, 24, 84, 114–15, 137, 239n35, 256n177

Madruga, Miguel Antonio de la, 84, 251n119

Malherbe, François de, 114

mammoths, Heredia on, 68–69, 247nn85–86

Manzano, Juan Francsico, 243n32

Marshall, John, 27

Meléndez Valdés, Juan, 72, 248n92

Milhoura, Francisco, 82, 120, 250n113

Milton, John, 26, 37, 241n11

Miralla, José Antonio, 11

Monti, Vincenzo, 147, 261n218

Moore, Ernest R., 236n7

Mora, Manuel, 164, 165

Mosquera, Mencía de, 55, 60

Navarro, Bernardo, 52, 75, 244n48

New Haven, CT, Heredia on, 115–17, 119
New Jersey, Heredia on, 74, 88–89
New York City, 5–6, 236n7; Heredia on, 70, 75, 77–78, 85–86, 88–89, 119
Niagara Falls, 14–16, 20, 28, 52, 56, 80–81, 104–12, 206–13, 255nn165–66, 255–56nn170–73, 263nn10–12
Norris, Norberto de, 86

Olmedo, José Joaquín, 20
Osés, Blas, 62, 63, 65, 72, 122, 123, 125, 135, 137–38, 140, 149–50, 161, 258n189; background of, 247n78
Ossian (James MacPherson), 6, 56, 57, 58, 85, 245n64, 251n120, 251n122

Pascal, Blaise, 114
Percival, James Gates, 20–21
Philadelphia, Heredia on, 66–70
Pinzón, José Gertrudis, 127, 128, 130–31
pirates, 28, 140, 260n209
Plato, 196–97
Plutarch, 262n7
Ponce de León y Espinosa, Francisco José Cirilo, 87, 129, 135, 258n193
Ponte y Cordero, Esteban, 149
Portillo, Manuel del, 82, 120, 250n113
Prado Ameno, Marquesa de, 45, 54, 243n32

Quintana, Manuel José, 85, 239n38, 251n121, 262n3

Racine, Jean, 114

Ramírez, Luis, 155, 261n225
Ramos, Luciano, 5, 43–44, 53, 72, 242n25, 244n42, 245n56, 259n202
Rivas Vértiz, Juan ("Señor de la Riva"), 41, 57, 71, 77, 130, 245n65, 258n196
Rocafuerte, Vicente, 86, 155, 236n8, 248n93, 252n125
Romanticism, 6, 14–16, 20, 26, 28, 240n42
Rueda family, 41, 76, 86, 241n20
Rueda y Ponce de León, Isabel, 58, 241n20, 245n67
Ruiz, Juan Francisco ("Pancho"), 81, 87, 155, 158–61, 250n112, 261n226

Saco, José Antonio, 87, 252n129
Sagra, Ramón María de la, 252n129
Santos Suárez, Leonardo, 5, 11, 114, 243n33
Savage, Annette, 74, 248n95
Scott, Walter, 28
Shakespeare, William, 5, 49, 243n39
slavery, 9, 17–18, 22, 26, 97, 170–71, 200–201, 237n22, 240n4, 243n32, 243n36, 244n45
Socrates, 202–3
Soles y Rayos de Bolívar, 4, 5, 6, 9, 23, 51, 240n4, 242nn20–21, 246n68, 251n119
Sterling, Micaela, 51, 244n44
Sterling del Monte, José Tiburcio, 80, 244n44, 250n107
sublime, the, 14–15, 28, 87, 102, 104–5, 108, 112, 206–7

Tacón, Miguel, 12, 13
Tapia García, Eugenio de, 99, 254n153

Tarrero, Mariano, 84, 130, 251n119
Telémaco. *See* Fénelon, François de
Teurbe Tolón, José ("Teurbillo"), 84, 131, 251nn118–19, 258n197
Ticknor, George, 20
Tió, Jaime, 50, 53, 57, 59, 245n62, 246n69
Titus, 145, 260n214
Toro, Marqués del, 122, 149, 257n184
Troy, NY, Heredia on, 93

Utica, NY, Heredia on, 100

Vanderlyn, John, 27
Varela, Félix, 5, 9, 11, 20, 236n8, 237n23, 243n33, 248n93, 252n129
verse forms, 30–31
Victoria, Guadalupe, 6, 155

Vidaurre, Manuel Lorenzo de, 236n8
Villaverde, Cirilo, 8–9, 29
Vives, Francisco Dionisio, 117, 240n4, 257n179

Warton, Thomas, 26–27
Washington, George, 10, 55, 62, 85–86, 157, 224–25, 262–63nn7–9; poem on, 6, 27–28, 30, 200–205
Webster, Daniel, 18–19, 20, 238n24
Whitney, Parkhurst, 255n161

Yáñez, Jacoba (wife), 6, 8

Zequeira y Arango, Ignacio, 47, 151, 154, 155, 159, 243n35, 261n223
Zequeira y Arango, Joaquín, 47, 243n35
Zequeira y Arango, Manuel, 243n35

www.ingramcontent.com/pod-product-compliance
Lightning Source LLC
Chambersburg PA
CBHW020641230426
43665CB00008B/273